THE CHANGING FACE OF ENGLISH LOCAL HISTORY

THE CHANGING FACE OF ENGLISH LOCAL HISTORY

edited by
R.C. RICHARDSON

Routledge
Taylor & Francis Group

LONDON AND NEW YORK

First published 2000 by Ashgate Publishing

Reissued 2018 by Routledge
2 Park Square, Milton Park, Abingdon, Oxon OX14 4RN
711 Third Avenue, New York, NY 10017, USA

Routledge is an imprint of the Taylor & Francis Group, an informa business

Publisher's Note
The publisher has gone to great lengths to ensure the quality of this reprint but points out that some imperfections in the original copies may be apparent.

Disclaimer
The publisher has made every effort to trace copyright holders and welcomes correspondence from those they have been unable to contact.

A Library of Congress record exists under LC control number: 00034852

ISBN 13: 978-1-138-74000-6 (hbk)
ISBN 13: 978-1-138-73995-6 (pbk)
ISBN 13: 978-1-315-18392-3 (ebk)

CONTENTS

ACKNOWLEDGEMENTS

Chapter 2 originally appeared in the *Proceedings of the British Academy*, xxxvii (1957) and is reprinted by kind permission of the author's executors, Stewart and Alison Sanderson.

Chapter 3 was first published in the *Journal of Historical Geography*, xi (1965) and is reprinted by kind permission of the author and of Harcourt Brace and Co. (Publishers).

Chapter 4 formed the introduction to the reprint of Thoroton's *Antiquities of Nottinghamshire* (EP Publishing, Wakefield, 1972) and is reprinted by kind permission of the authors' executors.

Chapter 5 formed part of *Archaeologia Cantiana*, cxi (1993) and is reprinted by kind permission of the author and of the journal.

Chapter 7 is from the *Local Historian*, 26 (1996) and is reprinted by kind permission of the author and of the British Association for Local History.

Chapter 8 was first given as an inaugural lecture at University College, Leicester in 1952 and is reprinted by kind permission of the author's executor, Mr A.G. Gostwick.

Chapter 9 was Hoskins's inaugural lecture at the University of Leicester in 1966 and is reprinted by kind permission of the author's executor, Susan M. Hewitt.

Chapter 10 was first given as an inaugural lecture at the University of Leicester in 1970 and is reprinted here by kind permission of the author.

Chapter 11 first appeared in the *Local Historian*, 25 (1995) and is reprinted here by kind permission of the author and of the British Association for Local History.

Chapter 12 is from the *Local Historian*, 21 (1991) and is reprinted by kind permission of the author and of the British Association for Local History.

LIST OF CONTRIBUTORS

MAURICE BARLEY taught in the University of Nottingham for nearly thirty years from 1946 and was Professor Archaeology there from 1971 to 1974.

ALAN EVERITT was Hatton Professor of English Local History at the University of Leicester from 1968 until 1982.

H.P.R. FINBERG was Reader and then Professor of English Local History at the University of Leicester from 1952 until 1965.

W.G. HOSKINS led English Local History at the University of Leicester until 1951 and returned there from Oxford as Professor in the subject from 1965 until his retirement in 1968.

PAT HUDSON is Professor of Economic and Social History at the University of Wales, Cardiff.

A.J. KIDD is Reader in History at Manchester Metropolitan University.

STUART PIGGOTT was Abercromby Professor of Prehistoric Archaeology at the University of Edinburgh from 1946 until 1972.

M.J. POWER lectures in economic and social history at the University of Liverpool.

R.C. RICHARDSON is Head of Research and the Graduate Centre at King Alfred's College, Winchester.

KEVIN SCHURER is a Senior Lecturer in History at the University of Essex

JOAN THIRSK was Senior Research Fellow in Agrarian History at the University of Leicester (1952–1965) and then Reader in Economic History at the University of Oxford (1965–1983).

K.S.S. TRAIN was Editor of the *Transactions of the Thoroton Society*.

1

INTRODUCTION: THE CHANGING FACE OF ENGLISH LOCAL HISTORY

R.C. Richardson

I want not arguments to recommend this undertaking to honest and worthy men who wish to see their native country illustrated or to prove that these studies afford the most agreeable and liberal entertainment. If there are any who wish to remain strangers in their own country and city, and children in knowledge, let them enjoy their dream.
William Camden, *Britannia*, ed. R. Gough (1789), I, ii.

[The] wider purposes of English local history ... I would suggest are essentially concerned with disentangling the ways in which, down to today, the English have related, though the local society or societies with which they have most immediately identified, to a more generalised notion of national belonging.
Charles Phythian-Adams, 'Local History and National History: The Quest for the Peoples of England', *Rural History*, 2, (1991), 20.

English local history has a long and varied pedigree. The earliest examples of it can be found in the historical writings of the Middle Ages. Bede and William of Malmesbury's histories – to cite just two instances – contain sections at least that deal with the specifics of individual places, though in ways that left no doubt of their authors' over-arching religious and moral purposes. The itineraries of William of Worcester in the late 1470s and of John Leland in the 1530s took the study of local history and topography to new lengths.[1] In the sixteenth and seventeenth centuries English local history experienced a remarkable flowering, usefully harmonising both with Bacon's concept of the advancement of learning and with rising preoccupations with English national (and Protestant) identity. English local history clearly participated in what F.S. Fussner has dubbed 'The Historical Revolution'.[2]

---

1   The texts of both writings are available in twentieth-century editions: J. Harvey (ed.), *The Itineraries of William of Worcester* (Oxford, 1969), Lucy Toulmin Smith, (ed.), *Leland. The Itinerary* (5 volumes, London, 1909–10).
2   F.S. Fussner, *The Historical Revolution. English Historical Writing and Thought 1580–1640* (London, 1962).

Its principal hallmark was an upsurge of interest in English counties, a trend grounded in the prevailing socio-political realities of the day since counties were the miniature worlds dominated by the gentry who provided most of the writers and readers of local history at this time. It was spurred on and facilitated by the Elizabethan Society of Antiquaries and the maps of Christopher Saxton and others.[3] William Lambarde's *Perambulation of Kent* came out in 1576. John Norden's *Middlesex* (1593) and *Hertfordshire* (1598) and Richard Carew's *Survey of Cornwall* (1602) were some of the other early examples. But the key figure in this 'discovery of England' – for it was no less – was William Camden (1551–1623). *Britannia*, his major work, offering a topographical survey of Roman and Anglo-Saxon Britain, was first published in a Latin text in 1586. Five successive editions had been called for by 1607, the last of them a folio. An English translation appeared in 1610 and took it to a much wider public than the scholarly circle which had first admired the original. It went on being reissued throughout the eighteenth and into the nineteenth century.[4] After Camden and his contemporaries the county history genre burgeoned further in the seventeenth century with William Dugdale's *Antiquities of Warwickshire* (1656) and Robert Thoroton's *Antiquities of Nottinghamshire* (1677) as the chief highlights. This publishing trend continued unabated in the following century. By 1800 only seven English counties still lacked their historians.[5]

Histories of English towns were slower in coming – an endorsement of the fact that the country was so incompletely urbanised in the sixteenth and seventeenth centuries. There had been some town chronicles, it is true, in the Middle Ages but John Stow's *Survey of London* (1598) ranks as the first substantial, fully-fledged urban history. William Somner's *Canterbury* (1640) and William Grey's *Newcastle* (1649) were two significant examples of urban histories produced in succeeding generations. But not before the late eighteenth century did urban histories really start to be produced in substantial numbers, a historiographical trend which coincided with the changing balance of an industrialising society and with the growth of travel and tourism. Urbanisation accelerated even further in the nineteenth century and middle-class consciousness was heightened. There was self-evidently a ready

    3   See May McKisack, *Medieval History in the Tudor Age* (Oxford, 1971); E.G.R. Taylor, *Late Tudor and Early Stuart Geography* (Oxford, 1934).
    4   D. Hay, *Annalists and Historians* (London, 1977), 151. See also R.C. De Molen, 'The library of William Camden', *Proceedings of the American Philosophical Society*, 128 (1984), 327–409. Inexplicably Camden receives only the most fleeting mention in W.G. Hoskins, *Local History in England* (London, 1959, 3rd ed., 1984).
    5   Hoskins, op. cit., 22–23. See also G. Parry, *The Trophies of Time. English Antiquarians of the Seventeenth Century* (Oxford, 1996); S.A.E. Mendyk, *"Speculum Britanniae". Regional Study, Antiquarianism and Science in Britain to 1700* (Toronto, 1989); C.R.J. Currie and C.P. Lewis (eds), *English County Histories*. A Guide (Stroud, 1994); J. Simmons, (ed.), *English County Historians* (Wakefield, 1978).

market for E.A. Freeman's series on *Historic Towns* when it was launched in 1877.[6]

The nineteenth century represents a rich chapter in the development of English local history which was bound up as one factor in the complex strivings of an expanding industrial and imperial power to find a new national identity, and in due course to cope with challenges to it. The underlining of 'Englishness' and the investigation of English local history were securely connected.[7] (From that point of view the Elizabethan and Victorian periods have an important common denominator and stand out as particularly decisive). But a development for which there was no precedent before the nineteenth century – the Railway Revolution – significantly promoted English local history by facilitating the exploration of the country and its heritage. Antiquarianism widened its social base to draw in more and more recruits from the rapidly growing professions to swell the ranks of the squires and parsons who, up to that point, had supplied the bulk of the authors and audience for English local history. The British Archaeological Association was set up in 1844. County-based publishing societies were founded. The newly-established Chetham Society, for example, dedicated to the publications of 'Remains Historical and Literary connected with the Palatine Counties of Lancaster and Chester' issued its first volumes in 1844.[8] Its activities were symptomatic of a general nineteenth-century trend to make historical source materials more easily accessible. The re-organisation of the British Museum, the opening of the new Public Record Office in Chancery Lane in 1862, and the launching of the Historical Manuscripts Commission seven years later are some of its major landmarks.

With vastly more primary sources at their disposal the nineteenth-century historians set to work. The sheer volume of their output is staggering. Some of it continued along the time-honoured path which had the pursuit of antiquarianism as its own sufficient and self-justifying goal. Other writers, however, and this was increasingly the case in the later decades of the century, used local history to illustrate the national picture. Thus the Rev. G.N. Godwin, for example, in his book on *The Civil War in Hampshire* (Southampton, 1882) modestly offered 'a useful aid' – so he said in his

6   Hoskins, op. cit., 24–25; Rosemary Sweet, *The Writing of Urban Histories in Eighteenth-Century England* (Oxford, 1997).

7   'Englishness' has attracted a considerable body of scholarly attention. See R. Helgerson, *Forms of Nationhood. The Elizabethan Writing of England* (Chicago, IL, 1992); R. Colls and P. Dodd (eds), *Englishness, Politics and Culture, 1880–1920* (London, 1986); A. Easthope, *Englishness and National Culture* (London, 1999).

8   The first Chetham Society volume was E. Hawkins, (ed.), *Travels in Holland, the United Provinces, England, Scotland and Ireland, 1634–1635 by Sir William Brereton Bart* (Manchester, 1844). On the Chetham Society see J. Tait, 'The Chetham Society: a retrospect', *Miscellany VII*, Chetham Society, new ser., 100 (1939), 1–26.

preface – 'to the recorders of the great events of English history'.[9] But not
all the products of nineteenth-century antiquarianism took the form of studies of individual places. Reference books like J.M. Wilson's *The Imperial
Gazetteer of England and Wales* published in six volumes in 1870 remain
today as monuments to the industry of these indefatiguable Victorian scholars. Philippa Levine has documented their activities in her book *The Amateur
and the Professional. Historians, Antiquarians and Archaeologists in nineteenth-Century England, 1838–1886* (Oxford, 1986).

Monumental is certainly the adjective that springs to mind in connection with another project, begun in the closing years of the Victorian
period and still very much in progress today. The *Victoria County History*,
designed as a 'scholarly comprehensive encyclopaedia of English local
history in all periods, a repository of essential information, and the starting point for further research', was launched in 1899.[10] It began as a
private enterprise with all the trappings and self-advertising of Victorian
entrepreneurialism. Such was the supreme self-confidence of its original
editors that they predicted that that the whole mighty enterprise could be
completed in 160 volumes in six years, and make a handsome profit into
the bargain! Some counties, it is true, were speedily covered; Hampshire
and Lancashire, for example, were completed by 1914. Christopher
Elrington, General Editor in 1992, was much less upbeat in his reflections
on the progress of the project; the 200 volumes produced in over ninety
years since the founding, he said, probably represented the half-way stage.[11]
For one thing modern expectations of English local history now called for
a different scale of coverage. Whereas Hampshire had been despatched by
1914 in five volumes ongoing county projects were now expected to result
in twenty-volume sets.

The *Victoria County History*, clearly and unavoidably, has changed in the
course of its hundred-year history, in the character as well as the scale of its
treatment. The general volumes now have noticeably different agendas from
those which characterised their predecessors and the topographical volumes
have different priorities and proportions. They give far less space than in the
past to architectural descriptions of parish churches and great houses, and
modern times are no longer crowded out by medieval and early modern
history.[12] Although it is still undeniably shackled by its own particular past,
the *Victoria County History* exhibits something of the changing face of
English local history. Differently organised and managed now, the *Victoria
County History* is firmly integrated to the Institute of Historical Research of

9   On Godwin see R.C. Richardson, 'Winchester and the Civil War' in S. Barker and
C. Haydon (eds), *Winchester in History and Literature* (York, 1992), 63–65.
10   The phrase is C.R. Elrington's in 'The VCH', *Local Historian*, 2 (1992), 128.
11   *ibid.*, 128, 133.
12   *ibid.*, 134.

the University of London which shares the running of the ongoing project with county councils and county committees.

Although the antiquarian outlook still persists in some quarters and the numbers of amateur local historians are larger than they have ever been in the past, English local history in the twentieth century has emphatically become professionalised. The formation of the County Record Offices since the end of the Second World War has meant that the principal archives used by local historians have been professionally managed. And in higher education English local history has secured its place as a partner, not just as a poor relation, in the academic study of history. Professional historians with university posts write about local history, university (and commercial) presses publish it, and a large proportion of postgraduate research students in history register for MPhils and PhDs in local history subjects. Scholarly journals devoted to local and regional history are firmly placed on the academic map. *Northern History*, *Midland History*, and *Southern History*, were launched in 1966, 1971, and 1981 respectively to supplement older publishing organisations such as the Lancashire and Cheshire Antiquarian Society and the Bristol and Gloucester Archaeological Society founded in the nineteenth century.[13] *CORAL* (the Conference of Teachers of Regional and Local history) was established in 1978.

In some of these developments the University of Leicester has played a major role as a power house of ideas and pioneering practice. W.G. Hoskins's decisive place in all this, from the early 1930s until his retirement in 1968 at the end of his second term at Leicester, has been justly celebrated, not least for his vital contribution to landscape studies.[14] Tributes have also been paid to the important work of H.P.R. Finberg and Joan Thirsk.[15] Alan Everitt and, later, Charles Phythian-Adams and Keith Snell at Leicester have each made a distinctive contribution to the concept and practice of English local history.[16] Once described as 'the Leicester School', these historians have

13   See J.W. Jackson, 'The genesis and progress of the Lancashire and Cheshire Antiquarian Society', *Trans. Lancs. & Ches. Antiquarian Soc.*, XLIX (1933), 104–12; Elizabeth Ralph, 'The Society, 1876–1976' in P. McGrath and J. Cannon, (eds.), *Essays in Bristol and Gloucestershire History* (Bristol, 1976), 1–49.

14   C. Phythian-Adams, 'Hoskins's England: A Local Historian of Genius and the Realisation of his Theme', *Trans. Leics. Arch. and Hist. Soc.*, LXVI (1992), 143–59; Joan Thirsk, 'William George Hoskins, 1908–1992', *Proceedings of the British Academy*, 87 (1994), 339–54.

15   M.W. Beresford, 'Herbert Finberg: An Appreciation' in Joan Thirsk, (ed.), *Land, Church and People. Essays presented to H.P.R. Finberg* (Reading, 1970), vii–xii, and bibliography of his writings, 1–6; Alan Everitt, 'Joan Thirsk: a personal appreciation', and the editors' introduction, J. Chartres and D. Hey (eds), *English Rural Society, 1500–1800. Essays in Honour of Joan Thirsk* (Cambridge, 1990), 1–26.

16   Everitt's collected essays – *Landscape and Community in England* (London, 1985) – indicate the range of his interests. See also Everitt, *The Community of Kent and the Great Rebellion, 1640–1660* (Leicester, 1966) and *Continuity and Colonization. The Evolu-*

certainly not thought and written as an undifferentiated, homogeneous group, and the messages on the nature of the subject which have been transmitted from Leicester have changed over time.[17] But central to the Leicester outlook on English local history has been a stress on the defining importance of community and, more recently, culture, and not simply place. Most fundamentally of all, the various Leicester historians have insisted on the key importance of their subject and have done more than any others to rescue it from the Cinderella status to which the rise of professionalised academic history in the late nineteenth century tended to consign it.

For Hoskins and Finberg exploring rhythms in the life-cycle of a single village community was, generally speaking, a sufficient objective for the English local historian to keep in view. For those who have followed them, however, it is not enough. Alan Everitt placed particular emphasis on the need to examine county communities, especially in relation to the origins, course and consequences of the English Civil Wars.

> In many respects, [he wrote in a widely admired local study], 'the England of 1640 resembled a union of partially independent county-states or communities, each with its own distinct ethos and loyalty... One important aspect of the history of the Great Rebellion is certainly the gradual merging or submerging of these communities, under the stress of revolution, in the national community of the New Model Army and the Protectorate.[18]

Joan Thirsk and Charles Phythian-Adams have moved towards comparative English local history and an appreciation of the dialectical interactions between the local and the national. English local history at the dawn of the twenty-first century is becoming demonstrably less inward-looking and particularising than it once was. When Charles Phythian-Adams says that English local history is ready for, and needs, a Braudel to take it forward,[19] he is recognising that the French *Annales* historians have directly influenced particular writings in the subject. (Margaret Spufford's *Contrasting Communities. English Villagers in the Sixteenth and Seventeenth Centuries* (Cambridge, 1974) and David Rollison's *The Local Origins of Modern*

tion of Kentish Settlement (Leicester, 1986). Charles Phythian-Adams's publications include *Desolation of a City. Coventry and the Urban Crisis of the late Middle Ages* (Cambridge, 1979). Keith Snell's output includes *Annals of the Labouring Poor. Social Change and Agrarian England, 1660–1900* (Cambridge, 1985).

17   A. Briggs, 'The Leicester School', *New Statesman and Nation*, (Feb. 1958). Margery Tranter et al. (eds), *English Local History: The Leicester Approach. A Departmental Bibliography and History 1948–1998* (Leicester, 1999) documents the various facets and phases of the Department's growth and activities in the fifty-year period and lists the publications of staff and research students. MA, MPhil and PhD theses are also recorded.

18   Everitt, *Community of Kent*, 13.

19   Phythian-Adams, 'Local History and National History: the quest for the peoples of England', *Rural History* 2 (1991), 3.

Society, Gloucestershire, 1500–1800 (London, 1992) are good examples). More generally, however, he is recognising the *Annales*'s impact on the changing frontiers of English local history.

The 'Leicester School' may have been pivotal in the process of re-defining the study of English local history in the last fifty years but there have been other centres, other influences as well. In the inter-war period when Hoskins was first establishing himself at Leicester some very notable local and regional histories were being produced elsewhere. The Lancashire schoolmaster G.H. Tupling published his pathfinding *Economic History of Rossendale* (Manchester, 1927). A.P. Wadsworth, editor of the *Manchester Guardian*, joined forces with the Oxford historian Julia de Lacy Mann to write their classic study of *The Cotton Trade and Industrial Lancashire 1600–1780* (Manchester, 1931). Another important contribution to English local and regional history came out in the following year in the form of J.D. Chambers's *Nottinghamshire in the Eighteenth Century* (London, 1932). More recently local and regional history has found a secure foothold in other universities – East Anglia, Exeter, Lancaster, Manchester Metropolitan, and Nottingham – and historians connected with them, such as J.D. Marshall have frequently voiced their views. Marshall, in particular, has been a forthright proselytiser for regional history, a relentlessly hostile antagonist to all forms of antiquarianism, and a critic of many features of the 'Leicester School' which he has accused of idealising the past. English local history, says Marshall, has damagingly shunned debate and controversy.[20]

Pragmatism has indeed usually been more conspicuous than problematics in English local history, and the foregrounded theorising about the subject by Charles Phythian-Adams is conspicuously exceptional. W.G. Hoskins, in contrast, declared that he had 'a temperamental allergy to such inventions' and was openly hostile to the concoction of 'vocabularies of esoteric jargon'.[21] And he was unashamedly an exponent of specificity, a believer in a sharply focussed approach to individual places and human settlements; it is revealing that Hoskins took such delight in the homespun, gossipy, and socially inquisitive text offered in Richard Gough's *Antiquities and Memoirs of the Parish of Myddle* in Shropshire written in 1700.[22] His collection of essays on *Provincial England* (London, 1963) gave pride of place at the

---

20   J.D. Marshall, *The Tyranny of the Discrete. A Discussion of the Problems of Local History in England* (Aldershot, 1997). On Marshall see Elizabeth Roberts and O.M. Westfall, 'J.D. Marshall: the making of the identity of a regional historian' in E. Royle (ed.), *Issues of Regional Identity in Honour of John Marshall* (Manchester, 1998), 226–39, and the bibliography of his writings, 240–47.

21   See below p. 137.

22   Hoskins talked about Gough's 'marvellous local history' in *Local History in England* (29), and produced a complete edition of the text in 1968. See also D.G. Hey, *An English Rural Community. Myddle under the Tudors and Stuarts* (Leicester, 1974).

beginning to a quotation from William Blake – 'To generalise is to be an idiot. To particularise is the alone distinction of merit'. It is a motto that emphatically would not be endorsed by Hoskins's present-day successors at the University of Leicester. The face of English local history has changed so much in the last generation.

There is no shortage of books on English local history currently available – Hoskins's among them.[23] They fall into three categories, the first two much more numerous than the third. The first consists of practical handbooks. Kate Tiller's *English Local History. An Introduction* (Stroud, 1992, 2nd ed., 1994) has proved very successful and offers basic, down-to-earth guidance to the local historian trying to cope with the practical problems of studying the medieval, early modern, and modern periods. David Hey's *Oxford Companion to Local and Family History* (Oxford, 1996) was designed as 'a starting point', addressed to both amateurs and professionals and aimed to provide a comprehensive, up-to-date and accessibly written reference work. It offered 'information on archives and where they can be found' and summarised 'present knowledge and academic debate'.[24] The second category consists of monographs of varying length, including the four series of Occasional Papers produced by the Department of English Local History at Leicester.[25] Amongst a very large accumulation of longer monographs those by Marjorie McIntosh on Havering, Essex and Mary Prior's *Fisher Row* (Oxford) might be singled out for special mention.[26] The third category – books dealing expressly with the concept of English local history – is not well stocked. Charles Phythian-Adams's *Rethinking English Local History* (Leicester, 1987) and J.D. Marshall's pugnacious *The Tyranny of the Discrete. A Discussion of the Problems of Local History in England* (Aldershot, 1997) are recent, but relatively lonely examples.

The present book attempts, therefore, to fill a real gap in the available literature of English local history by dwelling on its rich historiography. A blending of newly written with reprinted essays it collects together a series

---

23   Hoskins, *Local History in England* (London, 1959, 3rd ed., 1984) and *The Making of the English Landscape* (London, 1955, new ed., Harmondsworth, 1991) are both still in print.

24   Hey, *op. cit.*, v.

25   The Occasional Papers ran to about forty publications and included Joan Thirsk's *Fenland Farming in the Sixteenth Century*, Margaret Spufford's *A Cambridgeshire Community: Chippenham from Settlement to Enclosure*, Alan Everitt's *The Pattern of Rural Dissent: the Nineteenth Century*, Charles Phythian-Adams's *Fields and Fission: the Making of a Midland Parish*, and Keith Snell's *Church and Chapel in the North Midlands: Religious Observance in the Nineteenth Century*.

26   Marjorie K. McIntosh, *Autonomy and Community. The Royal Manor of Havering, 1200–1500* (Cambridge, 1986) and *A Community Transformed. The Manor and Liberty of Havering, 1500–1620* (Cambridge, 1991); Mary Prior, *Fisher Row. Fishermen, Bargemen, and Canal Boatmen in Oxford, 1500–1800* (Oxford, 1985).

of explorations of how English local history has been defined, approached, and practised at different stages in its development from the sixteenth century to the present day. Some of the essays focus on the work of individual historians, others provide overviews. Two deal with the sixteenth century, one with the seventeenth, two with the eighteenth, one with the nineteenth, and the remainder with the twentieth century. Three of the pieces reprinted here originated as inaugural lectures. The reprinted essays in this collection are selected from a time-span of forty-four years. Finberg's essay which forms chapter 8 was first published in 1952; A.J. Kidd's (chapter 7) appeared in 1996. There is a historiographical dimension, therefore, not only to the subject matter of this book but to the writing as well.

The book begins with William Camden and reprints Stuart Piggott's famous 1957 essay on the *Britannia*, Camden's *magnum opus*. Piggott explores the evolving nature of the text through its successive editions, the way in which Camden kept on incorporating fresh research in addition to the new county maps by Saxton and others as they made their appearance. Piggott also charts the resounding influence of Camden's work both at the time and in the next two centuries. This is an essay that provides more than a portrait of a key individual and his contribution to the emergence of late Tudor antiquarianism. Camden is firmly linked here with the intellectual milieu of Elizabethan London, with patronage and its pervasive power, with the Society of Antiquaries, the College of Heralds, and other scholarly circles.

John Stow, author of the *Survey of London* (1598) belonged to the same scholarly network as Camden, and is the subject of Michael Power's 1985 essay which forms chapter 3. London-born (and intensely proud of it) Stow provided a text which was a celebration of both the capital's past and present. Power's essay concentrates on Stow's painstakingly depicted topographical details to assemble an overview of the socio-economic geography of an already zoned and polarised London at the end of the reign of Queen Elizabeth.

Robert Thoroton ranks alongside William Dugdale as one of the great county antiquarians of the seventeenth century. Chapter 4 – first published in 1972 – examines Thoroton's indebtedness to Dugdale's model of a county history and critically assesses the end-product that this Nottinghamshire Royalist doctor and magistrate offered to his gentry readers. M.W. Barley and K.S.S. Train go on to show how Thoroton's text enjoyed a vigorous afterlife at the hands of John Throsby, its eighteenth-century editor.

Chapters 5 and 6 are wholly concerned with different facets of the antiquarian ethos of English local history in the eighteenth century. In the first of these, originally issued in 1993, Joan Thirsk provides a new assessment of Edward Hasted whose *History and Topographical Survey of the County of Kent* was published in four volumes between 1778 and 1799. Though his plodding, flat and rather colourless style and relentless recital of accumulated detail do not make for easy reading today, Thirsk pays tribute to the range of his coverage, his persistence in attempting to unravel the dense, complex manorial history of his county, and to his striving for accuracy.

Urban histories were joining county histories in increasing numbers in the late eighteenth century as the growth of towns, civic pride, and travel and tourism all registered their impact. In chapter 6, newly written for this volume, I examine one of them – the Rev. John Milner's *History, Civil and Ecclesiastical and Survey of the Antiquities of Winchester* (1798) – in relation to the self-consciously urban, and urbane, world in which it was received. Milner's *Winchester*, it is shown, became a local success story, surprising perhaps in view of the author's pronounced Roman Catholic bias and his open hostility to many of the genteel refinements and adornments of the age of the Enlightenment.

A.J. Kidd in chapter 7 surveys the flowering of English local history in the Victorian period as an important aspect of middle-class culture and takes a single county, Lancashire, as his example. (The article first appeared in *The Local Historian* in 1996). The Manchester Royal Jubilee Exhibition of 1887 and its 'heritage theme park' provide a convenient starting point. Kidd moves on to examine the inter-related activities and cross-membership of no fewer than four major publishing societies based in the county. Local luminaries such as John Eglinton Bailey (1840–88) and John Parsons Earwaker (1847–95) come under review.

Chapters 8 to 10 form a group. First delivered as inaugural lectures in the University College, later University of, Leicester in 1952, 1966, and 1970 by H.P.R. Finberg, W.G. Hoskins, and Alan Everitt, they underline that institution's lead in English local history; in a real sense these are *ex cathedra* statements about the subject. Finberg's 1952 lecture has been described as a kind of unilateral declaration of independence for the subject and a key statement about the need to understand the subtle rhythms in the development of localities.[26] The key emphasis here is firmly placed on communities, not simply places, and their life-cycles. Hoskins's 1966 inaugural lecture develops these themes further through a host of well chosen examples and makes clear the need for English local history to distance itself from a passive, unimaginative, fact-grubbing antiquarianism that was still far from extinct. Local historians, Hoskins insists here, need to be not only topographers but part sociologists, demographers, geographers, scientists, and environmentalists in their attempts 'to restore the fundamental unity of human history'.[27] Everitt's 'New Avenues in English Local history' – the title given to his 1970 inaugural lecture – includes not only an emphasis on the need to explore inner interconnections within whole individual communities but also the requirement that the subject must have a comparative dimension. His own native county of Kent is brought into play as one case

---

27   See p. 137 below.

study to open up these themes; the 1851 Religious Census and the 1860 enquiry into the distribution of landed property in England provide others.

Pat Hudson's essay (chapter 11), originally published in *The Local Historian* in 1995, takes us into methodologies and parameters of English local history which the University of Leicester professors could scarcely have envisaged at the time they were writing. She examines the impact of computer technology in cataloguing, cross-referencing, and accessing the local historian's archives and the ways in which advanced data retrieval systems have transformed the capacity to interrogate the sources and correlate and present the findings. Democratising the social range of English local history, Hudson argues, has been significantly promoted by the computer revolution.

Kevin Schurer's essay (chapter 12), first published in *The Local Historian* in 1991, takes stock of what by any standards might be described as the current 'boom' in English local history. It is critical rather than celebratory in tone and asks some uncomfortable questions. Is English local history still too parochial in its concerns? Are purely local explanations of the local past credible? Is English local history urgently in need of more conceptualisation and theory?

My own essay which forms the final chapter compares and contrasts the principal patterns in the development of local history in America with those manifested in the successive stages of the growth of English local history. The decidedly puritan strain in the formative phase of the American antiquarian tradition is highlighted. Attention is drawn to the different kind of academic leadership of local history in America today from that found in this country. There has clearly been no American equivalent of the 'Leicester School'. There have been significantly different emphases as well in what has been studied. The 'urban fixation' in American local history is examined as well as different working definitions of landscape history in the two countries. And – most general of all – the essay explores how the writing of local history in the two countries has often struck a different balance between past and present and the values attached to them.

The chronological limits of this book are represented by an English local historian, William Camden, writing in 1586, and by another English local historian, Charles Phythian-Adams, and an American local historian, Carol Kammen, writing more than four centuries later. Within that long time-frame, English local history – in tune with the changing ethos surrounding it as it has been written – has moved in different directions, adopted different working definitions, priorities, strategies and methodologies. Today English local history is widely recognised as having a fundamental and indispensable place in historical studies; it is not a self-contained and marginalised field of study obsessed with village small-talk and the parish pump. It is an approach to history that demonstrably matters. *The Changing Face of English Local History* explores the many vicissitudes experienced in its long and eventful journey through the last four centuries.

2

WILLIAM CAMDEN AND THE BRITANNIA

Stuart Piggott

The choice of the year 1951 for the inauguration of a series of archaeological lectures is a singularly happy one. The story of antiquarian studies in
Britain may fairly be said to begin with the New Learning, in Tudor and
Elizabethan times, and of the scholars of that period the acknowledged
leader in such researches, in his own day and for a couple of centuries later,
was William Camden, born just 400 years ago, in 1551. It is therefore fitting
that the first of the Reckitt Lectures should in part take the form of a
laudatio of Camden, appropriate to his quatercentenary, and that an estimation of the place of his work in seventeenth- and eighteenth-century
antiquarian scholarship should be made. His *Britannia* is his monument,
and the dates of its original publication in 1586, followed by those of the
two great revisions and enlargements by Gibson in 1695 and Gough in
1789, form significant milestones in the history of British antiquarian thought
from the Renaissance to the Regency.

The intellectual background of the Elizabethan antiquaries has been discussed by Sir Thomas Kendrick with characteristic scholarship and wit.[1] He
has shown how the myth of the British History invented by Geoffrey of
Monmouth in the twelfth century, in which the Trojan Brutus founded a pre-
Roman dynasty in these islands no less respectable than that of Aeneas, was
still dominating men's ideas about the early history of Britain in the beginning of the sixteenth century, and indeed the accession of the Tudors gave to
the legend an added propaganda value. But the Italian, Polydore Vergil, and
the Scotsman, John Major, had launched an attack on the British History
early in the sixteenth century that had soon gathered momentum, and by the
1550s the new objective and critical approach to the materials of British
history and archaeology had all but established itself, and certainly represented the prevailing intellectual temper among the antiquaries. In the first
half of the century, too, John Leland was making his tours, recording at first
hand the libraries, the topography, and the antiquities of town after town in

---

1   T. D. Kendrick, *British Antiquity* (London 1950).

England and Wales, gathering material for a great work that he seems to have visualised sometimes as a map, sometimes as an elaborate annotated gazetteer. But he died, his notes still in manuscript, a year after Camden was born, and it was he who realised a part of Leland's dream, in some measure with Leland's own materials.

William Camden was a Londoner, born in 1551 the son of a father described as *pictor*, and his markedly visual approach to antiquities may have owed something to a painter likely to have been engaged at least in heraldic draughtsmanship, if not in portraiture. He attended St Paul's School, and went up to Oxford in 1566 where, apparently partly as a result of his participation in religious controversy, he was refused a B.A., and came down in 1571. He was already interested in English topography and antiquities, and spent three years travelling about the country and evidently making notes which were later to be used in the *Britannia*. In 1575, at the age of twenty-four, he was appointed Second Master in Westminster School, a position he was to hold, as it happened, for the next twenty-three years of his life. Here was a position congenial enough for a young man of antiquarian tastes, and vacations afforded an opportunity for further travel – we know, for instance, that he made tours in Norfolk and Suffolk in 1578, when the plan for the *Britannia* was taking definite shape in his mind.[2]

He had determined on a study of antiquities as a schoolboy, when 'he could neither hear nor see any thing of an *antique* appearance, without more than ordinary attention and notice'. This enthusiasm had continued at the university, and although he seems to have made attempts, perhaps rather half-hearted, to give up these activities when a schoolmaster, yet 'whenever a Vacation give him liberty to look abroad, his thirst returned, and ... it was not in his power to restrain himself from making Excursions into one quarter or another, in quest of Antiquities'. Sir Philip Sidney and other men of taste and influence had encouraged this enthusiasm while he was at Oxford, and it is clear that while he was at Westminster his reputation as an antiquarian scholar had been spread abroad by his friends, so that when in 1577 the great European geographer Abraham Ortelius came to England, it was with Camden that he mainly discussed British topography and antiquities. He saw the notes that had already been collected and recognised in them and in their compiler a potential addition to European scholarship of no mean order, and after much persuasion induced the diffident Camden to complete the task he had set himself, and reduce his materials to a book. Nine years later the *Britannia* was published.

In the compilation of the material for this book, Camden seems from the first to have planned a course of studies for himself which would enable him

---

2   The main facts of Camden's life are contained in the Latin *Vita* prefaced by Dr Thomas Smith to his edition of the *Epistolae* in 1691. My quotations are from Gibson's translation of this printed in the 1695 and 1722 editions of the *Britannia*. For Camden as historian, H.R. Trevor-Roper, *Queen Elizabeth's First Historian* (Neale lecture in English history) (London, 1971).

to make the best use of his sources. 'He enter'd upon it', his biographer remarks, 'with all the difficulties, that could attend an Undertaking. It was a sort of Learning, that was then but just *appearing* in the world, when that heat and vehemence of *Philosophy* and *School-Divinity* (which had possess'd all hearts and hands for so many hundred years) began to cool'. Apart from the observations made on his travels, Camden was, of course, in possession of the necessary knowledge of Latin required for reading the medieval texts (mainly chronicles) on which he was to base his historical conclusions, but since, as we shall see, he was particularly concerned with the elucidation of contemporary English place-names, in relation to those recorded from the Roman Province, he recognised the necessity of acquiring a knowledge of a Celtic tongue, as well as of Old English.

To obtain a knowledge of Welsh was not difficult in Tudor England – 'he had the comfort to think, that it was a *living* language, and that he wanted not Friends, who were Criticks in it': Aubrey tells us he kept a Welsh servant for conversation in that language.[3] But Anglo-Saxon was another matter – 'a Language, then, which had lain dead for above four Hundred Years, was to be reviv'd; the Books, wherin it was bury'd, to be (as it were) rak'd out of the ashes; and (which was still worse) those Fragments, such as they were, exceeding hard to be met with'.

The beginnings of Saxon studies in Elizabethan England and the recovery of the language, have been described to the Academy by the late Dr Flower in a notable study of Laurence Nowell, for whom we can claim the distinction of the founder of Old English studies in this country.[4] It was to Nowell and his circle – Archbishop Parker, Sir Robert Cotton, William Lambarde[5] – that Camden would most naturally turn. He was in fact a close friend of Sir Robert Cotton, with whom he made tours in the north of England, and Lambarde, who had worked in close collaboration with Nowell and inherited his library, was on sufficiently intimate terms with Camden for the *Britannia* to be sent to him in manuscript for his comments in 1595. An even closer link can in fact be established. In his book of *Remaines* Camden quotes an Old English version of the Lord's Prayer from 'an antient *Saxon* glossed *Evangelists*, in the hands of my good friend Master Robert Bowyer'. Now this must be the collection of glossaries in what is now Cotton MS. Cleopatra A. iii which Dr Flower showed was used by Laurence Nowell, and later given by Bowyer to Sir Robert Cotton. Camden could not have learnt his Anglo-Saxon under more auspicious circumstances.

I should like, if you will permit me, to reserve, for a moment, discussion of the scope and content of the *Britannia* as originally planned and written,

---

3   Cf. Bromwich, *Bull, Board Celtic Studies* XXIII (1968), 14; ibid., 'Trioedd ynys Prydain' *in Welsh literature and scholarship* (Cardiff, 1969). No. IV below.

4   *Proc. Brit. Acad.* XXI (1935), 47.

5   Cf. R. M. Warnicke, *William Lambarde* (London, 1973).

and in the meantime to review, very briefly, the remainder of Camden's life, and to consider what we know of the man himself, his tastes, and his approach to antiquarian studies. He continued to make antiquarian tours after the publication of the book in 1586, collecting additional material which was to be inserted in the successive editions that appeared in 1587, 1590, 1594, 1600, 1607, and 1610. Between 1589 and 1596 he travelled in Wales, Devonshire, Wiltshire, and Somerset, and in 1599 he visited Cumberland and the Roman Wall with Sir Robert Cotton, though he had been to the Wall before the first edition of the *Britannia* appeared.[6] But meanwhile, in 1597, by which time he had become Headmaster at Westminster, he was offered and accepted the vacant post of Clarenceux King of Arms in the College of Heralds, which came as near to being an Institute of Antiquarian Research as could have been conceived of in Elizabethan England. So far as one can judge, Camden's interests were not in fact primarily genealogical, and indeed there seems to have been criticism from those concerned with family history that the *Britannia* did not contain enough pedigrees – 'There are some', he wrote in his revised preface, 'there are some peradventure who apprehend it disdainfully and offensively that I have not remembered this or that family, when it was not my purpose to mention any but such as were more notable, nor all them truly (for their names would fill whole volumes) but such as happened in my way according to the methode I proposed to myselfe'.[7] But a herald was at least an avowed and recognised antiquary, and once established as such, Camden could pursue his studies in any direction that interested him. The early and abortive attempts to found a Society of Antiquaries naturally concerned Camden, and it was no fault of his or his colleagues that the schemes were unsuccessful.

Sir Thomas Kendrick has reviewed the heraldic controversies in which Camden was involved almost immediately upon taking up his new duties, and they need not detain us here. In his later years he published two books containing materials gathered during the preparation of the *Britannia*, a collection of chronicles and the little commonpolace book of *Remaines concerning Brittaine* which, to judge by the succession of editions after its first publication in 1607, met with a receptive and appreciative public.

The *Remaines* do give us, I think, glimpses of Camden's own tastes, and some idea of his attitude to antiquities. In discussing the history of costume, for instance, he draws attention to the use of medieval effigies as evidence for contemporary dress and armour – 'what the habits both civil and military were in the time of King *John*, *Henry* the third, and succeeding ages, may better appear by their monuments, old glasse-windowes and antient

6   Cf. Haverfield in *Trans. Cumb. & West. Arch. Soc.* NS XI (1911), 343 for Camden and the Wall.
7   Preface to 1610 edition.

Arras, than be found in Writers of those times'. He gives an essay on British coins, which clearly fascinated him, and another on Anglo-Saxon, with examples; a very full list of proverbs current in his day, and two selections of medieval Latin verse, divided into *Poems*, in classical metres, and *Rhymes* in rhyming stanzas: in the *Poems*, too, he includes a long passage from Chaucer's *Nun's Priest's Tale*.

He obviously enjoyed the rhyming Latin verses, but in an age when the classical mode was the undisputed canon of taste among scholars, he finds it necessary to apologise – 'I could present you with many of them, but few shall suffice, when as there are but few now which delight in them', he writes. He gives us a remarkable selection of medieval secular Latin poetry, perhaps the most notable items being the extracts from Joseph of Exeter's *Antiocheis*, which, in default of surviving manuscripts, are our sole authority for the poem. In addition, we may notice the passages from John de Hanville's *Architrenius*, and, among the rhyming verse, the *Quisquis cordis et oculi* of Philip de Grève and the Goliardic *Prisciani regula penitus cassatur*. Best of all in this section are two passages from the masterly *Confessio* of the twelfth-century Archpoet.[8] He attributed many of the rhyming verses to Walter Map, as did subsequent editors up to the last century, and it is likely that he obtained many, and perhaps most, of the fragments of medieval Latin verse he quotes from those enormous compilations of texts made by Bale, Flacius Illyricus, and others for the purpose of anti-Catholic propaganda in the Reformation. But what is important about Camden's choice is that he is unconcerned with this attitude of the Protestant apologists, and prints the verses because they entertained and intrigued him. His anthology, then, must rank as the first printed collection of the secular verse of the Middle Ages presented to the reader for its own sake.

I have just used the phrase 'the Middle Ages', employing it, as we all do, as an essential part of our historical vocaulary. But it was Camden who, so far as it is known, was the first Englishman to make use of this term, and the concept it implied, in a printed work.[9] In introducing his collections of *Poems* he refers to contemporary Renaissance Latin verses, 'But' he goes on 'whereas these latter are in every man's hand ... I will onely give you a taste of some of middle age, which was so overcast with darke clouds or rather thicke foggs of ignorance, that every little sparke of liberall learning seemed wonderful; so that if somtime you happen of an uncouth word, let the time treat pardon for it'. As an Elizabethan, he cannot feel that the 'middle age'

British coins, from Camden, *Britannia, 1600.*

was anything but barbarous, but he does realise its existence, and recognises that it has qualities of its own which cannot be ignored.

Camden's work on British coins, contained in the *Remaines* and in the *Britannia*, is of pioneer importance. Leland had denied the existence of a native coinage at the time of the Roman Conquest, but Camden not only recognised the non-Roman coin types for what they were, but correctly appreciated the significance of the abbreviated titles and mints in the inscriptions of CVNOB ..., COM ..., VER ..., and CAMV .... His investigations were carried out with the assistance of Sir Robert Cotton, who 'with curious and chargeable search', formed the collection from which the engravings in the 1600 edition of the *Britannia* were made.

The chapter on *Inhabitants* is noteworthy for its complete omission of the Trojan myth, and for its enthusiasm for the Saxons. Here one can see the influence of Nowell and his circle, and Camden, relegating the Britons, now bereft of the glamorous Brutus, to a minor prefatory position, begins the theme of the greatness of England, and of the English language, with the *adventus Saxonum.*

> This warlike, victorious, stiffe, stout, and vigorous nation [he writes] after it had as it were taken roote here about one hundred and sixtie yeares, and spread its branches farre and wide, being mellowed and mollified by the mildnesse of the soyle and sweete ayre, was prepared in fulnesse of time

for the acceptance of Christianity. From this it is an easy step to discuss the origins of the English language – 'extracted (as the Nation) from the *Germans*, the most glorious of all now extant in Europe, for their moral and martial vertues', and to commend the thoroughness of the Saxon conquest – 'To the honor of our progenitors, the *English-Saxons*, bee it spoken, their conquest was more absolute here over the *Britains*' than anywhere in Europe where the Romance languages survived.[10]

Camden wisely refuses to accept any wild ideas on the remote origins of the English language, but does draw attention to Scaliger's observations of words similar to Germanic forms in Persian, and to the remarkable little vocabulary of surviving Gothic which Busbecq, the Dutch Ambassador at Constantinople, had fortunately recorded in his letters from conversation with men from the Crimea. All these, of course, are genuine parallel forms within the Indo-European language group, the significance of which were not to be appreciated until the end of the eighteenth century, but already the Renaissance scholars were approaching the subject from the right point of view.

To the chapter on the English language is added a delightful little eulogy on *The Excellence of the English Tongue*, by Richard Carew, with a list of all the

---

10   Cf. S. Piggott, *Ruins in a Landscape* (Edinburgh, 1976), ch. IV.

great contemporary writers ending – 'will you have all in all for prose and verse? take the Miracle of our Age, Sir *Philip Sidney*'. And Camden ends his chapter with a passage which would, I feel, please Sir Ernest Gowers:

> I may be charged by the minion refiners of *English*, neither to write State-English, Court-English, nor Secretarie-English, and verily I acknowledge it. Sufficient it is for me, if I have waded hitherunto in the fourth kind, which is plaine English.

It is in the grand Elizabethan manner that the book should end with *Epitaphs*, introduced in solemn prose that not only echoes Camden's contemporary, Sir Walter Raleigh, but curiously foreshadows the cadences of *Hydriotaphia*:

> And that we may not particulate, the Romans so far exceeded in funerall honours and ceremonies, with Oyntments, Images, Bonfires of most pretious wood, Sacrifices and banquets, burning their dead bodies until the time of Theodosius, that Lawes were enacted to restrain the excesse. Neither have any neglected buriall but some savage Nations, as Bactrians, which cast their dead to the dogs; some varlet Phylosophers, as *Diogenes*, which desired to bee devoured of Fishes; some dissolute Courtiers, as Mecaenas....
> Notorious it is to all, how the same *Lucian* bringeth in *Diogenes* laughing and out-laughing King *Mausolus*, for that hee was so pitifully pressed and crushed with an huge heape of stones under his stately monument *Mausoleum*, for the magnificence accounted among worlds wonders: But monuments answerable to mens worth, states, and places, have alwaies been allowed, yet stately sepulchres for base fellowes have always lyen open to bitter jests.

In the last years of his life Camden decided to endow a Chair of History in the University of Oxford, an idea which seems to have been in his mind since the compilation of the *Britannia*, and in 1622, the year before his death, the foundation of the Camden Chair was announced in Convocation. It involved reading lectures 'on Florus or other antient historians, twice a week, Mondays and Saturdays',[11] and was held in the first instance by Degory Wheare, nominated by Camden. During the ensuing couple of centuries the only Camden Professor of distinction was Thomas Warton, that learned and eccentric eighteenth-century historian of English poetry: after Warton's death, in 1790, one notes, with eyebrows mildly raised, that the Chair was held until 1861 by three successive Principals of St Alban Hall: this Society, now defunct and perhaps never over-endowed, doubtless saw in the Camden foundation an admirable sinecure for the Head of a House, But in the later nineteenth century, the Chair recovered its intended dignity with George Rawlinson and H.F. Pelham, and in Haverfield we have seen a Camden Professor who perhaps most of all would have delighted the founder.

---

11   Gough's *Life* of Camden, prefaced to the 1789 *Britannia*.

It is now time to turn from Camden to his *Britannia*, and to consider first of all exactly what was the intended scope and content of this work. And here we must clear our minds of the picture of the *Britannia* which we usually carry, and see not the great three-decker Gough in calf-bound folios, nor those of Gibson in two volumes or one; and not the rather smaller Philemon Holland translation, but the dumpy little quarto in Latin, with no maps and a woodcut of a medieval inscription as its only illustration, published in 1586.

Camden's first biographer, Dr Thomas Smith, who published a Latin life in 1691, revised and translated in Gibson's edition of the *Britannia* a few years later, had no doubt of the purpose of the book.

> *Italy* was the place [Smith wrote] where these *Topographical Surveys* were first attempted, for the more easier and delightful Reading of the *Roman* Histories; and there the difficulty was very inconsiderable. The express remains of the old names, preserved in the new ones, was a sufficient direction in many cases.... *France, Spain,* and *Germany* had not this advantage in so high a degree; but as they were subdued by the Roman Arms, so had they the good fortune to fall under the notice of the Roman Historians.... But Britain was *another world* to them; and accordingly ... their Accounts were unavoidably confused and imperfect. In the case before us, the best direction seems to be the *Itinerary* of Antoninus.

You will notice the insistence on two things, the Roman Empire and place-names, and we find them again when we turn to Camden's own words in his Preface, in the 1610 English version:

> Truly it was my project and purpose to seeke, rake out, and free from darknesse such places as *Caesar, Tacitus, Ptolemee, Antonine* the Emperor, *Notitia Provinciarum* and other antique writers have specified and *TIME* hath overcast with mist and darknesse by extinguishing, altering, and corrupting their old true names.

Camden goes on to say that the place-names of Roman Britain, 'as easier and elegant as they sounded, were generally barbarous, and of a pure *British* extraction'; this led him to acquire a knowledge of Welsh, and then, to follow the place-name development into the Middle Ages, Old English. He was particularly insistent on collating all the available documents on Roman Britain, and obtained details of the Peutinger Map (discovered in 1507), before its publication. Smith sums up the sequence of Camden's work:

> The old *Itinerary* being settled, the *British* and *Saxon* tongues in a good measure conquer'd, our ancient Historians perused, and several parts of England survey'd, he now began to think of reducing his Collections to method and order.

I do not think we can escape from the conclusion that the *Britannia* was originally planned to elucidate the topography of Roman Britain, and to present a picture of the Province, with reference to its development through Saxon and medieval times, which would enable Britain to take her rightful place at once within the world of antiquity and that of international Renaissance scholarship. Language and title alike declared its purpose: it was to have a European appeal, and, with the destruction of the myth of Trojan Brutus, was to establish Britain as a member of the fellowship of nations who drew their strength from roots struck deep in the Roman Empire.

It is for this reason, I suggest, that the framework of the *Britannia*, persisting through every edition, is that of the Celtic tribal areas of Britain as recorded in the classical geographers, with the English shires grouped within their accommodatingly vague boundaries. In such a scheme, too, the descriptions of British and Roman coins, and the recording of Roman inscriptions in growing numbers in each edition, so that by 1607 nearly eighty are included, would have significance, and not least of all, Camden's famous first-hand account of the Roman Wall, the most considerable monument in the Province, would form an appropriate climax, between the tribal area of the Brigantes and that of the Ottadini, the last tribe named before he reaches the remote regions of Scotia, and the outer Ocean.

If we accept this view of the original intention of the *Britannia*, we can also recognise that the scheme, in the simplicity outlined above, was not pedantically followed. To the Roman skeleton Camden added English flesh and blood. If some of his material was lifted, at times verbatim, from Leland's notes, it was none the less treated with so systematic a thoroughness, and subordinated to such a clearly conceived and individual pattern, that it takes on the character of original work.

Of the six editions of the *Britannia* which appeared in Camden's lifetime all were in Latin except the last, that of 1610, which was translated by Philemon Holland, the 'translator-general', and a second edition of this version appeared in 1637, after the author's death. By the 1607 Latin edition, the *Britannia* had already reached the status of a folio, and contained the well-known Saxton and Norden maps of the English countries, as well as the illustrations of British and Roman coins, and of Stonehenge, which had first been included in the edition of 1600, dedicated to Queen Elizabeth. The Stonehenge view is a version of a Dutch drawing of 1574, through the intermediary of an engraving dated a year later,[12] and Camden inclines to a cautious acceptance of the legend of Aurelius Ambrosius and Hengist which is engraved beneath the 1575 print.

The appearance of the English versions of the *Britannia* show in themselves a changing antiquarian public in this country. The original Latin work

---

12   E. H. Stone, *The Stones of Stonehenge* (London, 1924), 147.

was addressed to the world of European scholarship, as the interchange of
letters between Camden and his contemporary colleagues on the Continent
show. But by Jacobean times a new class of reader had grown up in England, anxious to read antiquarian literature written in English: a taste which
the *Britannia* itself had gone far to create. We have moved out of that Latin-
speaking fraternity of learning which, up to the time of Elizabeth, had
carried on the tradition of the scholars' *lingua franca*, and are in the new,
self-confident, national state in which, with the increase of literacy, an
interest in local history was no longer confined to the learned professions,
but was as likely to be found in the merchant or the country squire.

It is one of the greatest tributes that can be paid to Camden's sound
planning and construction, that when, at the end of the seventeenth century,
it was realised that a drastic re-editing of the *Britannia* would have to be
made in order to bring it into line with contemporary antiquarian thought, it
was possible to carry out this enlargement within the original framework
rather than to embark on a separate work *de novo*. This revised version
appeared in 1695, and we fortunately know the story of its progress and
achievement in some detail.

The 1695 *Britannia* is perhaps the best known of the editions, either in its
original one-volume form, or in the subsequent two volumes of 1722, and as
a work of that great figure of the Restoration church, Edmund Gibson,
Bishop successively of Lincoln and London, we probably most of us have
taken it without further thought, as the product of the ripe scholarship of a
dignified and mature churchman, his honours thick (and perhaps a trifle
heavy) upon him. But it is nothing of the kind. Gibson's scheme for re-
editing the *Britannia* orginated while he was still an undergraduate, and the
whole admirable achievement was the work of a young man who was
twenty-six years old when the book was published.[13]

The story begins, it is interesting to note, among a group of scholars
concerned with Old English studies who were, in the late seventeenth
century, taking up the tradition of Nowell, Lambarde, and Camden. They
were centred on Queen's College, Oxford, which became famous for its
'proluvium of Saxonists', led by Nicolson and Thwaites. Gibson came up
to Queen's in 1689, and at twenty-three published an edition of the *Anglo-
Saxon Chronicle*: in the same college he found, as a slightly junior fellow
undergraduate, Thomas Tanner, later to be 'one of the most erudite members of a learned Church',[14] and the two became fast and lifelong friends.
Gibson went down before Tanner, and it is from the letters written by him
in London to his friends in Oxford that we hear much of the progress of

13   For a Bibliographical Note on the 1695 *Britannia*, Gwyn Walters in facsimile ed.
(Newton Abbot, 1971), 14.
14   David Douglas, *English Scholars*, (London, 1939), 200 and *passim* for Gibson's
work.

the great task of re-editing the *Britannia* which he had taken upon himself.[15]

From the first, Gibson saw that the revision of the *Britannia* must be the work of a team of scholars under his general direction and editorship, as the task was far beyond the unaided efforts of a single individual. The initial problem presenting itself was that of translation, for it was generally agreed that Philemon Holland's version was in many ways unsatisfactory, and furthermore he had himself made unauthorised additions to the text. There appears to have been some discussion as to whether the new work should be in Latin or English, but the latter was decided upon, and it is interesting to note that Samuel Pepys, who was actively interested in the project, strongly recommended the use of English: here we presumably have the influence of the Royal Society's campaign for the use of the 'plaine English' which Camden had himself advocated, as we saw, as early as 1607. Gibson had met Pepys, on the introduction of Dr Arthur Charlett, Master of University College, Oxford, and would dine with him to discuss the work on the *Britannia* from time to time. New translations of the Latin text were therefore sponsored by Gibson, county by county, and he revised and collated the whole.

But more important was the question of additional material, similarly divided on a county basis. Here lay Gibson's main task as editor, and eventually he assembled some thirty contributors from among the antiquaries and historians of the day. They ranged in age from young Mr Tanner, not yet twenty-five, to old Mr Aubrey, who was nearly seventy, and included such famous names as John Evelyn, Samuel Pepys (who was responsible for the sections concerned with naval history), White Kennett, Ralph Thoresby, Robert Plot, Edward Lhwyd, and William Nicolson the Saxon scholar. It was a notable team, and it is a tribute to Gibson's charm and competence that he so successfully brought them together in the common enterprise. It is also significant of the growth of antiquarian interest since Camden's day that such a body of persons could be found.

The task of the editor was not however a uniformly easy one: contributors had to be handled with tact and firmness, or a rapid substitution made when an unsatisfactory choice had inadvertently been made. One of Gibson's triumphs was to secure from John Aubrey the use of material from his famous unpublished *Monumenta Britannica*, despite Aubrey's fear, voiced in a letter to Tanner in 1693, that the inclusion of extracts from the *Templa Druidum* section might prejudice its eventual publication as a complete work. But Tanner persuaded Aubrey to lend him the manuscript for transmission to Gibson in London, and his delay in sending it occasioned an

---

15   The letters to Tanner are in Bodleian MS. Tanner XXV, and those to Dr Charlett in Ballard V; some were published by Ellis, *Letters to Eminent Literary Men*, Camden Soc. XXIII (London, 1843).

amusing protest from the editor, with a lively sketch of the idle undergraduate's morning in Oxford –

> If you were to trot every day along *Cat-street* , and after a turn or two in the Schools quadrangle, to adjourn to Tom Swift's, I could excuse you for not sending your papers sooner. But when a man's cloysterd up in an old Monkish Lodge and the very Phys of his chamber is nothing but antiquitie itself; for such a one to make delays, is a little intolerable. If you knew how I am persecuted, you would not keep them a momʳ longer; old John Aubrey is dayly upon me, and the blame is as dayly layd upon poor Mr. Tanner.[16]

The papers arrived safely enough, but Gibson's reaction was one which will be appreciated by anyone who has tried to use Aubrey's still unpublished manuscript today:

> The accounts of things are so broken and short, the parts so much disorder'd, and the whole such a mere Rhapsody, that I cannot but wonder how that poor man could entertain thoughts of a present Impression.[17]

More serious trouble (but also, it must be confessed, some entertainment) was caused to Gibson by his unwary choice of that extraordinary character, John Toland, as the consultant on Ireland. Toland, whose books were to be burned by the public hangman and who was to be denounced with scandalised horror from every pulpit as the avowed champion of free thought, but whose enquiries into comparative religion show a mind of real anthropological acuteness, was at this time about Gibson's age, and already the centre of more than one scandal. There had been wild affairs with the students in Glasgow, and in Edinburgh (of which university he was a graduate) he had created a panic by declaring himself a Rosicrucian and setting off chemical flares which passed for the products of Black Magic; in London he had publicly burnt a prayer-book in a coffee-house. Gibson was intrigued and fascinated, and every piece of gossip was reported back to Tanner and Charlett in Oxford, where Toland was now living, but before any Irish memoranda were forthcoming they quarrelled – Gibson could not stand Toland's 'insolent conceited way of talking' – and this odd minor incident in the editing of the *Britannia* was closed.[18]

The work continued briskly in London and Oxford, with Gibson and Tanner in constant light-hearted consultation. The fact that the newly edited *Britannia* should be a paying proposition was not ignored:

---

16   Gibson to Tanner, 21 March 1693–4; Bodleian MS. Tanner XXV, f. 100.

17   Gibson to Tanner, 12 April 1694; MS. Tanner XXV, f. 134.

18   For the Toland gossip, see Ellis, op. cit., 226–9; Gibson to Charlett, 21 June 1694 (Bodleian MS. Ballard V, f. 48); Piggott, *William Stukeley* (Oxford, 1950), 99.

Hang't man, to lay too much stress upon *filthy lucre* is below the dispensa-
tion of Learning and a scholar; not but a great many good uses may be
made of 40 1. too.... After all, neighbour, it's a good honest way of getting
money[19]

wrote Gibson in connection with another literary project, and the editorial
business was conveniently discussed over beer at Mother Shepherd's in
Oxford, or wine at the Dog Tavern or Black Susan in London. Dr Gale was
helpful, Dr Bentley was interested, Ray was to do botanical notes – 'what
between herbs, camps, high-ways, families, etc. we shall have meat for all
palats'.[20]

After some discussion over the dedication, the new edition was published
early in 1695. It had been kept to one volume, despite the urgent desire of
the country gentry that the inclusion of all their pedigrees and details of
their estates should swell the work to several vast genealogical tomes.
Camden's newly translated text was followed by the additions, placed at the
end of each country. In Gibson's second edition, published in 1722 when he
was Bishop of London, the extra material was incorporated into the text,
though distinguished by enclosing it in square brackets, and the work had
grown to two folio volumes. As well as an introduction and a bibliography,
Gibson printed a translation of Thomas Smith's *Life* of Camden, originally
published in Latin together with Camden's letters in 1691, and the main
body of the work was prefaced by a transcript of the Antonine Itinerary
based on William Burton's edition. In addition to re-engraved plates of
British and Roman coins, a new section on Saxon coins was given, compiled by Walker and Thoresby. The county maps were by Robert Morden,
and the Stonehenge plate was re-engraved by Kip.

The new translation has precision, and a comfortable dignity, though one
regrets at times the enthusiastic, if wayward, style of Holland. We lose, for
instance, the charming phrase which describes Camden's visit to Hadrian's
Wall – 'Verily I have seene the tract of it over the high pitches and steepe
descents of hilles, wonderfully rising and falling', which is accurately, but
how flatly, rendered 'I have observ'd the track of it running up the moun-
tains and down again, in a most surprising manner'. But it is to Gibson that
we owe the exquisite rendering of the Elizabethan sentiment expressed by
Camden in his Introduction, in which Britain:

is the master-piece of Nature, perform'd when she was in her best and gayest
humour; which she placed as a little world by it self, by the side of the
greater, for the diversion of mankind.

---

19   Gibson to Tanner, 18 May [1694]; MS. Tanner XXV, f. 152.
20   Gibson to Charlett, 19 March 1693; MS. Ballard V, f. 14.

Here then was the *Britannia* adapted to the needs of the new school of antiquaries of the early eighteenth century, the circle of William Stukeley and the Gales, of Francis Wise, Ralph Thoresby and Sir John Clerk. Essentially, it was still Camden's work, with its Romano-British plan emphasised by the addition of the Itinerary and of Smith's new surveys of Hadrian's Wall given in the 1722 edition. But by this time the Act of Union of England and Scotland of 1707 necessitated an introductory essay describing this event, and after the word SCOTLAND in the title of the ensuing section are put in square brackets the significant words [OR NORTH-BRITAIN], and considerable additions based on Sir Robert Sibbald's work are given. There is also an account of the Antonine Wall, with half a dozen inscriptions and a plan of part of the Wall near Bo'ness by Timothy Pont, and a separate *Discourse Concerning the Thule of the Ancients* by Sibbald. *Britannia* now extended to the farthest bounds of the Roman Province.[21] Prehistory, too, had benefited, particularly by Gibson's summary of the seventeenth-century controversy on the date and origin of Stonehenge, and by the inclusion of a short description of Avebury from the *Monumenta Britannica*.

For nearly seventy years the 1722 edition of the *Britannia* was to hold the field, the third, and last, major revision being published in 1789 and reprinted in 1806. In the 1720s the great tradition of the Restoration historians was still alive, and works of outstanding scholarship in English medieval studies were being published; William Stukeley was carrying out his finest piece of field-work at Avebury, which would have set a new standard in the observation and record of a major prehistoric monument, had he published it then in its original form and not, twenty years later, as a religious tract involved in the fantasies of his Druidic Christianity.

But already by the middle of the century, and increasingly in its second half, the standard of historical and archaeological studies was sadly on the decline. Let me quote Professor David Douglas:

Medieval scholarship in England [he writes] underwent during the eighteenth century not a development but a reaction. These studies between 1730 and 1800 made no advance comparable to that which had been achieved in the previous seventy years. The stultifying of so promising a growth, the slackening of an endeavour which had been marked by such devoted labour was a phenomenon in the development of English culture which was very remarkable.[22]

So much for medieval research, the low state of which in the later eighteenth century Professor Douglas has shown in melancholy detail in the work from which I have quoted. In antiquarian or archaeological studies the story was

21 Cf. Piggott, *Ruins in a Landscape*, ch. VII.
22 David Douglas, *op. cit.*, 355.

much the same. Stukeley's own intellectual decline and fall after about 1725–30 is now familiar, and among its unedifying events stands out his acceptance of the forged Itinerary of Roman Britain by the bogus Richard of Cirencester, which bedevilled the study of Roman Britain for generations.[23] But Stukeley was not alone in acclaiming Richard as an authority equal to, or rather better than, the Antonine Itinerary, and the state of contemporary archeological scholarship and textual criticism is only too well shown by the enthusiastic election of Charles Bertram, the undergraduate who had invented Richard and written his Itinerary for him, as an Honorary Fellow of the Society of Antiquities of London in 1750.

It is, I think, in the second half of the eighteenth century that we really see the emergence of the antiquary as Sir Walter Scott saw him; Jonathan Oldbucks who eagerly identified Roman camps from hearsay rather than field-work, collectors of curios and old armour, uncritical and credulous, and ignorant of the essential disciplines of their scholarship in a way which would have horrified Gibson or Tanner or the young Stukeley. It was in this atmosphere of ponderous but ineffective dilettantism that the final editing of the *Britannia* took place.

Richard Gough, who undertook this work, was a country gentleman who, after going up to Corpus Christi College, Cambridge, had devoted his time to antiquarian travels in England. We today have reason to remember Gough with gratitude for his vast collection of topographical material – maps, drawings, plans, notes – which forms, in the Bodleian Library, a source of invaluable information still waiting for a detailed catalogue,[24] but we cannot come to his edition of the *Britannia* with the enthusiasm which Gibson's work unconsciously inspires in us. He began the task, he says, in 1773, when he was thirty-eight, and had already published his *Anecdotes of British Topography*, but it was sixteen years before the three folio volumes were published in 1789.

It is clear from Gough's preface that he regarded the task as one of antiquarian piety rather than the provision of a work of contemporary scholarship newly fashioned from the old stock. 'Without entering into the details of a county historian', he writes, 'or adopting the mode of a modern writer of a description of England I have endeavoured to do that for Mr. Camden, which Mr. Camden in the same circumstances, would have done for himself'. What we are to understand by 'in the same circumstances' is obscure, but the general tenor is plain. The approach is that of one who reveres the antique for its own sake, with the *Britannia* padded out with miscellaneous topographical notes; the annotating of a curious old book with affectionate antiquarian memoranda.

---

23   Piggott, *op. cit.*, 154.
24   For summary list see now M. W. Barley, *Guide to British Topographical collections* (London [C.B.A.] 1974), 95.

In his work Gough enlisted the help of his fellow antiquaries, but with very few exceptions the list he gives is one of nonentities. Pennant's help for Wales and Scotland must however be noted, and for the latter country Gough also received an important contribution from General Robert Melville, whose field-work first revealed the existence of Roman military works north of the Tay, and who encouraged and assisted Roy in the preparation of his great *Military Antiquities of the Romans in North Britain*, eventually published in 1793.[25]

The new edition continued to preserve the general form of the *Britannia* as contained in Gibson's recension, with the addition of a great deal of miscellaneous topographical information in the text, and the provision of a considerably enlarged number of illustrations. Maps of Roman and Saxon Britain are provided, the former unfortunately owing much to Richard of Cirencester, and prehistoric, Roman and Saxon antiquities bulk large in the engraved plates: in addition to those recorded in the text, there are over 220 Roman inscriptions and sculptures illustrated in the countries of Cumberland and Northumberland. The standard of the illustrations varies considerably – there is an excellent plan of Maiden Castle, Dorset, for instance, probably taken from that by Watson and Roy of 1756,[26] but the plans of Wiltshire hill-forts such as Yarnbury or Chiselbury are woeful. Yet there is a very great deal of material recorded in these plates, ranging from the Cerne Giant (unfortunately emasculated) to a plan of Silchester, from Kentish Saxon jewellery to Welsh Early Christian monuments and plans and details of major ecclesiastical buildings of the Middle Ages. Scotland is dealt with in greater detail than before, and Melville's notable additions to the knowledge of Roman antiquities in that region have been mentioned, while the Irish section contains illustrations of a very large series of Bronze Age antiquities, including the famous Irish Royal Crown (which is really a gold bowl of the Late Bronze Age illustrated upside-down).

But despite these important records, it is impossible to avoid the conclusion that Gough's edition of the *Britannia* is really a failure. It was undertaken too late, when the usefulness of Camden's great pioneer was diminishing with the appearance of detailed county or regional histories, and it was undertaken at a time when historical and archaeological studies were at a noticeably low ebb. By the opening years of the nineteenth century, when such studies were reviving, antiquarian topography was to be better served by such works as the Lysons' *Magna Britannia* series, by individual county histories, or such archaeological monographs as Sir Richard Colt Hoare's *Ancient Wiltshire*.[27] From the time of its first publication in 1586, Camden's *Britannia* had remained a source of inspiration to British antiquarian studies

25   G. Macdonald in *Arch.* LXVIII (1917), 161–228.
26   R. E. M. Wheeler, *Maiden Castle, Dorset* (Oxford 1943), 6.
27   Cf. Piggott, *Ruins in a Landscape*, ch. VI.

until their own decline in the first third of the eighteenth century, and Gibson's second edition of 1722 really marks the end of an epoch. The age of the great pioneers was at an end, after a century and a half of inspired and devoted labour which culminated, with the Restoration historians, in an achievement of scholarship and industry that we can still regard with respectful and astonished admiration. Then was to come the anti-climax, even though local history was less affected than the wider field of investigation of the English medieval past, and we must not forget that Edward Gibbon, having completed his Olympian study of the dying fall of the classical world, recommended in 1793 the systematic publication of English medieval records that was later to become a national undertaking. But this was at the end of the century, and Horace Walpole, to whom the Middle Ages was a bric-à-brac shop from which he could pick out material for an elegant (and inaccurate) historical essay, or Gothic rococo ornament that had 'the true rust of the Barons' Wars', is a more representative figure of the age. Richard Gough admired Camden, but did not appreciate that the time had come to begin afresh, as Camden himself had done as he stood with his back to the Middle Ages and set down the historical links that bound the topography of his England to the medieval world, the Saxon past, and to Rome herself.

3

JOHN STOW AND HIS LONDON

M. J. Power

In 1598 John Stow, a citizen of London, completed *A Survey of London* containing "the original, antiquity, increase, modern estate and description of that City". He described his motives in a dedication of the 1603 edition of the *Survey* to the Lord Mayor, commonalty and citizens of the City:

> Since the first publishing of the perambulation of Kent by that learned Gentleman William Lambert Esquier, I have heard of sundry other able persons to have ... assayed to do somewhat for the particular Shires or Counties where they were borne or dwelt ... And therefore ... I have attempted the discovery of London, my native soyle and countrey.[1]

Moved by the same impulse to describe and explain the appearance and history of his home ground that affected a whole fellowship of Tudor topographers he stands out among them because he tackled a town rather than a county. The result was a survey of incomparable detail and interest.[2]

Although all historians of medieval and sixteenth-century London depend heavily on Stow's *Survey* it has rarely been subjected to systematic scrutiny. The aim of this paper is to fill this gap by mapping the information that Stow gives about the sixteenth-century city.[3] Producing such a visual record will, it is hoped, allow three problems to be investigated: first the value of the survey to the historian of sixteenth-century London; second the physi-

---

1   J. Stow, *A Survey of London* (hereafter Stow), ed. C. L. Kingsford (Oxford, 1908) I, xcvii.

2   John Hooker was the only describer of a town, Exeter. For a brief survey of Tudor topographical writing see A. L. Rowse, *The England of Elizabeth* (London 1950) second prologue; and, on Stow, see H. R. Trevor-Roper, 'John Stow', *Transactions of the London and Middlesex Archaeological Society* (hereafter *TLMAS*) 26 (1975), 337.

3   C. L. Kingsford subjected the *Survey* to intense scrutiny in his edition, and his notes on individual London buildings are unrivalled but he did not draw back to consider the topographical pattern of London. The maps accompanying this paper were drawn by Jennifer Wyatt in the Geography Drawing Office in the University of Liverpool.

cal, economic and social morphology of the city at the end of the century; and third the extent of change in the Tudor capital.

An extended commentary on Stow himself is unnecessary because of the definitive account of his life pieced together by C. L. Kingsford. Born in 1525 of a tallow chandler who lived in Throgmorton Street, John Stow became a merchant tailor and set up in business in a house inside Aldgate in the eastern part of the City. He moved in the 1570s to another house in Aldgate Street in the parish of St Andrew Undershaft at about the time he began to exchange the craft of the tailor for that of the scholar. At first he worked on the history of the nation and it was only in his final years that he turned to the local study which resulted in his *Survey of London*. The first edition appeared in 1598 only seven years before his death.[4]

Stow's *Survey* tackles London in two distinct ways. The early and late chapters describe features of London as a whole, the wall, rivers, institutions, government and so on. The large middle chunk of the survey, 29 chapters long, contains a descriptive perambulation of each ward of the City, and of the suburbs and Westminster, with the boundaries, monuments and history of each small area closely examined. It is this central part of the survey, at the heart of the work and written first, which is the focus of our attention.[5] What kind of information does it contain, and how adequate an impression of London does it convey?

It is obvious that Stow gives much more attention to the City proper than to the suburbs or Westminster. Each of the City wards is given a chapter to itself (300 pages in all in the Kingsford edition), whereas the suburbs, the Liberty of the Duchy of Lancaster, and the city of Westminster, are dealt with in only three chapters (55 pages in all). Suburban Southwark is dealt with as one of the wards, Bridge Without (17 pages). This emphasis masks the fact that the suburbs were very populous and already approaching the point where their inhabitants would outnumber those of the City.[6] Stow's interest is therefore biased heavily in favour of the City, probably because of the greater interest and antiquity of the buildings there.

It was in buildings, the physical fabric of the capital that Stow was chiefly interested, but in recording them he provided a great deal of additional information about the commerce and industry, society, and sixteenth-cen-

4   Stow I vii–xxv, xxxvi–xxxviii; S. Rubinstein, *Historians of London* (London, 1968), 26–7.
5   Stow I xxxvii.
6   This had probably happened before 1640: R. Finlay, *Population and metropolis* (Cambridge, 1981), 61–2.

tury growth and development of London. It is our first task to assess how
adequate a picture he provides of each. To have recorded every building in
London would have produced a survey of immense length and tedium. Stow
avoided this by picking out only those he found interesting because of their
size or appearance. The great town palaces, Baynard Castle, Somerset House,
Arundel House, Whitehall Palace, Stow exulted over but more traditional
urban housing also caught his eye, particularly when handsome or deco-
rated, Goldsmiths' Row in Cheap, for example. Most houses, however, were
merged in Stow's description under such adjectives as 'many' or 'diverse',
which tell us very little about the quality of the number of the dwellings
involved.[7]

Just how selective Stow was in picking out houses for comment is difficult
to say. On only one occasion does he give an idea of the total number of
houses in an area, and then only indirectly. He tells us that there were some
1800 householders in the ward of Cripplegate outside the walls. The only
buildings he describes there are 'one Alley of divers tenementes' by St Giles
churchyard, 'many fayre houses' in Red Cross Street, 'beautifull houses of
stone, bricke &c timber' on Beech Lane, two almshouses outside the postern,
a watchtower and the Garterhouse along Barbican, a 'number of ... Dicing-
houses' in Grub Street, and 'many tenements of poore people' in Golding
Lane. We have, therefore, about eight sets of houses mentioned which must
have contained the 1800 households, and his descriptions 'some', 'a number
of' and 'many' must cover many hundreds of houses in each case.[8]

We can obtain a further perspective on Stow's description of housing by
comparing the *Survey* with the best map of London surveyed in his lifetime,
the 'Copperplate Map'. The comparison is apt because Stow himself probably knew the map well. It dates from 1558–9 and it has been argued that he
used it as a base map to guide him while he worked on the *Survey*.[9] If we
concentrate on three central streets in the area to which Stow paid most
attention (see Figure 1), Poultry (unnamed, running east-west at the top),
Bucklersbury (running roughly parallel below it), and Budge Row (turning
away southwards at the bottom), each source can be tested against the other.
Along the north side of Poultry the map shows a block containing a church
and four houses (counting doorways and roofs). Stow describes the church,
four houses, a prison, Coneyhope Lane, and a warehouse. Here Stow is
more comprehensive, describing at least one building and a lane not shown
on the map. In contrast, a comparison of the treatment of the north side of
Bucklersbury goes in favour of the map. It shows five or, perhaps, ten
houses (five doorways; ten roofs). Stow mentions only one house, a timber-

7   Stow I, 345.
8   Stow I, 301–03; II, 79–80.
9   M. Holmes, 'A source book for Stow', in A. E. J. Hollaender and W. H. Kellaway
(eds), *Studies in London history presented to P. E. Jones* (London, 1969), 279–84.

framed structure built to replace an old stone tower which Buckle, a grocer, had pulled down. Finally, along Budge Row, where the map shows eight or ten houses (eight doorways; ten roofs), Stow fails us completely. He ignores houses altogether, and mentions only two churches there.

We should not expect a sixteenth-century topographer or a mid-sixteenth century mapmaker to provide a complete survey of urban property, but the comparison of the two partial sources is instructive. Stow is clearly more informative about the character and history of those buildings he does describe but the map scores as a more comprehensive guide to the housing stock. A greater drawback to Stow for our purposes is that he is erratic, sometimes describing many houses, at other times mentioning few or no houses.

In describing dwellings Stow usually categorizes them as large or fair houses, houses, tenements or cottages. His use of the adjective 'fair' presumably indicates a handsome or well-kept house. 'Large' seems to indicate high. Along Cornhill he remarks on 'divers large houses especially for height'.[10] Tenement is a term Stow uses in two senses. On occasion he employs it in its modern sense, as a flat or apartment within a larger house. Thus, a great stone house on the south side of Bucklersbury, called the Old Barge, 'hath of long time beene divided and letten out into many tenementes'. More commonly he uses the term to describe individual smaller dwellings. The Earl of Shrewsbury demolished a great house on Dowgate called Coldharbour and 'builded a great number of small tenements now letten out for great rents to people of all sortes'. East of the Tower, tenement was used as a synonym for cottage. Possibly cottage and tenement were terms for dwellings too small to house a business or craft, unlike a house which was large enough for work and residence.[11] We should thus keep two problems in mind when using Stow's description of London housing, his erratic selection, and the undefined categories he uses.

Commerce and industry dominated the sixteenth-century city and are the subject of much comment in Stow's *Survey*. He carefully notes Company Halls, 46 of them in all.[12] The City markets are all mentioned: Leadenhall, the Stocks, East Cheap, Bakewell Hall and an additional cloth house nearby, Old Fish Street, Cheap, Newgate and Smithfield, nine in all.[13] Twenty river

10   Stow I, 194.
11   Stow I, 259, 237; II, 71; cottage was originally the description of a dwelling of cottars or farm labourers, house an all-embracing term for a building for human habitation: *Oxford English Dictionary*.
12   G. Unwin, *The gilds and companies of London* (4th edn London, 1963) mentions 28 company halls in the reign of Richard III and shows a total of 62 halls through the centuries on a map: 146, 185.
13   F. J. Fisher, 'The development of the London food market 1540–1640', *Economic History Review* V (1934–35) lists four major food markets at Newgate, Leadenhall, Cheapside and Gracechurch Street: 57–8.

Figure 1. Section from the "Copperplate Map" of London, c. 1558–59.

quays are named (there were 21 listed in an inquisition of 1584).[14] And major institutions, the Custom House, the Royal Exchange, the Guildhall, the Bridewell workhouse and 14 Inns of Court all receive mention.[15] Stow's list of such public or semi-public monuments seems comprehensive. His attention to private traders and craftsmen is more sporadic. He notes a range of dealers: drapers, grocers, skinners, haberdashers, mercers, vintners, stationers, apothecaries, ironmongers, salters and brokers, but seems to do this only when there were noticable groups of them living together, as in Bucklersbury, where the 'whole streete ... on both the sides throughout is possessed of Grocers and Apothecaries'.[16] Individual dealers elsewhere, perhaps trading anonymously behind domestic fronts, escaped mention.

The same is true of craftsmen. Where groups congregated they are noted: founders along Lothbury could hardly be missed, 'making a loathsome noise to the by-passers'; and on the south side of St Paul's Cathedral cutlers, licensed 'first to builde low sheddes, but now high Houses, which doe hide that beautifull side of the Church', receive the writer's censure. He notes, too, craftsmen whose premises caught the eye: shipwrights in Ratcliff, brewers along the Thames, brickmakers in Spitalfields, tenter grounds along Hog Lane, the armament foundry of the Owen brothers on Houndsitch.[17] But the 45 references to industrial premises in the *Survey* scarcely make up an adequate census of the number of craftsmen in London.

Similarly Stow's mention of food purveyors, bakers, fishmongers, butchers, cheesemongers, cooks, gives no idea of the numbers involved, though the areas where he mentions them may be presumed to be centres where their work was concentrated. He mentions inns only 27 times, surely only a fraction of the true number of residential hostelries, and an ever smaller fraction of the many humbler taverns and victualling houses.[18] In short, Stow gives us an impression of the obvious concentrations of traders, craftsmen and food and drink purveyors, not a thorough survey.

His approach to the social characteristics of his city is limited by the same practical limitation. The major social institutions are all noted: the six

---

14   B. Dietz, *The port and trade of Elizabethan London* (London Record Society 8, 1972), 160–1.

15   Sir John Fortescue described 4 Inns of Court and 10 Inns of Chancery in *De Laudibus Legum Angliae*: W. R. Prest, *The Inns of Court under Elizabeth I and the early Stuarts* (London, 1972), 1–2.

16   Stow I, 260.

17   Stow I, 277; II, 19; see, on this theme, P. Glanville, 'John Stow', *TLMAS* 31 (1980), 129.

18   In 1613 the Lord Mayor thought that there were over 1000 in the City: W. H. and H. C. Overall (eds) *Analytical index to the Remembrancia* (London, 1878), 541. By the 1620s there were estimated to be over 3,000 tippling houses in City and suburbs: P. Clark, The alehouse and the alternative society, in D. Pennington and K. Thomas (eds), *Puritans and revolutionaries: essays in seventeenth-century history presented to Christopher Hill* (Oxford, 1978), 50.

hospitals of Bedlam, Christ's, St Bartholomew's, the Savoy, St Thomas's
and the lazar house in Southwark; the workhouse at Bridewell; eight schools;
ten prisons; courts of law at Newgate, Southwark, Guildhall and Westminster Hall; and 21 almshouses with details of their endowments and
organization. But if we abstract from his survey mention of notable residents a very sketchy picture emerges. He mentions only 11 aldermen's
houses (there were 26 aldermen); he identifies 18 town houses of aristocrats
and 14 of gentlemen, surely underestimating the numbers of each group
with London houses (though he does refer to unspecified numbers of gentlemen living along Holborn and the Strand). Twelve government servants'
residences and four episcopal palaces complete the list of his notables.[19] In
only nine spots does Stow mention places of entertainment, principally
bowling alleys and bear pits. He totally ignores theatres and drinking houses,
apart from the inns he mentions. Such places cannot have been too anonymous or numerous to include, and we can only conclude that he ignored
them as uninteresting or unworthy of his notice.[20] We gain, at best, a partial
view of the social characteristics of London from the *Survey*.

New building, by contrast, was a phenomenon which fascinated and
concerned Stow. Within the City proper he seems to make a point of
identifying construction, often mentioning in detail who was responsible,
the character of the reconstruction, and the history of building on the site.
He even makes a point of commenting on repairs and additions made to
houses. We cannot be sure that he mentions every new building to be
erected in the sixteenth-century City, but the number of them (about 150
within the walls alone), and the fact that new buildings often elicit a
personal opinion from him, suggest they were of fundamental importance
in his *Survey*.

He not infrequently makes some implied or explicit judgement on the
builder. The builders of houses in Petty France outside Bishopsgate ob-
structed the City ditch, regarding more 'their owne private gaine than the
common good of the Cittie' for the cluttered ditch was in danger of
'impoysoning the whole Cittie'. He deplored unjust speculative builders,
such as one Russell, a draper, who rebuilt houses on Bishopsgate Street near
Shoreditch; 'and let them out for rent enough, taking also large Fines of the
Tenantes, neare as much as the houses cost him purchase, and building for
hee made his bargaines so hardly with all men, that both Carpenter, Brick-

---

19   L. Stone suggests that 30 peers owned London houses by 1560 and more rented or
leased London houses (59 by the 1620s). The number of gentry resident in London he
estimates to have been several hundred by the 1630s: *The crisis of the aristocracy* (Oxford
1965), 394–8. W. P. M. Kennedy lists 27 bishops in his *Elizabethan episcopal administration* (Alcuin Club XXV, 1924) I, xi, and we might expect this number of bishops resident in
London at time of synod or parliament.
20   Shakespeare and the dramatic scene are entirely ignored: H. R. Trevor-Roper,
'John Stow', *TLMAS* 26 (1975), 341; Stow, I, xl–xli.

layer, and Playsterer, were by that Worke undone. And yet in honour of his name, it is now called Russels Row'.[21]

In addition to new houses Stow points out the new institutions, churches, company halls, almshouses, water pumps and cisterns, industrial concerns, places of entertainment and gardens which made the sixteenth-century capital change and grow so rapidly. Most new building must have occurred in the suburbs where there was room for expansion and Stow's unease about the suburban sprawl is very obvious. Whitechapel Road, outside Aldgate, was described as 'no small blemish to so famous a city, to have so unsavery and unseemly an entry'. And he decries the fashion for 'fayre summer houses, and as in other places of the Suburbes, some of them like Midsommer Pageantes, with Towers, Turrets, and Chimney tops ... for shew and pleasure, bewraying the vanity of mens mindes, much unlike to the disposition of the ancient Cittizens, who delighted in the building of Hospitals, and Almes houses for the poore'. We hear the sober tone of a writer well into his seventies for whom development was not necessarily progress, even in his own beloved city, living in 'the most scoffing, carping, respectlesse, and unthankeful age that ever was'.[22]

What has been said so far might suggest that Stow should be read only to gain a general impression of the topography of the capital at the end of Elizabeth's reign, and that to attempt to map his *Survey* would be to express in exact form evidence that is partial and impressionistic. This view would carry weight if one views maps as valid only if they represent the exact and comprehensive truth about an area. However maps always represent partial truth, the aspects of an area that the cartographer notices as significant and chooses to represent. Stow's view of London represents an amalgam of what was visually arresting to an observer who perambulated the city streets and his particular concerns and prejudices. Though less comprehensive in his survey of housing than a cartographer would be Stow's noting of occupations, élite residents and rebuilding make his record of the city more three-dimensional.[23]

---

21   Stow I, 164; II, 74–5.

22   Stow II, 72, 78; I, xli; most commentators agree on Stow's nostalgia and his disapproval of the hardship caused to the poor by the speculative builders of the late-sixteenth century: see R. Ashton, 'Stow's London', *TLMAS* 29 (1978), 137; V. Pearl, 'John Stow', *TLMAS* 30 (1979), 132.

23   Overall, the impressions left by maps and by Stow are comfortingly similar. The distribution of housing described by Stow fits well with that shown on Braun and Hogenberg's map published in 1572. This displays the ribbon development along the major streets out of

Because he is selective, maps derived from his *Survey* will lack quantitative precision, but this does not mean that they will be misleading. With certain exceptions, such as theatres, Stow was an omnivorous observer and there is reason to suppose that he looked at each parish in the same way. He systematically describes the church, the notable buildings street by street, and particular residents or clusters of tradesmen which characterized each. There is no reason, therefore, to suppose that mapping will not give a fairly reliable view of the differences between different districts. Moreover, it is only by mapping the *Survey* that an overall view of the distribution and juxtaposition of topographical elements in London can be obtained. A reading of his text, if it is not to stop at an impression of the parts, naturally leads one on to an attempt to see the whole, most easily and conveniently on maps. It is with this aim, of assimilating the overall morphology of London in the late-sixteenth century, that the rest of this paper is concerned.

To begin with housing, Figure 2 records Stow's description of the physical appearance of the London he studied. He saw it as a gracious city, with a preponderance of 'fair' and 'large' houses. The City within the walls is dominated by them, though a few groups of humbler houses and tenements are obvious to the north and east of St Paul's, by the north wall inside Cripplegate, around Cornhill, and by the river west of London Bridge. As one moves into the West End and Westminster a number of very grand houses stand out; some were residential institutions, Bridewell, the Temple, Lincoln's Inn and the Savoy Hospital; others were aristocratic and royal palaces, Somerset House, Arundel House, Scotland Yard and Whitehall Palace. What most disturbs the overall impression of fair housing is the number of humbler houses and tenements to the north and east of the city walls, and in Southwark. Along and around the main streets leading out from Aldersgate, Bishopsgate and Aldgate into the suburbs humble dwellings are common, particularly in the East End and Southwark where the tenement and the cottage are the norm. The overall pattern does not conform to the suggested natural form of a preindustrial city, with wealthy centre and poor periphery.[24] Instead London seems to possess a wealthy centre and western suburb and uniformly poor eastern and southern suburbs.

The economic morphology of London is more complex and in many ways more interesting than the pattern of housing. Figure 3 plots Stow's references to commerce and industry. The most immediate impression is the heavy concentration of activity inside the city walls. This effect is partly explained by the situation of every company hall but one (the Cooks') in

---

London so evident in Stow, and within the walls the map shows gardens in areas of the City in which Stow mentions few buildings, west of Austin Friars, near the Tower and in Blackfriars, for example: A. Prockter and R. Taylor, *The A to Z of Elizabethan London* (Lympne Castle, 1979), 32.

24   G. Sjoberg, *The pre-industrial city* (New York, 1960), 97–8.

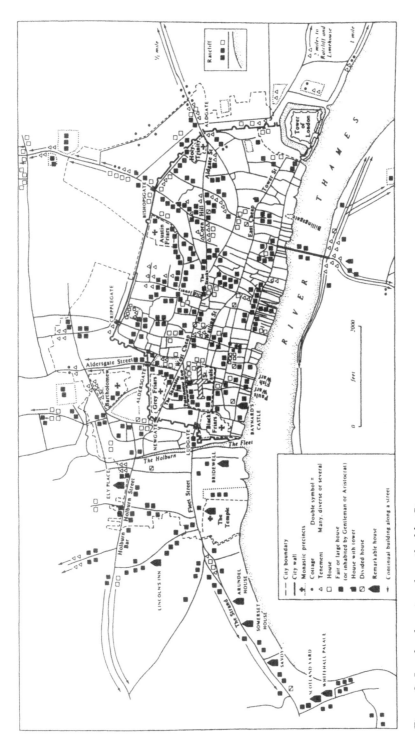

Figure 2. London housing described by Stow

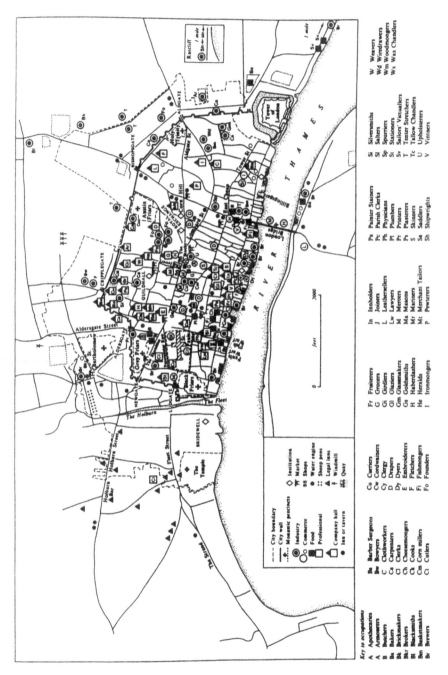

Figure 3. London commerce and industry described by Stow

this central area. These were most heavily concentrated north of Cheap (22 halls) and south of Cheap, especially near the river (18 halls). East of Gracechurch Street there were comparatively few (only 6). No obvious pattern emerges from this distribution. Merchant company halls mingle at random with craft company halls. Some halls are situated where one would expect the trade or craft to be concentrated: the halls of the vintners, fishmongers and woodmongers are near the Thames; those of the mercers and grocers are near Cheap, the main commercial street. But others, the Brewers' Hall inside Cripplegate, for example, far away from the river, are not. Some halls are surrounded by the members of the company: founders on Lothbury, butchers by Greyfriars, fishmongers by London Bridge, vintners on the riverside east of Queenhithe. But in other cases Stow does not mention members of a company anywhere near their hall. One possible explanation for this lack of coherence is the small-scale world of London within the walls. Wherever one lived would not be far from the company hall. Furthermore, movement of groups of traders or craftsmen in search of a better market was not uncommon and was not usually followed by moving the company hall.

That groups of traders and craftsmen moved Stow himself tells us: 'men of trades and sellers of wares in this City have often times since chaunged their places, as they have found their best advantage'.[25] The tendency for occupational groups to cluster together was long-established, being noted by FitzStephen in his description of London in the reign of Henry II, and has been seized upon by modern scholars as one characteristic of a medieval city.[26] Some 64 groups of commercial and industrial workers noted by Stow in his perambulation are transcribed on Figure 3. Commercial groups, mercers, drapers, haberdashers, and skinners predominate in the centre, particularly along the major streets, Cheap and Watling Street, where as dealers they no doubt 'found their best advantage'. Stow seldom mentions shops, but where he does, they too are in this central area. Comparatively few dealers are found towards the edge of the City (mercers by Ludgate, mercers and haberdashers on London Bridge), and only two groups appear outside the walls, brokers near St Bartholomew's and leathersellers in Southwark.

Industrial groups, by contrast, are more common towards the City perimeter: brewers, millers and dyers line the riverside; founders, silversmiths, printers, carpenters and curriers cluster to the north by Aldersgate and Cripplegate; and basketmakers, wiredrawers, carpenters and glassmakers are found towards Aldgate. The central area is not devoid of craftsmen: goldsmiths and upholsterers live along Cheap, and curriers and cordwainers

25   Stow I, 81.
26   Stow II, 222–24; J. E. Vance, 'Land assignment in pre-capitalist, capitalist and post-capitalist cities', *Economic Geography* 47 (1971), 115.

on Soper Lane show that craftsmen infiltrate there too. But the general pattern of dealers monopolizing the City centre and craftsmen the periphery is clear, and the pattern is accentuated by the presence of brickmakers, tenter grounds, carpenters, founders, armourers and shipwrights outside the walls in the east, which appears to be an early industrial suburb. In sharp contrast, the area to the west of the City has all the appearance of a professional suburb, dominated by lawyers.

The disposition of markets and food purveyors is equally striking. Four food markets lie along the central axis of the city from Newgate to Aldgate, running along Cheap and Cornhill: Newgate, Cheap, the Stocks and Leadenhall. Two cloth markets are to the north near the Guildhall. The two fish markets are situated near the river, along Old Fish Street and in East Cheap. And the meat markets are at Newgate (the Shambles) and outside the walls at Smithfield. The concentration of markets along the major east-west street, and the absence of markets outside the walls (with the exception of Smithfield where slaughtering took place) is striking. London may have been expanding, a mile west towards Westminster and a mile east to Ratcliff, but markets remained highly centralized.

Food purveyors, on the whole, follow the markets: butchers cluster near the Shambles inside Newgate; fishmongers live near the fish markets in East Cheap and Old Fish Street; and grocers are found along Poultry near the Stocks market. Bakers are more isolated, selling probably from shops to the south of St Paul's and near the Tower. Two groups of food purveyors are found in the suburbs: bakers north-east of the Tower in the Navy Victualling Office, and alongside the river in Southwark; and ships' victuallers along the riverside of Wapping towards Ratcliff.

Two other economic features are worth comment. Quaysides which served the London commercial and craft fraternities line the riverside, 14 situated upstream of London Bridge, 6 downstream, and 1 on the south bank. Inns are found along the major roads into the City, the Strand, Holborn, near Smithfield, Bishopsgate Street, Aldgate Street, and to the south of London Bridge in Southwark, where they could best catch their trade.[27] Within the walls there were groups of them lining the major north-south route from Bishopsgate to London Bridge, and in the area of Bread Street.

The overall economic picture, therefore, is of a very dense concentration of commercial and industrial activity in the City within the walls, with dealers and markets monopolising the major central streets, and craftsmen towards the periphery, and all served by a concentrated quay system. The only significant exceptions to this concentration of economic activity are the crafts in the East End, professional groups in the West End, and inns surrounding the City. The flight of industry to the suburbs, if we trust Stow's

---

27   P. Clark, *op. cit.*, 48–9, on nature of inns.

evidence, is a phenomenon that had hardly got under way in the sixteenth century.[28]

To complement this economic morphology of London we should take account of the social characteristics of the capital described by Stow, mapped in Figure 4. We can get some idea of the location of the social élite in London by his occasional reference to aristocracy, gentry and government servants. As we might expect Westminster and the West End here come into their own. The natural leaders of society live in a suburb whose social tone must have been quite different from that of the City. It was more socially exclusive than the City, a street such as the Strand monopolized by the houses of the great, Lord Burghley, Sir Robert Cecil, the Earl of Bedford and the Lord Chancellor. A physical characteristic that promoted this exclusiveness was the absence of back-yards and alleys in the West End where poorer groups might have lived.[29]

In the congested City, with its many back-alleys and yards as well as major streets, society was more mixed. All the aldermen mentioned by Stow lived within the walls; so too did some landowners and government servants, often near the walls in monastic precincts: Holy Trinity Aldgate had housed the Duke of Norfolk; Austin Friars the Marquis of Winchester, for example. With these governing groups lived the traders, craftsmen and labourers who made up a majority of the City's population. We lack an occupational or social census of the City in Stow's time but analysis of hearth tax evidence in the 1660s shows at that date a considerable intermingling of rich and poor, commerce and craft, skilled and unskilled, in the same parishes and even in the same streets.[30]

Stow is disappointing as a guide to society in the East End and Southwark. We know from parish register evidence that the East End had a poor working society dominated by mariners, ship repairers and victuallers, with few wealthy merchants and even fewer landowners.[31] In Southwark, Stow's noting of prisons is suggestive if we assume that they set or reflect the social tone of an area.

The distribution of social institutions differ with their function. Of eight schools six were centrally placed within the walls, one was at Westminster, and one at Ratcliff. In addition Gresham College was established inside Bishopsgate. The great hospitals, in contrast, formed a ring around the

28   V. Pearl, *London and the outbreak of the Puritan Revolution* (Oxford, 1961), 15–16.

29   M. J. Power, East and West in early-modern London in J. J. Scarisbrick *et al.* (eds) *Wealth and power in Tudor England* (London, 1978), 177–82; Braun and Hogenberg's map of London in Prockter and Taylor, *op cit.*, 32.

30   Poor people tended to concentrate in back-yards and alleys: M. J. Power, 'The social topography of Restoration London', to be published in *The making of the metropolis*, eds R. Finlay and A. L. Beier.

31   East London History Group, 'The population of Stepney in the early-seventeenth century', *East London Papers* 11 (1968), 83–4.

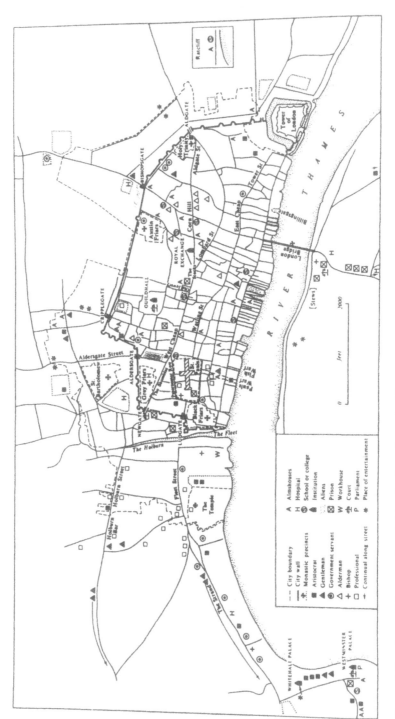

Figure 4. London residents and social institutions described by Stow

walls, reflecting their monastic antecedents: Bedlam, for the insane, was outside Bishopsgate; Christ's Hospital, the City orphanage, and St Bartholomew's, for the sick, were by Newgate; Bridewell, the workhouse, was outside Ludgate; and St Thomas's, for the sick, was sited at the south end of London Bridge. The Savoy Hospital, rebuilt by Henry VII for the poor, was further out, along the Strand, as was the lazar house in Southwark. The 21 almshouses were more evenly spread: 15 within the walls, 1 outside the wall near the Tower, 2 to the north of Cripplegate, and 3 in Westminster. Interestingly, no almshouse was situated in the western suburbs apart from Westminster, an inverse reflection, perhaps, of a relatively wealthy population.[32] Prisons were situated in groups: the two compters of the sheriff of London were north of Cheap; a large group, the Clink, the Surrey compter, King's Bench, Marshalsea and White Lion, were in Southwark; and the Fleet and Newgate prisons nestled in the area between the city wall and the Fleet river. The City compters apart, all were sited in areas apparently considered undesirable by the national and civic élite.[33]

Places of entertainment, insofar as Stow noted them, were found in Southwark (two bear pits), outside Aldgate (bowling alleys), outside Cripplegate and Aldersgate (bowling alleys and dicing houses), and in Westminster (tennis courts, bowling alleys and a cockpit attached to Whitehall Palace). A mushroom growth of the sixteenth century, they could perhaps be sited only in suburbs where there was room for such development. If any generalization can be hazarded about the situation of all these institutions it might be that those serving regular and respectable members of the community, schools and almshouses, were centrally placed, whereas those for the deviant, sick or boisterous, hospitals, prisons, entertainments, were on the periphery, where aliens also tended to settle.

The overall impression given by the mapping of the physical, economic and social morphology of Stow's London is of two prosperous centres: the City with its substantial housing and its busy commercial and industrial life, albeit slightly ragged around the walls, and the West End and Westminster with its landowners, government servants and lawyers. Counterbalancing these were two less prosperous suburban areas, the East End and Southwark, each characterized by humble housing, industrial development, and a mixture of prisons, hospitals and places of entertainment which, perhaps,

---

32   W. E. Jordan, *The charities of London* (New York, 1960) 146 mentions no almshouses in the West End either. Between 1541 and 1500 he claims that 21 were established in London and Middlesex.

33   The area surrounding the Fleet and Newgate prisons should have been a West-End poor area though Stow gives no indication of this. It had certainly become a black spot by 1638: see E. Jones, 'London in the early-seventeenth century: an ecological approach', *London Journal* 6 (1980), 129–32. And by 1666 it contained as many poor as the rest of the City put together: Public Record Office E 179/252/32.

mark them out even at this early date as areas of urban deprivation, inhabited by a poor working population. Such a pattern distinguishes London as a far from typical preindustrial city, more complex than a simple model such as that of Sjoberg allows for. It may be that historians need to consider capital cities in a quite separate category from other towns and cities.

Perhaps the most thought-provoking aspect of Stow's *Survey* is the evidence he gives of sixteenth-century development in London. Though he wrote his survey in the 1590s he viewed his city with the perspective of one who had watched it change from the time of the Reformation onwards. His response was a complex mixture of pride in the growth and vitality of his home town, and an old man's disapproval of the side-effects of growth, the greed of developers, the deterioration of the fields around the city, the ostentation and levity displayed by the new rich of the Elizabethan age.[34] All the new developments described by Stow are mapped in Figure 5. What major features stand out?

The dissolution of the monasteries was a process which had a profound effect on English towns, and in this London was no exception. Miss Jeffries Davis has investigated the fortunes of monastic property in London in detail and her work makes it unnecessary to develop the theme at length.[35] But there is no doubt that the dissolution removed the physical presence of the church to a marked degree. The houses of St Katharine's, Holy Trinity, Austin Friars, St Mary Spital, Holywell, Elsing Spital, St Martin-le-Grand, Jesus Commons, St Bartholomew's, the Charterhouse and Whitefriars became the sites of secular housing. St Mary Graces, the Minories and Crutched Friars, all towards the east, were used for industry. St Thomas of Acon became the Mercers' Hall. St Mary of Bethlehem, St Bartholomew's Hospital and the Greyfriars were transformed into secular hospitals. Stow does not strike any obvious attitude over this revolution but instead unemotionally recounts the fortunes of each site, unless the new development was of a kind he disapproved.[36]

The secularizing trend is reflected, also, in the disappearance of the great episcopal palaces from London. Those lining the medieval Strand were all but taken over by secular statesmen: the Bishop of Salisbury had been displaced by Lord Buckhurst, Lord Treasurer; the Bishop of Exeter's place

34 A point developed by R. Ashton, 'Stow's London', *TLMAS* 29 (1978) 137–9.
35 E. Jeffries Davis, 'The transformation of London', in R. W. Seton-Watson (ed.) *Tudor Studies* (London, 1924), 287–311.
36 But his general disapproval of destruction by reformers and puritans is emphasised by A. J. Taylor, 'Stow and his monument', *TLMAS* 25 (1974), 316–18; and H. R. Trevor-Roper, 'John Stow', *TLMAS* 26 (1975), 338–41.

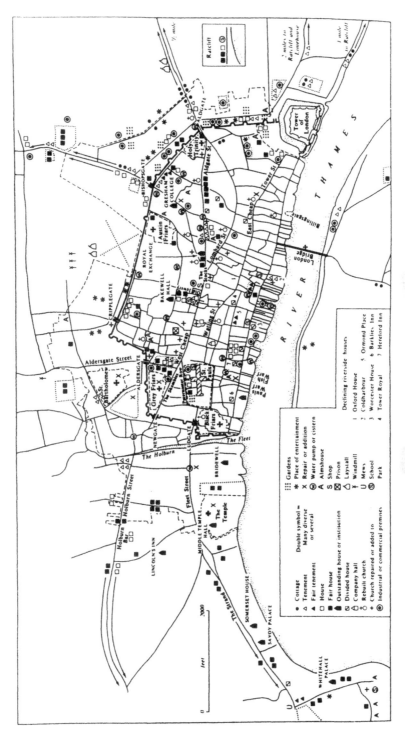

Figure 5. Sixteenth-century development in London described by Stow

by the Temple had passed to Thomas Paget, and later to the Earl of Leicester and then to the Earl of Essex; the Bishop of Bath's house became the residence of Thomas Seymour, and later the Earl of Arundel, becoming Arundel House; the residences of the Bishops of Llandaff, Coventry and Worcester were all levelled by Protector Somerset for his new house in 1549; the Bishop of Carlisle gave way to the Earl of Bedford; the Bishop of Norwich's house passed first to the Archbishop of York, and by the date of Stow's *Survey* into the hands of the Lord Chancellor. Only the Bishop of Durham seems to have held on to Durham House. There could be no clearer visible sign of the transfer of political power from religious to secular hands than the fate of this desirable Thames-side property in the sixteenth century. From the evidence of Stow we might even assume that the bishops had fled London altogether. He mentions only four episcopal residences in London: in addition to Durham House (he does not make clear whether the bishop still inhabited it after 1581) he mentions the Bishop of St David's house next to Bridewell; the Bishop of London had his palace north-west of St Paul's; and the Bishop of Winchester still held his traditional station in Southwark, hemmed in by the Clink and Surrey compter prisons.

If the princes of the church seem in retreat church building certainly was not. The most notable ecclesiastical building was the Henry VII chapel in Westminster Abbey, begun in 1502, and the re-roofing of St Paul's Cathedral after the great fire of 1561 which destroyed the steeple. More significant, some ten City parish churches were completely rebuilt, and eleven extensively repaired or added to during the sixteenth century by their congregations.

A more dramatic feature of the capital's development was the erection of great buildings, public and private. Several public institutions were erected: Sir Thomas Gresham built the Royal Exchange in 1566–7; Bakewell Hall was rebuilt in 1588; and Gresham College was established in the 1570s. These were matched by royal building: Henry VII rebuilt Baynard Castle in 1501 and the Savoy Palace as a hospital in 1509; Henry VIII built Bridewell as a palace to receive Charles V on his visit to London in 1522, and undertook his extensive additions to Whitehall Palace. Protector Somerset's house on the Strand vied with royal palaces in ambition. And the great hall of the Middle Temple built in 1572, and the gatehouse and Chancery Lane wing of Lincoln's Inn, built by Sir Thomas Lovell in Henry VIII's reign, complete the list of ten grand buildings which must have been the sights of sixteenth-century London.

At a humbler level there were many developments which benefited the community. Six of the eight schools mentioned by Stow were built in the sixteenth century: four of them were in the City, St Paul's 1512, the Mercers' school after 1541, Richard Plat's school in the Vintry in 1601, and the Merchant Tailors' school in Dowgate in 1561; Westminster school was established in 1559 and Avice Gibson's school in Ratcliff was built in Stow's youth. Of the 21 almshouses listed by Stow some 12 were sixteenth-century foundations, 7 in the City and 5 outside. And sixteenth-century Londoners put great efforts into improving the water supply of the capital, some 12 cisterns, pumps or taps being installed within the City and 3 outside in the suburbs. Taken together these suggest a century when Londoners were strongly committed to civic and community improvement.[37] It is small wonder that Stow enthused about the development of his home town and such works of philanthropy surely balance the ostentation and levity of the bowling alleys and summer houses which the writer deplored.

A glance at the pattern of development shown in Figure 5 suggests some conclusions about the general trend of sixteenth-century change in London. The development to the east and west, which occurred in the course of the century, created a suburban sprawl which was the origin of the Greater London of later centuries. As we have seen the fair and grand housing of the west contrasted sharply with the humble housing in the east, reflecting the occupations and social status of their respective residents. Each suburb was socially exclusive, the West End monopolized by people of quality and learning and the East End by manual working people. The phenomenon bears repeating because such occupational and social segregation was a development new to the Tudor period and contrasts sharply with the heterogeneous mixture of occupations and of rich and poor living within the walls of the medieval City.[38]

J. E. Vance has suggested a model of modernization in seventeenth-century London which involves a transition from a medieval system in which occupation determined location to a modern system in which wealth became the deciding factor. London evolved from a situation where all the mercers lived together, and all the cordwainers gathered in an area, and so on, to one where the wealthiest members of each group moved out to socially exclusive suburbs.[39] Without getting enmeshed in the general validity of the theory we can say that sixteenth-century suburban development as described by Stow fits that interpretation imperfectly. It is certainly true that wealthy groups lived in the West End and poorer groups in the East. But a determining factor in this pattern was still occupation. If one was a lawyer one would settle along Holborn or Chancery Lane with one's fellows. Conversely, ships' victuallers congregated on Wapping Wall or Ratcliff Highway in a characteristically 'medieval' pattern. A further complication is provided by the fact that many new suburbanites were immigrants from the rest of England, not Londoners relocating within their own city, as Vance suggests in his model. In the epilogue to the *Survey* it is stated that 'the Gentlemen of all shires do flie and flock to the City'; and the 'Retaylers and Artificers ... do leave the Countrie

37 W. K. Jordan, *op. cit.*, 19–24; see comment on Stow as protector of the environment in V. Pearl, 'John Stow', *TLMAS* 30 (1971), 131–2.

38 M. J. Power, 'East and west in early-modern London', 177–82.

39 J. E. Vance, *op. cit.*, 115–16.

townes, where there is no vent, and do flie to London, where they be sure to finde ready and quicke market'.[40] That each group settled in different suburbs according to its occupation and wealth was a natural continuation of the settlement pattern of the medieval city into the suburbs.

Such occupational segregation was not confined to the suburbs, however, for if the City within the walls is examined it is possible to discern the process of separation of the landowning élite from the commercial and craft citizenry proceeding apace. In particular it is possible to discern on Figure 5 that the area close to the Thames was becoming poorer and more business-orientated; humble property, divided houses and the spread of commercial and industrial enterprises suggest this conclusion.

This impression is much strengthened if one looks more closely at the changing occupation of notable houses near the river.[41] It is quite clear that the early-Tudor City, especially by the Thames, was occupied by the land-owning and governing élite, of bishops and earls, lords and ministers, even of kings. By the 1590s the prestige had all but gone. For some houses social decline was slight from landowner to alderman. Along Candlewick Street, Oxford House, once the residence of the Earls of Oxford, was now the home of Alderman John Hart.[42] For many others the decline from graciousness was more drastic. Coldharbour, a great medieval house on the river front in Dowgate, passed from Cuthbert Tunstal, Bishop of Durham, to the Earl of Shrewsbury who rebuilt it as tenements for 'people of all sortes'. A similar fate befell Worcester House in Vintry, 'sometime belonging to the Earles of Worcester, now divided into many Tenementes'. The Tower Royal, just south of Watling Street, once the home of Richard II's mother and a lodging for the king himself, was first turned into stabling for the king's horses and later divided into tenements. Ormond Place in the Vintry, the possession of Edward IV's queen, was taken down and replaced with tenements, one a tavern. Barklies Inn, near Baynard Castle on the Thames, the home of the Earl of Warwick under Henry VI, 'is now all in ruine, and letten out in severall Tenements'. And the Bishop of Hereford's Inn in Queenhithe, though repaired by Bishop Booth in 1517, had fallen into ruin and was divided into many small tenements, with the great hall used as a bakery.[43]

Such examples are not the only such cases. The houses of Lord Nevill and Lord Souche inside Aldgate were taken over by City merchants, the Earl of Oxford's house in Lime Street was divided into tenements, Thomas Cromwell's house on Throgmorton Street became the Drapers' Hall, North-umberland House inside Aldersgate became a printing house. All suggest the same trend, the social élite's abandonment of City residences to merchants or more humble tenants, or to commerce and industry. If the riverside area stands out in this process it does so because the flight seems more pronounced from there, and the deterioration in the use of the property more drastic. There is some reason to suppose that the urban deterioration which was to afflict the riverside parishes upstream from London Bridge in the seventeenth century was already taking hold.[44]

The loss of aristocrats and government servants from the City was, of course, a gain for the West End and Westminster. The social character of the capital was discernibly changing throughout Stow's lifetime, the City becoming more business orientated as the social élite colonized a new suburb. The process was slow, and even when Stow wrote the city retained a few of its titled residents, particularly near the walls where monastic precincts provided space for gracious accommodation. Whether, at the same time, the East End drew people out of the City from the other end of the social scale, unskilled and semi-skilled workers, it is impossible to tell from Stow's pages. If it did we might go further in hypothesizing about change in the City as a centre which became increasingly taken over by 'middling people', traders and skilled craftsmen, the independent mercantile and industrial businessmen at the heart of London's prosperity. Even with Stow's limited evidence it is possible to suggest a sixteenth-century trend towards increasing occupational and social segregation in London.

One can forgive Stow for the information he fails to give because of the copious detail he does provide. Our picture of London at the end of the reign of Elizabeth is patchy but a good deal more subtle than for cities that lack their Stow. If there is one underlying feeling of unease that a reading of the *Survey* induces, however, it is that in all his close description very little of the struggle and dislocation that accompanies urban change comes through. The population of London increased by perhaps three times in the sixteenth century. There was massive immigration, and considerable rebuilding within the City and large-scale new building in the suburbs to accommodate it. The problems of feeding, employing and controlling the growing mass were sufficient to cause the City Corporation unimaginatively to attempt to suppress the growth from 1580 onwards.[45] Yet Stow gives little hint of such strain or the fear accompanying it. We can only conclude that Stow, despite his age and occasional doubts, must have seen his city through rose-tinted spectacles.[46]

---

44   As in St Anne Blackfriars, for example: see B. Burch, 'The parish of St Anne's Blackfriars, London, to 1665', *Guildhall Miscellany* III (1969), 14.

45   N. G. Brett-James, *The growth of Stuart London* (London, 1935), chapters 3 and 4

46   Though in a paper read to a conference on London History at the Institute of Historical Research on 25 June 1983 D. Keene suggested that London growth was slow before 1580. If this is true Stow's experience of the strain of growth would have been comparatively short.

ROBERT THOROTON

M. W. Barley and K. S. S. Train

Local history is now a well-recognised mode of historical writing: increasingly popular, and a source of pleasure to many who attempt research in it
and who read the results. Fashions have changed over the centuries, and new
classes of source material have been discovered or exploited. Nowadays, a
county history is most likely to take the form of a narrative of political
events and an elucidation of social and economic changes. Both Thoroton
and Throsby followed another pattern, now pursued only by those who
compile guide books. They saw local history as a matter of parishes and
villages, their landowners and the vicissitudes of land ownership; the old
and new buildings of public interest. Their work is worth attention, not
merely from piety and for the picture they present of the interests and
attitudes of their time, but also as an indispensable work of reference.

To explain how a country doctor in Nottinghamshire came to write a
history of his county, and only the second of its kind to be published,
requires an understanding of the society to which he belonged as well as an
account of the author himself.

Robert Thoroton was born on 4 October 1623 at Car Colston, a member
of a family which had lived at Thoroton, Screveton and, from the beginning
of the sixteenth century, Car Colston. They were descended from a branch
of the great Norman family of Lovetot, by a marriage with a daughter of
John Morin of Car Colston in the late fourteenth century.[1] In spite of this
descent, of which Robert was so proud, they were only yeomen and minor
gentry but, during his lifetime, they were rising in the social scale. He was
the first of the family to go to Cambridge, where he entered Christ's College
in 1639 and became a B.A. in 1643. In his *Antiquities* Thoroton says that he
was at Newark in March 1644 when Prince Rupert relieved the town, and it
was probably there that he married Anne, daughter of Gilbert Boun or
Bohun, on 27 October 1645.[2] His father-in-law was a serjeant-at-law and
M.P. for Nottingham in the Short Parliament of 1640. He had been turned

---

1   For further details of Robert Thoroton's life and ancestry see M. T. Hildyard, 'Dr.
Robert Thoroton', *Transactions of the Thoroton Society*, LXI (1957), 8–20.

2   Date on a loose sheet of paper in Thoroton's notebook at Flintham Hall.

Dr Robert Thoroton
From the Frontispiece to Volume I of The Antiquities of Nottinghamshire *(2nd edn 1790)*

out of his house, Bugge Hall on High Pavement in Nottingham, at the beginning of the Civil War for his Royalist sympathies, and in 1645 was Recorder of Newark.

In 1646, Thoroton, aged twenty-two, was granted by Cambridge University licence to practise medicine: not such an unusual choice for the eldest son of a country gentleman as it might seem, as several of his family were London apothecaries, though he was to become a physician, then the highest rank in the medical profession. Nothing is known of where he obtained his medical experience or when he settled down as a physician and country gentleman at Car Colston, but his three daughters were baptised there between 1650 and 1654. Thoroton became friendly with Gilbert Sheldon who had been expelled from the wardenship of All Souls' College, Oxford, by the Parliamentary commissioners and lived at East Bridgford for three or four years in the 1650s. When Sheldon became Archbishop of Canterbury in 1663 he conferred the Lambeth degree of M.D. in that year on his younger friend.[3] Something is known about Thoroton's patients because many of the notes and materials which he used for his *Antiquities* are in the possession of the Nottinghamshire Record Office.[4] Among the papers are twenty-four letters from or about his patients. These, obviously only a small part of his correspondence, happened to survive because he used their backs on which to draw up pedigrees or to trick shields of arms; they throw an intimate light on his relationship with his patients between 1662 and 1670. They included members of the gentry and the professions over a wide area: Elizabeth Byron of Bulwell Hall, George Cartwright of Ossington, Godfrey Clarke of Somersal near Chesterfield, Sir Gervase Clifton of Clifton, George Lacock of Woodborough, Joseph Sedgwick, headmaster of Repton, and others from Newark, Nottingham and Southwell. He was obviously an intimate friend of his patients and, strangely enough, one of his best friends was Gervase Pigot of Thrumpton Hall who had been an active Parliamentarian while Thoroton was a convinced Royalist. He stated in the preface to his *Antiquities* that he expected no more glory from these researches than he had 'gotton Riches' from his practice as a physician, but his practice brought him enough money to rebuild the family home, Morin Hall (I, ix; I, 240), and to finance the publication of his book.

Another aspect of his life, though not such an attractive one, was his career as a magistrate. Thoroton is first mentioned in this capacity on 11 January 1694/5[5] and, with his neighbour Peniston Whalley of Screveton,

3 Lambeth Palace Library, F11/1663, Flc. f. 139v.
4 Notts. County Record Office, hereinafter Notts. CRO, M493, 494. These important notes were once owned by Peter Le Neve (1661–1729), then by the Plumptre family who took them into Kent and, finally, by W. E. Doubleday, who sold them to the Library in 1923: 'An Important Literary Find', *Notts. Weekly Guardian*, 10 Nov. 1923.
5 Notts. CRO, QSM 14.

was most persistent in prosecuting Dissenters, particularly Quakers.[6] The Conventicle Act penalised, by a fine of 5s., anyone present at a meeting for religious worship – other than Church of England – and, by fines of £10 or more, the owner of such premises and also the preacher. If anyone was too poor to pay, others had their fines increased. Thoroton was alleged to have encouraged informers who received one-third of the fine, to report these cases and urged the constables to be severe in distraining on the goods of offenders. However, the constable at Blyth and a churchwarden of Mattersey were so appalled at the treatment of Quakers at Blyth by Thoroton and Whalley that they actually appealed to the Privy Council, which in 1677 ordered the justices to answer the charges.[7] The Quakers believed that the King ordered some restraint but Thoroton was actually prosecuting for conventicles in July 1678, over a year later.

Robert Thoroton obviously became ill soon after his last attendance at court, on 1 October 1678, as he made his will on 30 October and was buried in a stone coffin which he had prepared six years before.[8]

For the title-page of his work, published in 1677, Thoroton adopted almost exactly the words of William Dugdale (1656): *The Antiquities of Warwickshire, illustrated; from Records, Leiger-Books, Manuscripts, Charters, Evidences, Tombes and Armes: beautified with Maps, Prospects and Portraictures.* Thoroton modelled his work on that of the scholar who had more than once stayed with him at Car Colston,[9] who persuaded him to attempt to write the history of his county (I, vii) and to whom he dedicated the result. The true reading of the dedication, apart from Thoroton's proper modesty and his respect for the author of several works which had achieved immediate distinction, is that William Dugdale and Gervase Pigot persuaded Thoroton to put into systematic and comprehensive form and for the whole county the notes he had already begun to make, for his private pleasure, on villages and families in Nottinghamshire. The visitation return contains pedigrees certified by Thoroton and dated 1662 or 1663.[10] His notes contain pages of his drawings of shields found in windows of various churches, dated August and September 1662; there is also a preliminary draft of Car Colston, and partial accounts of Screveton, Staunton and Sibthorpe. That for Car

6   Many instances in H. Copnall, *Notts. County Records, seventeenth century*, 141 (from QSM 14); P. J. Cropper, *The Sufferings of the Quakers in Notts.*; Notts. CRO, Q 30 C, Mansfield Sufferings.

7   Notts. CRO, DD4P, 67/78.

8   Date of burial, 23 November, Car Colston Register; on coffin lid, now in church, 21 November, which may have been the date of death. Dugdale noted his death as 28 November (W. Hamper, *Life, Diary and Correspondence of Sir William Dugdale* (1827), 140), perhaps the date when the news reached him.

9   For instance in July 1670, when Dugdale broke his journey from Belvoir to Haddon; Hamper, 132.

10   Thoroton Society Record Series, XIII (1950).

Colston contains more topographical information than he eventually printed.[11] There are pedigrees for Thoroton and Whalley ending in 1663. If the project was being pursued systematically by the mid-1660s, as the dedication implies, it must have gone on until 1675 (II, 241; III, 269; II, 161, 24 May 1675).

Dugdale, writing to Daniel Fleming of Rydal Hall, Westmorland, on 1 September 1677, just after he had bought the *Antiquities*, states: "I do esteem the book well worth your buying though had he gone to the fountain of Records it might have been better done".[12] Dugdale had pressed Thoroton to stay at York and examine the archbishops' registers and other archives, but he was unable to go and had to rely on agents, some of whom proved unsatisfactory (I, vii). His rough notes contain some excerpts from the registers as well as a booklet giving a list of all the benefits in the county, with other particulars,[13] both of which he used, the latter being ascribed to J. M.[14] He was unable to follow Dugdale's example and give list of clergy.[15]

Thoroton was equally unable to leave his practice and spend time in London searching the public records. He was therefore dependent on what was already in print, or on transcripts and notes put at his disposal by friends and acquaintances. He was able to use the three volumes of Dugdale's *Monasticon Anglicanum* which appeared in 1655, 1661 and 1673. He had Dodsworth's notes of Nottinghamshire items in the public records down to the end of Elizabeth's reign. His father-in-law, Gilbert Boun, had transcribed the Nottinghamshire section of Domesday Book (I, vii).[16] The account of Sherwood Forest is almost entirely due to Boun; there are many other references ascribed to him, and at Thrumpton Hall Thoroton had been shown his attempt at a description of the county.[17] Much material had been collected by J. B., almost certainly John Boun, his deceased brother-in-law (III, 126). Thoroton also used extensively the collection made by St. Lo Kniveton (d. 1628), third son of Thomas Kniveton of Mercaston, Derbyshire, and brother of Mary the wife of the first Viscount Chaworth, whose grandson (I, xviii) had let Thoroton have some of the volumes.[18] Other helpers who are mentioned as supplying information for several parishes

11   Notts. CRO, M493; M494, ff. 154–68.

12   *Hist. MSS. Comm.* 12th Report, App. VII (Fleming), 139–40.

13   Notts. CRO, M494, ff. 94–5, 132–9.

14   From statements in I, II, 12, 18, it might appear that his agent was John Marler, rector of Normanton on Soar; in the booklet the name of the rector of this parish is given in the form John Morley, possibly the same.

15   Now compiled by K. S. S. Train for the ancient deaneries of Nottingham and Retford, Thoroton Society Record Series, XV (1955), XX (1961).

16   Part of this is in Notts. CRO, M494, ff. 212–27.

17   For the first chapter of this, probably compiled in 1641 (f. 143v.), see Notts. CRO, M494, ff. 140–53.

18   Burke, *Extinct and Dormant Baronetcies of England* (1841), 292; N. Denholm-Young and H. E. E. Craster, 'Roger Dodsworth and his circle' *Yorks. Arch. Journal*, XXXII (1934–6), 14–15.

are: Robert Atkinson of Newark, to whom two of the Newark illustrations are dedicated, Charles Lacock of Woodborough, Reason Mellish of Ragnall and Thomas Rosell of Radcliffe-on-Trent. He also acknowledges the help of Samuel Roper; this must be the son of the Samuel Roper who had encouraged Dugdale as a young man, and who died at Heanor in 1658.[19] Thoroton calls Robert Saunderson, who came from a Blyth family and was bishop of Lincoln in 1660–3, 'the most diligent collector of genealogies I ever knew in these parts' (III, 427), but there are no acknowledgements to him as a source. Thoroton has earned the greatest praise from a modern historian, of Nottinghamshire origin, for his treatment of Domesday Book and the way he exploited its evidence as the key to manorial history.[20] Beyond Domesday Book, he had at his disposal, and could use in the comfort of his own study, all those monastic and private cartularies which we know to have existed, and many smaller collections of deeds. He was perhaps fortunate in that the Nottinghamshire monastic houses, all of post-Conquest foundation, had not had occasion to forge charters, and so he was not faced with problems of diplomatic criticism. He rarely used medieval chronicles, for they would have led him into paths of historical writing that he did not choose to follow.[21] Thoroton borrowed all the monastic cartularies which were available, was fortunate enough to have access to that of Lenton Priory which is now lost, and actually owned the Sibthorpe cartulary. He used a register or cartulary of Worksop Priory (III, 387 ff.) but there once must have been another because Dugdale 'tells the sad story of the losse of the Worsop Leigier-books'.[22] Francis Leeke, prebendary of Southwell, had lent him 'our Chapter booke' and asks for its return by the messenger.[23] If the references which he was so careful to make are examined, it will be seen that he used the deeds and other documents in possession of most of the landowners in southern and central Nottinghamshire. The one important collection which he might have been expected to use, that of the Willoughby family of Wollaton Hall, was in fact inaccessible to him.[24] Thoroton was

---

19   Hamper, 8, 10, 103.
20   Sir Frank M. Stenton, in *V. C. H. Notts.* 1, 246: 'It is perhaps the greatest merit of Thoroton's work that he fully grasped the essential fact that the key to all manorial history lies in the distribution of land recorded in Domesday, and ... as far as the work of identification is concerned independent investigation can often do little more than confirm his minuteness and accuracy'.
21   He refers in his account of Nottingham to John Rous, *Historia Regum Angliae*, presumably from notes supplied by Dugdale, and to the Chester Chronicle; he also used the Worksop Chronicle which was in the St. Lo Kniveton Collection.
22   Letter from Gervase Pigot, 20 October 1666, Notts. CRO, M494, f. 36v. See also G. R. C. Davis, *Medieval Cartularies of Great Britain*, under names of religious houses.
23   Letter 10 April 1667; Notts. CRO, M493, f. 24v.
24   Mrs. M. Welch, Keeper of Manuscripts, University of Nottingham, writes: 'A serious fire at Wollaton in 1642 seriously damaged the living accommodation, and after the death of Sir Percival Willoughby in 1643, his son, Sir Francis Willoughby, continued to live

obviously less intimate with the owners of estates in the north of the county, for his accounts of many of those villages are surprisingly brief and there is a marked absence of references to manorial documents.

Thoroton's formal acknowledgements and casual references show how a circle of country gentry and professional men must have shared his interests and admired the industry involved in not much more than ten years' work. Those descriptions and histories of counties which achieved print[25] are only a sample of works conceived or projected in that age. Dugdale and Dodsworth had been compelled to pawn manuscripts to raise the money to publish the first volume of *Monasticon*. Dugdale's *Baronage* (1675–6) sold readily, and we can guess that Thoroton's *Antiquities*, with its strong genealogical element, also found a ready market. Now that so many estates have been broken up, so many country houses demolished or institutionalised and so many collections of family papers deposited in record offices, it is hard for this generation, to whom property rarely means more than a mortgaged house and the wasting asset of a motor car, to enter the mind of the propertied classes of the seventeenth century. Their sense of continuity from past generations and of responsibility to their descendants must have been fulfilled by Thoroton's work. He himself regarded it as no more than a work of reference: 'it cannot expect many more thorough Readers than a Dictionary' (I, ix). Before we condemn Thoroton for aridity, and for the things that he failed to say, let us realise that the opening sentences of the Preface represent deep feelings, and not merely an attempt at wit. Many of those who nowadays attempt local historical research are moved by pride of place and pride of family; change in society have largely destroyed that pride and sense of responsibility for property which filled Robert Thoroton and the small public for which he wrote.

---

at the more modest Middleton House in Warwickshire, where he was already residing. This latter house remained the main family home during his lifetime and that of his son Francis Willoughby the Naturalist, who died in 1672 leaving three young children. Wollaton had been closed apart from brief visits by the Naturalist, and when his widow married Sir Josiah Child in 1676 and removed her family to her second husband's home in Essex, Middleton also was closed. The two houses remained shut up until the younger heir, Sir Francis Willoughby, the first baronet, and his sister Cassandra, went to live at Wollaton and began repair work in 1687. After his premature death the following year, his brother Thomas, the second baronet and first baron Middleton, took up residence at Wollaton in 1689, again with his sister Cassandra as housekeeper, and the two young people brought from Middleton their father's library and his natural history collection. No special reference is made to manuscripts. It is assumed that the older documents at least had remained at Wollaton during the seventeenth century, though current records would obviously have been at Middleton. Under the circumstances, in neither place would they have been available for consultation by Thoroton'.

25   Richard Carew, *Survey of Cornwall* (1602); William Burton, *Description of Leicestershire* (1622); Robert Plot, *Natural History of Oxfordshire* (1677) and *Staffordshire* (1686); James Wright, *History and Antiquities of Rutland* (1684).

Nevertheless, we can regret that the broad intentions with which Thoroton started evaporated somewhat by the end of the first section. He began by describing and explaining the divisions of the county and the classes of men; his approach illustrates 'the deep interest in the structure of society' shared by these early historians.[26] Once he started on the detailed history of each parish, Wapentake by Wapentake, he clearly intended first to identify the meeting-place of each Wapentake. He did it for Bingham (I, 138), but not again, perhaps because he found that he lacked evidence. He also intended to explain the name of each village. He certainly appreciated that most place-names have a personal name as their first element (I, 20), and this is one of several respects in which a reader coming to Thoroton with some knowledge of modern scholarship is made to realise the achievements of the scholars of the seventeenth century. Unfortunately, Thoroton largely abandoned, once he had finished Rushcliffe Wapentake, his comments on place-names. In the few he made he was far more often right than wrong, but he was unable to distinguish between place-names of Anglo-Saxon and Scandinavian origin.[27] Perhaps Thoroton's greatest shortcoming, compared with his model Dugdale, was his lack of interest in what would now be called the archaeology of the county. He can be forgiven for not noticing the very few prehistoric barrows; no doubt those in the Trent valley and occasionally elsewhere visible on aerial photographs had already been ploughed down. But he is almost silent on Roman antiquities and had clearly not given much thought to them. He had picked up from Camden[28] two forms of the name of one Roman site, *Agelocum* and *Segelocum*. The former he equated with Eaton (III, 257) without comment, and the latter with Littleborough, under which (III, 292) he refers to Roman finds. This was the beginning, as far as Nottinghamshire is concerned, of the long arguments enjoyed by antiquaries of the eighteenth century and since, and which are quoted by Throsby,[29] attempting to locate on the ground those Roman towns named in the Antonine Itinerary. Thoroton does not explicitly state the Roman origin of the Fosse Way, though he must have known it. He makes no reference to a Roman site (*Margidunum*) near his own home, though he certainly intended to do so, according to the surviving draft entry for Car Colston.[30] We can only conclude in general that the enormous task of elucidating the manorial history of every village made him abandon attempts at more varied and

<hr>

26 H. A. Cronne in L. Fox (ed.), *English Historical Scholarship in the Sixteenth and Seventeenth Centuries* (1956), 74.
27 Thoroton refers to W. Somner's *Dictionarium Saxonico-Latino-Anglicum*, published in 1659.
28 Camden, *Britannia* (1587).
29 See p. 38.
30 Notts. CRO, M494, f. 154.

topographical descriptions. It is easy to reproach Robert Thoroton for the
things he did not do or say. He makes no more than casual reference to the
Civil War,[31] and certainly does not reveal Royalist sympathies; his remarks about Newark (I, 391) show complete detachment. In addition to
the gentle warmth about Lady Hutchinson and her garden, or the reference
to his schoolmaster at Thoroton (I, 228) he included a classic and moving
account of the last hours of his patient and friend Sir Gervase Clifton (I,
108).

Thoroton's comments on the effects of enclosure in his time and before
are a unique source for the economic historian, because in this matter alone
did he allow his emotions to dictate what he wrote. The evil sprang in his
view from dissolution of the monasteries ('that stupendous Act'[32]), but all
the examples he gives lie in the Vale of Belvoir.[33] This is partly due to his
closer familiarity with his own part of the county, and we can now name
other villages which declined or disappeared in the sixteenth and seventeenth centuries,[34] but the enclosure and conversion to grass of the strong
soils of the Vale were a local interaction of environmental and agrarian
conditions. So too was 'the abominable destruction of Woods' in Sherwood.
There is rare humanity in Thoroton's remark (II, 161) about the value of the
bilberries there to the poor.

Robert Thoroton was not inhuman; he had a clearly-seen goal, and he
reached it. He certainly took a narrow view of local history, but we must be
thankful that he did so much and so well. Like all pioneers he made mistakes – places were wrongly identified, Christian names incorrectly given
and errors made in constructing pedigrees.[35] The best clue to his object is
his massive index of personal names, with about 2,700 entries.

Thoroton tried in one other respect to model his work on *Warwickshire*.
Dugdale had set an unprecedented standard in the illustrations to his work.
He included maps, of the county, of separate Hundreds, and of the towns; he
illustrated coins found in the county and other archaeological finds, as well

---

31   His account of the imprisonment of Gilbert Boun by the 'first setters up of the late
horrid Rebellion in these parts' (II, 37) may be compared with his comment on Lady
Hutchinson, the widow of Sir Thomas Hutchinson, a Parliamentarian, taking 'great delight'
in her garden on High Pavement, Nottingham (II, 38).

32   I, xvi. Throsby altered this to 'stupendious', the more fashionable spelling of his
time.

33   I, 217 (Elton), I, 200 (Tithby); I, 234, 241 (Car Colston), I, 247 (Screveton), 323
(Flawborough), 332 (Sibthorpe), 344 (Cotham), 356 (Hawton). He refers to rebuilding at
Flawborough; if he had been writing a few years later, he could have mentioned the revival
of Langford.

34   See M. W. Beresford and J. G. Hurst, *Deserted Medieval Villages* (1971). Beresford
has noticed (p. 50) that Dugdale in his map of Warwickshire used a special symbol for
deserted villages.

35   The W. E. Doubleday Index (Local Studies Library, County Library, Angel Row,
Nottingham) notes many instances.

as monuments in churches; most strikingly of all, he included prospects of towns, castles and country houses. In this respect he stands at the head of a tradition which the camera and development in printing have made a commonplace. The large number of plates, engraved by Wenceslaus Hollar, added to the cost of the work, but Dugdale must have thought them essential; a contemporary (Somner) said *Warwckshire* was expensive because of 'the many curious and chargeable cutts'.[36]

Thoroton followed Dugdale's example, and thus helped to establish the tradition of illustration in local historical and archaeological publication. He included prospects of Newark and Nottingham, views of country mansions and great churches, and elevations of many church monuments. He was able to procure a map of the county, the first on which roads are shown, and of the city of Nottingham, but from whom we do not know. Thoroton himself was no artist, though he could draw shields of arms competently. For many of the plates he commissioned drawings by Richard Hall, who may possibly be the same as the Nottingham 'tombe-maker' of that name who had in 1642 contracted to make a wall monument for St. Peter's church.[37] The drawings were engraved by Wencelaus Hollar, who also worked for Dugdale. The cost of illustration was no doubt offset by contributions from those landowners to whom particular plates were dedicated.

A century after its publication, copies of Thoroton were scarce and expensive enough to provoke ideas of reprinting. W. Whittingham of King's Lynn, who had reprinted histories of Kent and Norfolk and W. Burton's *Description of Leicestershire* (1622, 1777), sent to the proprietors of the *Nottingham Journal* a specimen page of a proposed reprint dated 20 November 1777. They suppressed his advertisement and instead of his print at six guineas advertised one of their own, at two guineas, with new engravings and additional material. In the end, each proposal defeated the other; nothing further is heard of the *Nottingham Journal* venture, and Whittingham got no further, apparently, than producing in 1781 a few copies of a first

---

36   Hamper, 310. The maps Dugdale had to purchase. It is safe to assume that some of the drawings of monuments and small objects are his own, for he was certainly capable of 'taking a prospect' of a castle or a town. On the other hand he had help in this respect, and no original drawings for the volumes are known to have survived. For references to Dugdale's own activity with a pencil, and to his assistants, see Hamper, 97, 107, 167, 177, 186, etc. The drawings done by Dugdale in the summer of 1641 of glass in Newark church are reproduced in C. Brown, *History of Newark* (1904), I, 288 *et. seq.* See also L. C. Loyd and D. M. Stenton, *Sir Christopher Hatton's Book of Seals* (1950), xxiv.

37   The monument was to George Cotes, rector of St. Peter's (II, 96–7); Thoroton transcribed the inscription (p. 507), but it had presumably disappeared by Throsby's time. The contract is to be printed in *Trans. Thoroton Soc.*, a forthcoming volume. Although there is an interval of thirty years between the contract and work for Thoroton, the identification seems worth proposing. No artist named Richard Hall occurs in any dictionary, except that Thieme-Becker, *Künstler-Lexikon* (Leipzig, 1922) lists a view of Westminster Abbey as by him and engraved by Hollar. We have been unable to locate a copy of it.

instalment. It contained Rushcliffe Hundred, the first page of Bingham Hundred and ten new engravings of Thoroton's plates.[38]

In 1790 the task was taken up by John Throsby of Leicester. Very little is known about him.[39] He was born in 1740, and his only known employment is as parish clerk of St. Martin's, Leicester, from the age of thirty till his death. His father, Nicholas Throsby, was alderman of the town, and mayor in 1759. One may suspect either that John Throsby was not strong, or that a fond father encouraged him in his ambition to render himself 'conspicuous as a draughts-man and topographer' (Nichols). From 1777 onwards he published historical works on the city and county of Leicester, one of them contained engravings of his own drawings.[40] His appointment as a parish clerk, even in a rich and busy town church, must have left him with both the leisure for other things and the need to supplement his stipend and fees. Nichols said of him that 'later in life he attempted many expedients to maintain his family'. The Leicester City Museum possesses a copy of his *History and Antiquities of Leicester* in which has been pasted a copy of a printed notice of a public subscription on his behalf, dated 1802. It states that 'in addition to a local derangement of his general circumstances he is now labouring under extreme bodily afflictions'. The first phrase suggests that his 'many expedients' had landed him in greater financial and possibly other difficulties. He died in the following year. Nichols, who made extensive use of Throsby's work in his large *History of Leicestershire*, spoke kindly of his 'strong natural genius', but he or someone else discovered that Throsby was a very inaccurate transcriber of historical documents; the copy of the *History of Leicester* in the Museum was evidently corrected for Nichols.

Throsby began 'following the track of Thoroton' (I, 6) in August 1790. How often he travelled alone we do not know; he only tells us incidentally that at Staunton on the Wolds (I, 81) his companion was 'a reputable grazier'. One hopes that he regularly had company, for like other travellers of this age he found the minor roads, especially in the clay areas, very bad. He gives the problem an unexpected slant when he says that the roads round South Leverton (III, 272) were 'intolerable for poor curates', who were obliged to travel, and that round Misterton III. 331) bad roads were only 'light impediments to the truly religious mind' of Catholic, Methodist and Calvinist sectaries.

In some parts of the county, Throsby was even discouraged by the land-scape. Round Widmerpool it was 'comfortless in winter, in summer only

---

38   There are copies in Bromley House Library, Nottingham, the Belper Library in the Nottinghamshire County Record Office, and in the Local Studies Library, Angel Row, Nottingham.

39   See *D.N.B.* We are indebted to Professor Jack Simmons for biographical notes.

40   *Memoirs of the Town of Leicester* (1977); *Select Views in Leicestershire* (1789); *History and Antiquities of Leicester* (1791).

tolerable' (I, 79) and he contrasted it with a neighbouring county, no doubt Derbyshire, which he found 'splendid, grand and awful'. He admired, as did his contemporaries, the prospect from an elevated point such as the church-yard of St. Nicholas, Nottingham (II, 100), but he looked most eagerly for the improving hand of man. On agrarian changes which we now regard as revolutionary he makes no more comment than to state whether a parish had been enclosed; he notes special local crops such as hops at Wellow and Tuxford and Retford (III, 203, 25, 278). His main interest as an observer was in buildings, especially 'the seats of the Nobility and Gentry', and their environs. He praised a church which appeared, 'as all should do, decent and respectable' (Stapleford, II, 197); the church at Staunton on the Wolds was condemned as 'below description, the most despicable place I ever beheld' (I, 81); at Laxton the results of 'impious neglect' were described in detail (III, 212). On the other hand a new church, which he could have been expected to admire, might have 'no food for the mind of the antiquary' (Ollerton, III, 349), and did not keep him long from the 'comfortable re-freshment for the body' at the Hop Pole Inn.

Parsonage houses were naturally picked out for comment. Most of those he praises still survive, even if no longer used for their original purpose – for example Cromwell, 'one of the best parsonage houses in the midlands' (III, 171). Ordsall had 'a good rectory' (III, 453), Normanton on Soar had 'internal elegance and convenience' (I, 13). The greatest condemnation fell on Edwalton (I, 123), 'one of the most wretched habitations I ever saw' with 'walls of dirt'. The highest praise was reserved for Eakring (III, 198) which 'stands on a desirable site, is a handsome building, and adorned with exten-sive pleasure grounds and water'.

Here we begin to see what pleased Throsby most – a handsome house, suitable planting and a lake or stretch of water. Given all these three, he did not stint his praise, especially if the water had a boat or two. Beesthorpe Hall (III, 142) has a sailing boat in the foreground, though in the text there is only 'a rivulet at the bottom of the pleasure grounds'. One suspects that just as he admitted to adding a plantation or improving a screen at Kelham Hall (III, 120), he was also prepared to invent a lake and a boat. He had no praise for Nuthall Temple, which was demolished in 1929 and is mourned by architectural historians;[41] for Throsby it was 'a modern looking building', 'in a style of singularity, unsheltered from storms and tempests' (II, 255). His taste was not so much wayward as typical of his age. Ossington Hall had 'more magnitude than splendour' (III, 174). Thoresby was damned because it was built of brick, lacking 'harmony and elegance' (III, 344). Throsby's judgments were influenced by the status of the occupants of a country house. Averham Park Lodge, which had been a popular attraction in

---

41   e.g. N. Pevsner, *Buildings of England: Nottinghamshire* (1951), 143.

the 1720s,[42] was now 'occupied by a farmer' (III, 112); Holme Pierrepont, 'large but not magnificent' (a description which conceals a house partly of the fifteenth and partly of the seventeenth centuries) was 'inhabited, I believe, now only by servants' (I, 181); Langar Hall had 'become the abode of shepherds' (I, 209). Farmhouses were rarely worth mention, but one at Bilsthorpe (III, 193) was 'of a pleasing appearance', perhaps because it belonged to Sir Robert Sutton, and he comments on those at Wiseton built by Jonathan Acklom (III, 310). In any case he was prepared to sacrifice a sight of the interior, if he thought there were no 'pictures of note', in order to finish his own drawings of the exterior (I, 36).

It would be somewhat unkind to call Throsby a snob, but his comments on a house were certainly coloured by whether he was allowed inside. Visiting country houses was as popular in the eighteenth century, for those who had the necessary means of travel, as it is today,[43] but it was perhaps easier for the Hon. John Byng, a viscount's heir, to get inside than for John Throsby. The housekeeper could no doubt smell out a parish clerk, accompanied perhaps by a reputable grazier, as well as her master. Throsby evidently got inside Wollaton Hall – even into the housekeeper's room (II, 215), but he fared less well in what later was known as the Dukeries. He did not get inside Clumber, and complained at being turned out of the park (III, 406–7). At Clifton Hall he walked the gardens, but 'the house in its present state is not shown to strangers' (I, 113).

This scrutiny of Throsby's tours is not intended to denigrate his work, but rather to assess its particular qualities. We must be grateful for his industry, even if, like Thoroton's, it was spread somewhat unevenly over the country. His additions for the Wapentake of Rushcliffe, nearest to his home in Leicester, are much ampler than for the north of the county. He admits, when writing of a northern village (East Drayton, III, 241), that he did not visit a place if he was 'informed that there was nothing within it of ancient note'.

Throsby included an up-to-date map of the county which reflects the cartographic standards and the public demands of his time. It was provided by J. Cary, who specialised in road maps. It has the mileages from London along the Great North Road and between towns marked to correspond with milestones. Turnpike roads are marked by a bold line, and open roads distinguished from enclosed. Country parks and gentlemen's seats are clearly distinguished. There are trifling errors – Stockholm for Sookholme, Ansterfield for Austerfield, and Bathley is marked as well as Barlow, an alternative form current in the eighteenth century.

Throsby also set himself to provide an almost entirely new set of illustrations. For some subjects he used older drawings, or engravings: Robert

---

42   See *Trans. Thoroton Soc.*, LXV (1961), 47–56.
43   See John Harris, 'English Country House Guides 1740–1840', in J. Summerson (ed.), *Concerning Architecture* (1968), 58–74.

Smythson's plan of Nottingham castle, which he took from C. Deering's *Nottinghamia Vetus et Nova* (1751), and Thomas Sandby's drawing of the Town Hall and Prison (1741), from the same source. For the 'Papish Holes' on what is now Castle Boulevard (a sight very popular with tourists) he used an anonymous drawing made in 1778. Most of the engravings were made from drawings done by Throsby himself, and it must be admitted that he was no more than competent as an artist. He also took liberties with his subject in at least three cases, Stanford Hall (I, 9); Annesley Hall (II, 270); Kelham Hall (III, 120), in a way that casts doubt on the topographical value of his drawings of country houses. He expected that 'every Gentleman of Taste must commend' the liberties taken (I, xix), but the modern age would have preferred him to let his subjects and views speak for themselves.[44] Wigley, who was a Nottingham engraver (I, 130), did a 'Field Picture' for Throsby (I, 366), as well as some drawings of church monuments, a prospect of Nottingham and drawings for two plates of coins (II, 144, 148). Hayman Rooke of Mansfield Woodhouse, F.S.A., who had published various papers in *Archaeologia* on ancient remains in his part of the county, and with whom Throsby was in correspondence while working on Nottinghamshire, provided drawings of antiquities and of Papplewick Hall.[45] There remains a number of engravings, especially of the great houses of the county to which Throsby had no access, and the small oval vignettes, whose authorship is unknown.

Throsby could not afford as many illustrations as he would have wished (III, 449, note). His full-page drawings of country houses were engraved by W. and J. Walker of London, at various dates between 1791 and 1794, and sold separately. The public support of the print-seller and popular demand for prints had replaced the private patronage of Thoroton's time. Whatever the quality of the illustrations, the range of subjects – coins and ancient earthworks, ruined medieval buildings as well as country houses, church monuments and Nottingham characters – shows how much interest in the past and in the countryside had expanded in the previous century.

Certainly Throsby felt called on to sort out the Roman sites of Nottinghamshire. He was able to draw on several eighteenth-century antiquarian and historical works, such as John Horsley's *Britannia Romana* (1732) and the great enlargment of Camden published by Richard Gough in 1789. He also used 'the learned Dr. Gale' (II, 7), as printed by Nichols in *Bibliotheca Topographica Britannica* (III, 1780) and Stukeley's *Itinerarium Curiosum*. Indeed a reader who pursues Throsby's comments on Roman Nottinghamshire through the various places in which they occur, under Willoughby (I,

---

44   His drawings were done in pencil (I, 350) and have not survived. The Leicester Museum (Newarke Houses) has one pencil drawing by him.
45   See A. G. Sherratt, 'Hayman Rooke, F.S.A. – an eighteenth century Nottinghamshire Antiquary', in *Trans. Thoroton Soc.*, LXIX (1965), 4–18.

71), Hickling (I, 147), Nottingham (II, 7, 10), Collingham (I, 374), Southwell (III, 87), thanks to his adherence to Thoroton's arrangement, will be bored by their tedious and disorderly length. He copied from others at length, and his account of the origins of Nottingham, including Mr. Baxter 'speaking for himself' (in Latin!), is lifted bodily from Deering. He also drew on Leland, whose *Itinerary* had been published by Hearne in 1711, and Samuel Rastall on Southwell (published in 1787). At the end, noting that Throsby in this part of his work did no more than copy from printed sources, one can understand a contemporary comment that he was 'a modest and well-meaning man, though not a profound clerk'.[46] In remarking on historical buildings, he does not more than note, for example, that Mrs. Bainbrigge of Woodborough 'lives in an old hall house, in a plain stile' (III, 35). The phrase 'hall house' is itself of some interest; it seems to denote something lower in social status than a manor house, but Throsby nowhere puts a date, or a period designation, to any old houses. Indeed this could not have been done, in Throsby's time, by any recognition of the style of a period, either in domestic or ecclesiastical buildings. Throsby confessed in a paragraph on 'ancient church architecture' (II, 16) that he could not distinguish Saxon from Norman architecture,[47] but nor could anyone else for another generation. Throsby would have been ahead of his time if he had made a critical scrutiny of earthworks in the county. He noticed the remains of Civil War fortifications at Newark (I, 400) but did not attempt to describe them, and he was slightly contemptuous of Gough for drawing attention to lynchets at Barton in Fabis (I, 101).

The only documentary research done by Throsby was the scrutiny of parish registers, the type of historical document with which he was most at home. He liked to see them for their own sake, and to measure the growth of villages, but he was aware that they were an unreliable guide to population figures since Dissenters did not have their children baptised in parish churches (I, 112). For the rest, he was content to use scissors and paste to take what he wanted from other historians of the eighteenth century. For Bingham, which had no historian from whom he could borrow, he reproduces some amusing stories. He also transcribed some epitaphs from monuments in the churchyard, for as a parish clerk he appreciated their homely originality.[48] One respect in which he shows as a man of his time, and reflects a decline in standards of historical scholarship from Thoroton's time, is in the section he added on Robin Hood (II, 164–70). Thoroton's contemporaries certainly

---

46   The Rev. Samuel Pegge (1704–96), vicar of Whittington, Derbyshire, in a letter to Rooke: *Trans. Thoroton Soc.*, LXIX (1965), 15.

47   Cf. m, 395, where he stated that Worsop Priory is 'after the zig-zag Saxon architecture'.

48   See *Trans. Thoroton Soc.*, LII (1948), 76, for comments on the local school of monumental masons.

knew of him (see II, 170), but Thoroton had no place for him. The legends about him throve particularly in the eighteenth century, and Throsby reproduced them, including that of the cave at Papplewick 'used by that celebrated predator' (II, 287) and the stone at Bilsthorpe 'vulgarly called Robin Hood's p-ss pot' (III, 193).

Whatever Throsby's shortcomings as an historian or an observer, he earns good marks as an editor. In most of the later editions of classic works of the first age of historical research, the original is lost in the continuation or enlargement. It was no doubt Throsby's modesty which led him to claim that 'the Reader may expect a faithful Copy of Thoroton' (I, xix); we must be grateful that in the accounts of villages it is easy to tell Thoroton from Throsby. He reprinted accurately, merely turning Thoroton's marginal references into footnotes, and using roman and italic type for personal and place names instead of italic and gothic. It is probable that the printers set up the new work direct from Thoroton's printed page. It is possible to pick out a few errors of transcription but no more than a modern author would regard as inevitable. Leaving so much responsibility to a printer, or an engraver, led to sad confusion over Thoroton's pages of shields (printed in II). Thoroton had included eight pages of shields and a narrow slip of arms containing eight more – 520 in all. These were reproduced by Throsby in Volume II in four folding sheets but the last ten shields were omitted and one other, making 509. In addition to minor mistakes, such as incorrect spelling and wrong numbering (plate 4), there is a very serious error in Throsby's plate 3. His index to these plates follows Thoroton and reads from left to right, but the shields are transposed so that they read from right to left, making nonsense of their identification.[49]

When it came to the borough of Nottingham, Throsby thought that he could improve on his original by rearranging as well as continuing. Hence Nottingham fills most of the second volume, which also includes 'all that is valuable in Deering'. In parts of it Thoroton's text is placed within quotation marks, but this is not done quite consistently. Nevertheless, we can accept Throsby's claim that Thoroton is all there.

The work eventually came out, as far as can be judged, in 1796. Essentially, there were two editions. For the first, a title-page was used bearing the date 1790, though the dates of engraving range from 1791 to 1796, no doubt because they were offered for sale separately as and when they were produced. In some copies the date on the title page of Vol. III has been altered,

---

49   Throsby Plate 3, first line no. 19 is no. I in index of plates, no. 18 is no. 2, etc.; second line no. 38 is no. 20, and so on down the line. In addition, his last line of this plate has the shields muddled so that the ascriptions are incorrect in any case. For comments on Thoroton's shields see V. W. Walker, 'Thoroton's Illustrations of Coats of Arms', *Trans. Thoroton Soc.*, LXX (1967), 55–8, but her identifications apply to Thoroton's plates, not to those of Throsby.

by hand, to 1796. In Vol. II of this printing the engravings at p. 83 (St. Andreas) and p. 149 (Ventriloquist and Musician) were tinted by hand. There was a second edition in 1797, printed in Nottingham by G. Burbage, in which no engravings were tinted. This reprint has been done from a copy of the 1790–6 printing. Throsby in 1795 also published separately the borough of Nottingham: that is, Vol. II without Broxtow Hundred but including Sherwood Forest. For neither version did he collect subscriptions in advance, as Whittingham had proposed to do in 1777, and as did a great many authors and publishers of works of local interest. The second edition of 1797 must be a measure of the success of Throsby's venture. Even if we cannot measure his financial gain, the modern reader can gauge for himself his workmanlike approach to his self-appointed task. We can also discern the modesty which occasionally reveals itself (I, xix) and which in particular allowed the character and achievements of Robert Thoroton to remain visible.

5

HASTED AS HISTORIAN

Joan Thirsk

Passing judgment on Hasted as a historian is a subjective exercise, deeply influenced by the time and the viewpoint from which it is carried out. Fashions in historical investigation come and go. They are most effectively revealed when authors, seeking facts that are essential for new research, find the data they require summarized in an old work that has for long been disregarded. When this happens, it is clear that the wheel has turned again; our historical vision of the past has shifted, and attention is directed at facets of history which long neglected authors of the past also viewed perceptively. The precise viewpoint of those earlier writers will have been in some way different, but at least it set them in search of the same facts.[1]

Assessing Hasted's *History of Kent*, therefore, is like holding a mirror to the prejudices and preferences of the person and the age that judges him afresh: the exercise has to be carried through with a clear view of the bias contained in that judgment. Furthermore, since no single individual has the knowledge or insight to evaluate with the same discernment every page of Hasted's massive work, every attempt at an assessment is partial. The present writer is especially diffident on that score. Hasted has been studied much more intently by Alan Everitt, who wrote the introduction to the new edition, when it was reprinted in 1972. He was studied more thoroughly still by John Boyle, who pored for countless hours over Hasted's manuscripts and final text, and brought to light a great deal that was hitherto unknown about the man and his methods. At the end of a fine detective story, he uncovered much original information about Hasted as a historian.[2]

Nevertheless, fresh insights are always possible. One of the least offered here derives from an experience not entirely unlike that of Hasted, that of being involved for nearly forty years in a large publishing venture. Work of a prolonged kind, on a similar scale, teaches many of the same lessons

---

1   The essay is the revised text of a lecture originally given at a one-day symposium on Edward Hasted, arranged by the Kent Archaeological Society at Sutton-at-Hone, November 23rd, 1991.

2   Alan Everitt, Introduction in Edward Hasted, *The History and Topographical Survey of the County of Kent*, Reprint of the second edition (Canterbury, 1972); John Boyle, *In Quest of Hasted* (Chichester, 1984).

learned by Hasted. While the work itself leads to fresh discoveries, it also steadily alters viewpoints; yet, the toiler in the field must of necessity adhere to the structure of the original plan. In his long march to the end of the history of every parish in Kent, Hasted must often have wished that he had arranged things differently, even perhaps wished to step aside and do other things.[3]

In Hasted's persistence, however, lay one of his strengths; the highest tribute has to be paid to him for completing his heroic work. Historians who have worked in detail on counties (like Lincolnshire), which lack such a county history, know the good fortune of those who study Kent.[4] The tribute to Hasted must be even more fulsome when the unusually complex manorial history of Kent is recognised. The parish of Hadlow, for example, far from unusual in its structure, has some seven to ten small manors;[5] it poses an entirely different historical problem from parishes in some Midland counties where one manor often spans the whole of one parish, and where, at worst, parishes generally have no more than three or four manors. The contrast illuminates the magnitude of Hasted's task in trying to identify all the owners in all Kent parishes through all the ages.

A further tribute needs to be paid to Hasted's striving for accuracy. Some of his informants expressed harsh words about his mistakes, but no matter how many errors of fact one may find, Hasted undoubtedly strove hard to supply a correct record. Corrections at the end of volume IV demonstrate an almost finicky concern. One correction tells us that at the burial of Matthew Parker, Archbishop of Canterbury in 1575, his bowels were deposited near the remains of his wife in the Howard chapel in Lambeth church. The main text shows this to be a somewhat fussy correction. In fact, Parker instructed in his will that his bowels be buried in the Duke's chapel in Lambeth church, and his body in the chapel of Lambeth Palace.[6] The change was evidently deemed necessary, in part to correct the name of the chapel, show the separation of bowels from body, and also, perhaps, because no one could

3   The author is General Editor, volume editor, and part-author of *The Agrarian History of England and Wales* (8 vols., Cambridge, 1967–).

4   The author's first published work surveyed the agriculture and society of Lincolnshire. See *English Peasant Farming. The Agrarian History of Lincolnshire from Tudor to Recent Times* (London, 1957).

5   Hasted, 2nd edn., [henceforward = O for octavo] V, 177–93.

6   Canterbury Cathedral Archives (= CCA) Irby Deposit, U11, 430, pages unnumbered; Hasted, 1st edn., [henceforward F for folio] IV, p. 46 of corrections at end of vol., and p. 741. Hasted's accuracy in text and maps is examined in considerable detail, and favourably judged, in G.H. Burden, 'A Critical Appraisal of Edward Hasted's *View of the Geography of Kent, 1797–1801*, in the light of other Material relating to eighteenth-century Kent', M.Phil. Arts thesis, London University, 1973. But the survey does not distinguish between the contents of the first and second editions. Robert Pocock, the historian of Gravesend, 1760–1830, claimed to have found 2,000 errors. – Everitt, Introduction, *op. cit.*, xviii.

be certain that the testator's wishes were actually carried out. Hasted's work required thousands of facts to be discovered, transcribed, and checked, calling for monumental dedication and patience. Like every other historian, he must often have wished he were a novelist.

Hasted's *History* poses a further problem, since, as John Boyle has shown, the first edition was his work, but not all of the second, which was much revised and rearranged by others. Yet, the second edition is the most readily available, and the first edition relatively rare. Close reading of the second edition produces self-revealing sentences, which have to be checked in the first edition to see if Hasted really wrote them. In the account of Waldershare church in Eastry Hundred, for example, judgment is passed on an altar tomb, with figures of a man and woman described as being 'out of all proportion and conspicuously absurd', while in the east window appear 'several female figures, which seem singularly indecent, at any rate very improper for the place'. Was this Hasted's observation, or someone else's? It proves to have been Hasted himself, though in the first edition the sentence appeared less conspicuously in the footnotes. In the second edition it was given the more prominent position in the main text, perhaps in a deliberate attempt to awaken the reader from an otherwise dull narrative.[7] But to attribute even those words to Hasted is a bold conjecture for, as John Boyle has shown, Hasted incorporated whole passages that were contributed by others, and in this Hundred he was especially indebted to William Boys and William Boteler for their help.[8] So while such unusually outspoken comments were inserted by Hasted, they may not have been his original ideas.

The pure and unadulterated Hasted, even in the first edition, is an elusive character. Nevertheless, to dwell overmuch on this point involves distortion, for a great deal of the first edition survives in the second. At the parish level, however, the two texts needs to be read with some care, in order to collect all the factual information available. Statements in the first edition were omitted in the second, sometimes to economize in length, sometimes because they were no longer true. Wives' names and identities were frequently omitted, the editors of the second edition brushing them aside more readily than did Hasted. At Waldershare a long list of rectors and vicars going back to the thirteenth century in the first edition was omitted in the second edition, where the list of vicars only started in the early eighteenth century. On the other hand, a noticeable addition was made in the second edition, namely, the number of poor supported constantly, or casually, in each parish. The acquisition of new information, coupled with a certain shift of interest, allowed the inclusion of these figures in the second edition, whereas

---

7   Boyle, 92–101; Hasted, O–X, 59–60; F–IV, 193.
8   Boyle, 18–24, 98.

Hasted's analysis of the social classes in the first edition had not acknowledged the existence of poor in Kent.[9]

Although an assessment of Hasted as a historian rests squarely on his
published work, his manuscripts reveal him also as the failed historian of a
History of Sequestrations in the Civil War. His notes contain a large quantity
of transcribed documents on Parliament's sequestrations of the property of
royalists in the 1640s, covering many countries of England, and not only
Kent. The Hasted manuscripts, bought by the British Library, include the
text of the work he intended, with an Introduction, and interspersed comments as Hasted set out the documents relating to different counties. If this
work had been published as it exists in manuscript, it would not have
enhanced Hasted's reputation as a historian of judgment. It shows him to
have been a diligent transcriber, but lacking in the skill needed to weave the
documents into an integrated history of the whole subject, and to make a
judicious, objective assessment at the end. His introduction to the sequestration is obsessed with the notion of plunder. 'The many actions of these
men', he wrote, 'are the subject of the following sheets, which are transcribed from their own papers, wherein it will be seen how much they
abused their trust, how difficult it was to bring them to account, how often
they were changed, what immense estates most if not all of them acquired
by this plunder, and the whole of their iniquitous proceedings will be laid
open'. The text then begins with many pages of the sequestration ordi-
nances, followed by random documents county by county. One of these,
which Hasted intended to print in full, was an inventory of the goods of the
Earl of Cleveland at Toddington, Bedfordshire, in 1644. It is a revealing list
of a nobleman's possessions, but not relevant to a history of sequestrations.[10]

It would be unjust, however, to judge Hasted on the basis of a manuscript
which he may have regarded only as a preliminary draft. Moreover, it was
doubtless a work planned in his younger days. But the absorption in documents for their own sake, and a one-sided view of the subject as a whole
recurs in a modified form in the *History of Kent*. There, however, both
characteristics are more acceptable, since the history of a county on the
eighteenth-century model called for documents to be assembled in mass,
and in all such cases authors were inspired with the same fierce local pride
that Hasted expressed for his native county of Kent.[11] In describing
sequestrations during the Civil War, however, no scholar who dismissed

9   Comparing the wives' names, see, e.g. Hasted, O–V, 179–81, with F–II, 312, 314–
5; for names of rectors and vicars, see O–X, 61 with F–IV, 193–4. For poor relieved, see e.g.
O–V, 194. For Hasted's silence on the existence of poor, see O–I, 301–3.
10   BL Add. MS 5491, ff. 2ff, and Add. MSS 5494, 5508.
11   Pride in Kent is at its most fulsome in F–I, dedicated to William Pitt in 1798, and
describing Kent as 'the county which stands foremost in the rank of all others, so deservedly
proud of its preeminence in every respect'. Hasted, F–I, Dedication.

them at the outset, and without qualification, as plunder could claim to be a balanced historian of sound judgment.

The *History of Kent* was the product of Hasted's riper years, and, as he explained, resulted from the encouragement he received when meeting Dr Littleton, Bishop of Carlisle and President of the Antiquarian Society, and Dr Ducarel, librarian at Lambeth Palace. His many friends, and the many helpers who subsequently supplied him with documents and summaries, led him to arrive at more mature conclusions. The fact remains, however, that the final work was of a kind calling more for the diligent collection of documented facts than for spacious, long-considered judgments. Hasted is best judged, therefore, on the task to which most of his energies were devoted, namely, the collecting and presenting of documentary evidence. With this agenda, the following remarks are divided among three headings: first, under literary style; second, under content; and, finally, under absent content, where regard is paid to what one might reasonably expect to find in Hasted's work, but which is missing.

Style is a major attribute in the writing of history, for a narrative can make dull reading, or can bring a subject to life in a phrase. Hasted does not emerge well from this test. His style is flat and virtually colourless. Occasionally, a sardonic remark creeps in, but only furtively. Referring to Archbishop Cranmer's surrender to Henry VIII of some of the best church lands, Hasted explained that it was by way of exchange, 'if it could be called so', he added.[12] He would, doubtless, have liked to call it plunder, as did W.G. Hoskins in the title of his book on Henry VIII's reign, *The Age of Plunder.*[13] But perhaps maturity in his later years restrained him. The remarks already quoted about Waldershare church briefly light up another narrative, but such occasions are rare. In other parishes, the family descents proceed unrelentingly (in Sevenoaks, for example), and on page after page fact is piled on fact without a stirring of curiosity, or an aside expressing interest in an individual, to break the boredom. In the account of Sevenoaks Hasted referred to 'some famous silkmills' at Bradbourne of Peter Nonaille. Plainly a Frenchman, Nonaille's identity stirred no questions, not even a brief reference to the association of the French with silkmaking in Kent.[14] The Earl of Dorset *circa* 1612 sold Sevenoaks manor and Knole, with its park and more besides, to Henry Smith, citizen and alderman of London. Smith was astonishingly generous in his benefactions to the poor in many Surrey parishes, as Hasted made clear. He recited all the money sums and many of the names of the parishes, taken (one assumes) from his will. Yet,

---

12 O–VI, 66.
13 W.G. Hoskins, *The Age of Plunder. The England of Henry VIII, 1500–1547* (London, 1976).
14 O–III, 61.

no questions are asked about the origins, the career, or even the trade of this unusual man.[15]

Not only is Hasted's style flat; his descriptions of people are formal. Even when they are more discursive, even florid, they are in conventional language, showing no personal engagement in depicting the character of a breathing, human being. Mentioning the Sackvilles, Hasted referred to Sir Richard and his son, Thomas Sackville, first Lord Buckhurst at Knole. Thomas he described as having been 'a very fine gentleman as well in his person as in his endowments both natural and acquired. He was in his youth without measure lavish and magnificent'. The description continues in the same vein, and it does not sparkle. In fact, Hasted is paraphrasing a contemporary description of Lord Buckhurst and his family, which is found in Sir Robert Naunton's *Fragmenta Regalia*. But Naunton's language was infinitely livelier. Naunton reported Richard Sackville's nickname as Fillsack because of his great wealth and vast patrimony. Thomas, in his turn, was excellent with his pen, and, wrote Naunton, 'his secretaries did little for him … [for] he was so facete (*sic*) and choice in his phrases and style.' Naunton offered a yet more colourful anecdote. Thomas was unusually decorous in handling his suitors; his attendants kept a roll of their names with the date of their first approaches to him. Thus, they received a hearing in strict order 'so that a fresh man could not leap over his head that was a more ancient edition except in the urgent affairs of the state.' Here is a lively, memorable thumbnail sketch, far superior to Hasted's lump of lead. Yet, Hasted must have known Naunton's text for one of his volumes of manuscript notes was the whole text, now preserved in the British Library.[16]

On content Hasted scores a far higher mark. It is plain from John Boyle's book and from Hasted's own notes that he scoured such documents and catalogues as were than available in the British Museum, in the Tower of London, at Lambeth Palace, in the cathedral archives at Canterbury, in private collections, and in printed books. He engaged in personal correspondence with landed families, as well as relying heavily on professional informants and searchers.[17] The pages of information on the descents of property readily reveal the quantity of facts which he unearthed and managed to weld together into an orderly narrative. In west Kent where his knowledge and sources of information were weaker than in east Kent, he found material from a multitude of scattered sources, and, through his manuscript notes, it is possible to see how he welded disparate facts together to make a continuous narrative, refraining, frequently, from drawing attention to the gaps of many years, perhaps a century and a half between

---

15   O–III, 71–2.
16   Sir Robert Naunton, *Fragmenta Regalia* (ed.) J.S. Cerovski (Washington, 1985), 78–9; Hasted O–III, 77; BL Add. MS. 5499.
17   Boyle, *passim*.

each fact. In Hadlow, for example, he followed the ownership of its many small manors by diligent search in the Exchequer and other public records, and a neat filing system in his finely-written notebooks, arranged alphabetically by parish, reminded him of the source for every fact. It may be called scissors and paste work, but that is nine-tenths of the task involved in compiling a county history.[18]

With regard to content, it is sometimes said that Hasted was obsessed with the genealogies of landed families and with the church.[19] But it was the convention of the age, and Hasted depended on the gentry to buy his books. Since these families fed him with a mass of valuable information, he needed their co-operation, and was obliged to requite them with a certain prominence in his text. It is true that he spread himself on the well-known and influential families, and was content to throw in a name and move on when meeting the lesser known landowners. But two hundred years later, when we have access to far more documents, the problems remain of uncovering the identity of the modest families who did not spawn a great kindred, or survive over many generations. Historians still skirt around the task, even though current interest in the social structure of village communities makes it a more urgent necessity. At least, Hasted offers the family name to start a further search.

Hasted's obsession with landed families seems less of an obsession when all his manuscripts are surveyed. The British Library has only 62 out of 122 volumes, but they suggest other interests which never emerged as publications. He collected documents on several themes, not only on the sequestrations of the Civil war, but on the seizures by the Commissioners for Prizes taken in the Dutch war, and on stores and ammunition sent to Ireland in the Commonwealth period.[20] One might reasonably describe him as obsessed with certain aspects of the Civil war and Commonwealth period. But they were not some of the central political issues, as seen at the time or since. Rather, they were eccentric, outside the mainstream of current interests among his contemporaries, and in the end no book emerged.

In the late twentieth century historians may welcome, rather than criticise, Hasted's minute concern with landed families. Some of his information was readily available to him then, which we do not find so readily now. But another stronger reason lies in the shifting sands of current historical concerns. A common complaint was directed in the 1950s–1970s at the format of the *Victoria County History*, that it shed the brightest light on the landowners and their genealogy, and on the church, leaving economic life and other social classes out of sight. But a significant change of attitude is becoming discernible. When economic and social development receives

---

18   See e.g. Add. MS. 5537.
19   Everitt, 'Introduction', p. xviii.
20   BL Add. MSS. 5500, 5501, 5508.

attention nowadays, a deeper understanding is shown for the influence
which landowners exerted, in the short and long term, over the social structure, and economic organisation of individual parishes. From the very
beginning of any study of an individual parish, therefore, it is essential to
know the principal landowner. The family network is the bedrock of primary information on which to build an understanding of the shape, structure,
and development of the village community. If the owner was non-resident,
he usually exercised a fairly slack oversight over the tenantry. Though this
was not always true of ecclesiastical owners, nor of all lay landlords, an
absentee could never control matters as closely as a resident. If non-resi-
dence persisted over many generations, it could leave a permanent stamp on
the settlement pattern and structure of the parish. Similarly, a change from a
non-resident to a resident manorial lord could produce a dramatic transformation.[21] A new book by Lawrence Biddle on the village of *Leigh in Kent,
1550–1900*, well illustrates this turn of events. Hasted in 1778 believed that
'the village [of Leigh] hath nothing worth notice in it'. At the time of
writing, he could perhaps have justified this drab description: it was a poor
village, the centre of a number of farms occupied by tenants who paid rent
to non-resident owners. But soon afterwards a gentleman moved in, the old
manor house was pulled down, a new Georgian manor house was built, and
the poor hamlet became a Victorian estate village. In short, a radical change
was wrought in the appearance and the social structure of the place.[22]

Viewed more broadly still, landowners can be seen to have influenced the
sizes of farms, the farming specialities on their estates, the numbers of
labourers, the numbers of poor, and the presence or absence of industries.
The significance of studying the gentry when considering the development
of local resources is further underlined if their fluctuating numbers are taken
into account. A historian of Somerset has counted the numbers of gentry in
the county at different dates, showing 150 families in 1569, and 352 in
1623. These are rough and ready figures only, but they imply profound
changes in those villages which acquired a resident gentleman where none
had lived before. Others even acquired a cluster of gentry at this period,
either living in different hamlets in the same parish, or competing for power
in one village. More counting of this kind remains to be done in the future,
but already interest in this subject has produced a study of Norfolk and
Suffolk showing significant change in the numbers of gentry in those two
countries, rising to a peak in the mid seventeenth century, and declining

21   For recent work, see B.A. Holderness, 'Open and Close Parishes in England in the
eighteenth and nineteenth Centuries' *Agricultural History Review*, 20, ii (1972), 125–39;
D.R. Mills, *Lord and Peasant in nineteenth-century Britain* (London, 1980); S.J. Banks,
'Nineteenth-century Scandal or twentieth-century Model? A new Look at "open" and "close"
Parishes' *Economic History Review*, 2nd Ser., XLI, i (1988), 51–73.
22   Lawrence Biddle, *Leigh in Kent, 1550–1900* (Leigh, 1992).

after 1700.[23] Hasted, in short, laid an essential foundation for the late twentieth-century historian of economic and social development: one of the first questions to be asked in any parish concerns the identity of the land-owners in shaping its development.

In another respect, Hasted offers information which falls into line with rising current interests. He gives long lists of the incumbents of the churches in Kent. These offer invaluable raw data for the study of pluralism in the church, a subject which has not hitherto attracted research, even though the computer offers a fine opportunity to measure its scale statistically. It could shed much fresh light on the religious and educational consequences in individual parishes of an incumbent's absence. Now the opportunity is being seized at Leicester University: a large investigation into pluralism is starting, and the computer can devour the information in Hasted, which has lain inert for so long.[24]

The absence of certain themes from Hasted's *History of Kent*, when set against the background of his age, yields further insights into his personality, and the breadth of his historical concerns. Certain omissions are conspicuous and regrettable. Every local historian nowadays is expected to start the history of a parish with a description of its location, soils, farming specialities, indus-tries, and, if possible, its social structure. An account of the whole population is required, giving some guide to the size of farms, number of husbandmen, cottagers, and poor as well as the landowners. Hasted gave an expansive account of the whole county in volume I, written in a mood of county pride, and claiming that Kent had everything. He described the main regions in general terms, obviously basing his remarks on careful enquiry, but he offered only the briefest words to describe the agricultural or geographical situation of individual parishes. Similarly, his discussion of Kent's social structure is couched in general terms, and not parish by parish; it is thus curiously lacking in balance. Gregory King in 1695 divided the lower ranks of the population (below the gentry) into freeholders of £50 per annum, freeholders of £10 per annum, farmers, cottagers, day labourers and paupers, and (separately in the towns), tradesmen and professions. Hasted described a much leaner structure which was at odds with the real world of his day. He considered yeomen, common yeoman (we would call them husbandmen), and labourers, but the labourers were the sons of yeomen, who by gavelkind would one day inherit family land. There ended his listing of the classes in society. He emphasised furthermore the social harmony between gentry and yeomen, 'the good will and kindness from the one sort to the other', as he phrased it, and he did not

23   The subject is discussed in Joan Thirsk, 'The Fashioning of the Tudor-Stuart Gentry', *Bulletin John Rylands Library*, 72: 1, (1990), 73–5. For the Norfolk and Suffolk gentry, see Nigel Wright, 'East Anglian Gentry Homes', *Newsletter of The Centre for East Anglian Studies*, University of East Anglia (July 1988), 2–3.

24   *Newsletter of Friends of the Department of English Local History*, no. 4 (1991), 7.

take even a first look at the poor. Plainly, he was deeply interested in gavel-kind, and it received ten full pages of discussion, showing that Hasted had read as fully as possible on the matter. He even listed all the private acts disgavelling the lands of individual landowners, prompting in the reader the question, though Hasted did not raise it himself, why forty-four Kent landowners were gathered together in one act in 2–3 Ed. VI to disgavel their lands, when usually such acts were procured singly.[25] But in his view of the agricultural situation and the social composition of Kent villages Hasted was plainly out of line with some of his contemporaries, and out of line with some earlier writers whose books lay before him as he prepared his own. From the very beginning of his work he had among his models Robert Plot's *Natural History of Oxfordshire* (1677), and *A Natural History of Staffordshire* (1686). Plot, moreover, had a special claim on Hasted's attention, for he came of a Kentish family, of Sutton Barn, in Borden, and had himself planned to write a *Natural History of Kent*. Hasted had the benefit of his MSS which lie in Hasted's own collection.[26]

Plot in his work had announced firmly: 'I intend not to meddle with the pedigrees or descents either of families or lands'. Instead Pliny's *Natural History* was his model, with the result that he had chapters on waters, earth, stones, plants, and antiquities. Plot sent out questionnaires in order to gather local information, asking about soils, grains, crop rotations, farm implements, minerals, and industries, and his approach was so much in the same tradition as that established, and accepted, by members of the Royal Society from its foundation in 1660, that Plot was elected a Fellow of the Society after his Oxfordshire volume appeared. Indeed, he became the Society's Secretary in 1682.[27]

Plainly, Hasted did not move in a circle which included members of the Royal Society. If he had, it is likely that his plan for Kent would have been modified to accommodate more of what was called at the time the natural history of the county. He was not unaware of this alternative viewpoint. John Thorpe of Bexley sent him several pages on rare plants found in Kent, explaining exactly where each grew. But the information went unused.[28]

So while Hasted must have seen many of the newly published works on agriculture and natural history as he scanned the libraries for books which

25   Hasted O–I, 265–71, 293–302, 311–21. Hasted evidently reminded himself to take notes on soil, situation, and husbandry. See Boyle, 107. On social structure, compare Gregory King, in *Seventeenth-Century Economic Documents* (eds.) Joan Thirsk and J.P. Cooper (Oxford, 1972), 768.

26   BL Additional MS. 5537; O–VI, 69–71, esp. 70 footnote; Everitt, Introduction, *op. cit.*, p. xvi; D.A. Baker, 'A Kentish Pioneer in Natural History: Robert Plot of Borden, 1640–96', *Trans. of Kent Field Club*, III, part 4 (1971), 213–24.

27   R.A. Butlin, 'Plot's Natural History of Staffordshire: an Appraisal', *North Staffs. Journal of Field Studies*, 2 (1962), 89.

28   BL Additional MS. 5490, f.2v.

he did read, like Somner or Robinson on gavelkind, they plainly did not engage his particular interest. Yet, Kent was in the forefront of improving agriculture; the very first farmers' club known to historians was the Faversham Farmers' Club, set up in 1727. And when John Banister, a gentleman farmer of Horton Kirby, Kent, published his *Synopsis of Husbandry* in 1799, he mentioned the spate of treatises on agriculture issuing from the press. It is almost as if Hasted read Plot's announcement that he was concentrating on natural history and not pedigrees, and Hasted resolved to do exactly the reverse.[29]

Yet, Hasted's decision did not pass without opposition. An implied criticism from his contemporaries lies in the changed content of the second edition of his *History of Kent*, over which Hasted himself had less control. John Boyle believes that Hasted may have had a hand in reducing by about a third the historical matter in the second edition. But others made additional changes in line with new policies, and those resulted in a notable lengthening of the agricultural descriptions of the parishes. John Boyle reckons that 56 out of 80 parishes in volume I of the first edition, and 67 out of 115 in volume II were virtually described afresh in the second edition. Moreover, lively descriptions and local colour crept into those new accounts, in contrast with some of the drab statements by Hasted about parishes that in his view had nothing worthy of notice. Especially lengthy were the new accounts covering Wealden parishes.[30]

Knowing the way farming procedures were being enquired into, and written about, in the 1780s and 1790s, we should not be surprised that the revisers of Hasted for the second edition silently expressed their criticism of him by giving much fuller accounts of the agricultural situation of individual parishes. The Board of Agriculture had embarked in 1793 on a plan to publish a general view of the agriculture of every county, and every writer which it commissioned started by sending out questionnaires to local informants.

The author commissioned for Kent to write its *General View of Agriculture* was John Boys, and the first edition of this work appeared a year later, in 1794. John Boys was presumably a member of the large Boys clan, as John Boyle suggests, but the Boys had seventeen branches. John was not closely related to William who was one of Hasted's leading informants, and the writer on Sandwich: a note in the Irby deposit rather deliberately disclaims any relationship.[31]

John Boys was a farmer at Great Betshanger, the Boys family home, and had been farming there since 1771. In his *General View*, Boys leaned heav-

29   *Agrarian History of England and Wales, V, ii, 1640–1750*. (ed.) Joan Thirsk, 574; John Banister, *Synopsis of Husbandry* (London, 1799), v.

30   Boyle, 93 ff.

31   John Boys, *General View of the Agriculture of the County of Kent* (1st edn. 1794; 2nd edn, 1805); Boyle, 67; CCA, Irby Deposit, U11, 430, letter dated 25 Feb., 1800.

ily on Hasted's *History* when he had to make generalisations about Kent as a whole, when writing, for example, on Estates, Tenures, and Population in broad terms. Indeed, he quoted Hasted verbatim in many places. On Minerals he quoted him for three and a half pages, but the quotations diminished as he plunged deeper into farming matters.[32]

For his part Hasted's second edition showed full awareness of John Boys's existence. Additions in volume 10 of the second edition mentioned that Boys had written the *General View of Agriculture*, and identified the manor farm at Betshanger where he was living. Volume 9 had been even more fulsome, mentioning under Northbourne that Little Betshanger manor was in the hands of the Boys family, and naming John Boys as the present occupant whose scientific knowledge in husbandry was well known, especially through the publication of the *General View* (though the writer evidently did not have the book beside him because he did not know the correct title). A letter in the cathedral archives, however, corrects some of this information about John Boys.[33]

Who was the author of the changes in the second edition? John Boyle offers discerning remarks about the identity of this anonymous person, deciding that two different people were at work. One writer, in Boyle's opinion, was more cultured, and less prone to use clichés. The second editor he calls Mr Cludge because he uses the word 'cludgy' for the first time to describe the soil at Boxley. As this sounds like the usage of someone from a farming background, it is tempting to wonder if John Boys had a hand in this re-writing, thus explaining the sensitive and colourful descriptions of landscape. But although John Boys cited Hasted so much in his own book, he gave no hint of having contributed anything to Hasted's work, nor did Hasted's work thank him for any help. Boys called himself in his *General View* unlettered, though plainly he was not, or he would not have written his book. But he also added that he was 'immersed in the cares of a numerous family and an extensive business', which we may well believe. Finally, he seems to be ruled out of the role of editor, part editor, or author of passages in the second edition, because he would have known the correct title of his own *General View*; surely, he would not have allowed that blunder to pass?[34]

Nevertheless, an indirect association between the Boys and Hasted publications cannot entirely be ruled out. Boys proceeded on his agricultural survey by way of a prior questionnaire. Many descriptions of parishes must have fallen onto his desk from informed local people. He acknowledged being better informed on east Kent than on west Kent, and on west Kent

32   Boys, 6–8, 22–5, 37, 207.
33   Hasted, O–X, 440, O–IX, 592; CCA, Irby Deposit, U11, 430, 'Corrections and Additions to 9th vol.', dated 25 Feb., 1800.
34   Boyle, chapter 6, 92ff.; Boys, Preface.

explained that he had the help of a middle Kent farmer. It may be significant here that John Boyle notices the rich descriptions of parishes in the Weald. It is not impossible, then, that some of Boys's collections of notes assisted the editors of Hasted's second edition. This speculation cannot be pressed far, but it poses a question to alert future researchers.[35]

Scrutiny of the Hasted volumes in the British Library, in fact, reveals some of Hasted's personal informants. A more thorough search through these notes could possibly identify more, as could a search for more of the 59 volumes of Hasted which the British Library did not buy. They might well tell more about the whole enterprise. The Irby deposit relates, as John Boyle explains, to the period after 1770 in the writing of the history, and it is strongly focused on east Kent parishes. The history of west Kent was another world, and called for someone offering quite different information, notably, on the Honour of Clare. Seeing how much help was given to Hasted by two men in east Kent, William Boteler and William Boys, we may justly suspect the existence of other informants supplying information in west Kent. Yet, that world is closed to us, apart from the evidence of documentary references which Hasted himself collected.[36]

The Hasted story plainly calls for more research from the point of view of its information on west Kent. Scholars writing on east Kent always command the heights of Kentish history because they have far superior ecclesiastical and other records. East Kent, moreover, had a social structure harbouring many gentry who carefully preserved their archives. Even now, John Boyle perpetuates the tradition of historians inspired to look at Kent from a bastion in the eastern half of the county. It is important to underline this emphasis on east Kent in Hasted, in order to galvanise the west Kent historians into looking at his work with this imbalance of knowledge in mind. Hasted's sources of information in west Kent are unclear. The whereabouts of half the Hasted archive is unknown. The two problems are probably interconnected, and should be pursued together.

Among summary judgments of Hasted's work, one of the most waspish was that of Egerton Brydges, one of Hasted's contemporaries and neighbours: 'he had no imagination or sentiment, nor any extraordinary quality of the mind unless memory'. In paying tribute to the work of Hasted, John Boyle, who penetrated deeply into the way Hasted worked, has given the most recent summary, but that, too, is couched in harsh language. He calls

---

35   Boys, 11; Boyle, 95–7.
36   Boyle, 66–91. John Boyle identifies many of Hasted's informants, who appear in letters to him, and some came from west Kent. But other names appear in Hasted's parish notes (see BL Add. MS. 5537), and have yet to be identified. Boyle notes that three notebooks in Maidstone seem to correspond with volumes not bought by the British Library, but altogether 59 out of 122 volumes of manuscripts (not all, of course, relating to Kent history) were passed over by the British Library.

him a scissors-and-paste man, energetic at seeking out his sources, but attempting no synthesis.[37] He had a second-hand wit, and a dormant imagination. Every damning phrase has truth. But the present-day editors of the *Victoria County History* would say that no compiler of a county history has much chance to show his imagination. And as for offering a synthesis, those who embark on a large work, and publish as they go, know that the most original insights are gained at the end, not at the beginning. Authors are not the main beneficiaries of their own encyclopaedic work unless they live long enough to write a sequel. The main beneficiaries are the generations that come after and stand on the shoulders of the first author.

37   Everitt, Introduction, p. xliii, citing Sir Egerton Brydges, *Autobiography*, I (1834), 50–51; Boyle, 92.

6

WRITING URBAN HISTORY IN THE EIGHTEENTH CENTURY: MILNER'S *WINCHESTER*

R.C. Richardson

The History, Civil and Ecclesiastical, and Survey of the Antiquities of Winchester, to give it its full title, by the Rev. John Milner was published in 1798. A second edition, corrected and much enlarged, appeared in 1809. A third, posthumously edited and updated, was issued in 1839. The eleventh edition of the work (1851) is the last entered in the British Library catalogue. But the publishing history of Milner's *Winchester* is more complicated and impressive even than this. The original publication in 1798 quickly produced offspring of a different kind, in the form of abridgements and extended extracts. *A Short View of the History and Antiquities of Winchester*, forty-seven pages long, first appeared in 1799 and reached its seventh printing by 1820. Milner's *Historical and Critical Account of Winchester Cathedral*, which first saw the light of day in 1801, sold so well that no fewer than twelve impressions had been called for by 1840.[1] Clearly all this represents a local phenomenon of some importance and it is worth investigating it from a number of different, but closely related perspectives. Winchester itself at this time as well as Milner and his *History* all need to be examined. At a more general level issues connected with the growth of towns, provincial culture, and urban historiography claim our attention.

1851 was the first census year in which it was recorded that the majority of the population of this country lived in towns and cities rather than in the countryside. In the eighteenth century urbanisation accelerated but London remained highly exceptional in every respect, and with a population of 900,000 by the end of the century it was in fact the largest capital city in the

---

1 The third edition of Milner's *Winchester* carried a biographical notice of the author by the Rev. F.C. Husenbeth. The publisher claimed that the *Short View* was 'faithful and accurate' to the original from which it was drawn and that its publication was necessary to counteract other 'superficial and erroneous' guides then circulating.

whole of Europe.[2] But whereas in 1700 only one provincial English city (Norwich) had a population in excess of 25,000, a century later there were fifteen towns in this position. A further twenty-four English towns had populations of 5–10,000; Southampton was one of their number. Perhaps as many as fifty more had populations of between 2000 and 5000 inhabitants;[3] Winchester belonged to that group. Ports, dockyard towns and spas went through a significant stage in their development in the eighteenth century and industrial centres like Birmingham, Manchester, Halifax, Leeds, Nottingham, and Leicester became increasingly conspicuous. Urban growth and national economic expansion went hand in hand and internal trade operated through fewer, larger hubs rather than, as before, through many small ones. County fairs declined relatively as a medium of trading; specialised shops and exchanges – regularly, rather than occasionally, functioning institutions – increasingly took over.[4] Towns, in other words, were the pace-setters in the eighteenth century and so many of the virtues and refinements cultivated and admired in that period were quintessentially urban; towns were relied on to set the standards of 'civility' and (self-evidently) of 'urbanity'. Life in towns had a variety and pace that the countryside could not rival. William Hutton's exhilaration on first encountering (in 1741) the bustle and energy of Birmingham is well known.

> I was surprised at the Place [he recalled later] but more at the People. They were a Species I had never seen. They possessed a Vivacity I had never beheld. I had been among Dreamers, but now I saw Men awake.[5]

But urban change in the eighteenth century was not restricted to the physical extension of towns and their more emphatic economic profile. The quality of life in towns, the urban aesthetic, their architectural appearance, were all transformed as well. An 'urban renaissance', indeed, has been claimed for the eighteenth century by historians such as Peter Borsay.[6] In a now well-known study published in 1989 Borsay presented his compelling case that a major transformation occurred in the character, ambience and status of towns be-

---

2   See E.A. Wrigley, 'A simple model of London's importance in changing English society and economy, 1650–1750', *Past & Present*, 37 (1967), 44–70.
3   C.W. Chalklin, *The Provincial Towns of Georgian England. A Study of the Building Process, 1740–1820* (London, 1974), 4–5.
4   On these trends see P.J. Corfield, *The Impact of English Towns, 1700–1800* (Oxford, 1982); P. Borsay (ed.), *The Eighteenth Century Town. A Reader in English Urban History, 1688–1820* (London, 1990); P. Clark (ed.), *The Transformation of English Provincial Towns, 1600–1800* (London, 1984).
5   Quoted in Corfield, *op. cit.*, 3.
6   P. Borsay, *The English Urban Renaissance. Culture and Society in the Provincial Town, 1660–1770* (Oxford, 1989); J. Barry, 'Provincial town culture, 1640–1760: urbane or civic?' in J. Pittock and A. Wear, (eds.), *Interpretation and Cultural History* (Basingstoke, 1991), 198–234.

tween the later years of the seventeenth century and the last quarter of the eighteenth. London and Bath were the most prominent and compelling examples of the trend, but it was without doubt a trend and it was observable in varying degrees throughout the whole country. The quality of the urban environment was significantly changing with much rebuilding of both public edifices and private housing; town halls, assembly rooms, elegant terraces and squares all made their appearance. Significant improvements were made to paving, street lighting and water supplies. In the course of the century a wider and more systematic provision for leisure activities was offered. Horse racing, parks and gardens, concerts and plays were all made available on a scale never before witnessed. Provincial theatres, coffee houses, subscription libraries and reading rooms proliferated. The urban service sector expanded. Shops, rather than markets, became increasingly characteristic and extended in range; confectioners, grocers, booksellers, tobacconists, newsagents, and hairdressers all became regular features of the eighteenth-century urban scene. The professions expanded; there were more lawyers, doctors, chemists, architects, civil servants than ever before.[7] Regional social capitals in the eighteenth century became more clearly delineated and provided a focus which they had not done before in the same way. Resort towns were very much the creations of the eighteenth century.[8] To look upon the eighteenth century as no more than the 'aristocratic century' and to indulge an exclusive fascination with the 'Namierite aridity of high politics', as an older generation of historians was content to do, is clearly inadequate. Borsay, Barry, Porter and other historians today have performed a valuable service in directing attention away from the social and political elite to the 'middling sort', the 'polite and commercial people' and the 'urban renaissance'.[9]

Winchester displayed these features of the 'urban renaissance' which Borsay and others have depicted. With a population approaching 4000 it was still only two thirds of its size in its heyday in the twelfth century, and the glorious prospect of renewed royal patronage which had seemed to be opening up in the 1680s had been abruptly terminated in 1685 by the death of King Charles II. His project of a new royal palace was never completed and Winchester abruptly lost its chance of becoming another Windsor.[10]

---

7   See Borsay, *The Eighteenth-Century Town, passim*; Corfield, *passim*; C.W. Chalklin and M.A. Havinden (eds), *Rural Change and Urban Growth, 1500–1800. Essays in English Regional History in Honour of W.G. Hoskins* (London, 1974), 202 *et seq.*

8   Corfield, *op. cit.*, 51–65, 82–98; Phyllis Hembry, *The English Spa, 1560–1815. A Social History* (London, 1990); R.S. Neale, *Bath, 1680–1850. A Social History* (London, 1982).

9   Borsay, *op. cit., passim*; R. Porter, *English Society in the Eighteenth Century* (Harmondsworth, 1982); Rosemary Sweet, *The Writing of Urban Histories in Eighteenth-Century England* (Oxford, 1997), 276.

10   Adrienne Rosen, 'Winchester in Transition, 1500–1700', in P. Clark (ed.), *Country Towns in Pre-industrial England* (Leicester, 1981), 180–81.

Even the most cursory inspection of present-day Winchester, however, shows unmistakably from the surviving buildings that the eighteenth century was a crucial and prosperous phase in the city's development. Georgian Winchester had its impressive town houses, its theatre, market hall, assembly rooms, circulating library, and so on. The documentary evidence confirms the visual.

The first Winchester guidebook appeared in 1760, and by the end of the century it had gone through many editions and had been joined by others, Milner's included. As well as celebrating Winchester's illustrious medieval past, care was taken in the guidebook to highlight the new prosperity, refinements, and comforts of the eighteenth-century present. The 1780 edition of the guidebook, for example, boasted of improvements in trade and navigation and of consequent reductions in the price of essential commodities such as coal. Paving and street lighting, it was proclaimed, had been transformed 'after the example of the metropolis'. (Provincial imitation of London in this period was increasingly common).[11] Winchester, the guide went on, was both 'populous and well inhabited... [and] the great number of genteel families that reside in it contribute to make it polite and agreeable'. Winchester's social gatherings were 'brilliant and fashionable'.[12]

The first trade directory for Winchester is that of 1784 and it is instructive to analyse it. It depicts a weak industrial base but a very strong and diverse service sector. Included in the directory as the most numerous occupational category were thirty-six innkeepers and victuallers. Way below them in terms of numbers, but still representing sizeable sub-groups, were fourteen shoemakers and thirteen grocers. Eleven drapers and the same number of milliners were listed. Six hairdressers and five wig-makers were included. Also part of the listing were four confectioners and four gardeners and nurserymen. Smaller numbers of hatters, wine merchants, mantua makers, booksellers and printers still made their mark in the directory. A single tobacconist, coffee house keeper, china and glassman, cabinet maker, and dancing master were also included in the occupational census and provide significant clues to the kind of place Winchester had become by the late eighteenth century. The fact that there were also fourteen attorneys, six surgeons, two physicians, five chemists, apothecaries and druggists is also highly revealing. Winchester was firmly established on the map of southern

11   See P. Borsay, 'The "London Connection": Cultural Diffusion and the Eighteenth-Century Provincial Town', *London Jnl.*, XXIX (1994), 21–35. Roy Porter and Donald Read have taken the view that the eighteenth-century provinces did not really exert a cultural distinctiveness of their own but slavishly followed the lead of the capital. (R. Porter, 'Science. provincial culture and public opinion in Enlightenment England' in P. Borsay (ed.), *The Eighteenth-Century Town* (London, 1990), 243–67; D. Read, *The English Provinces c.1760–1960. A Study in Influence* (London, 1964), 1–22. Sweet, *op. cit.*, 238–39, disagrees.
12   *The Winchester Guide, or a Description of the Antiquities and Curiosities of that Ancient City* (Winchester, 1780), 89, 91.

England not simply as an ecclesiastical centre and as a marketing hub but, ever more insistently, as a social focus for its region. The city provided a social and recreational supplement to Bath and London even though, self evidently, it was not capable of rivalling them.

One obvious dimension of the 'urban renaissance' portrayed by Borsay and others was the heightened self-consciousness which towns experienced as they grew in size, prosperity, diversity, and as they paraded increasing signs of genteel comforts and elegance. Writing histories of towns and cities was one very clear expression of this new cultural ethos. Rosemary Sweet has produced a full-length study of the phenomenon. 'To buy an urban history', she says, 'was a demonstration of local feeling; to undertake to write it demanded some sense of commitment to and pride in the town'.[13] The enhanced role and status of towns in the eighteenth-century present gave an added impetus to studying their past. Jostling for precedence among provincial towns and emulation of the metropolis were both powerful factors stimulating urban historiography. Not that individual towns consisted of unified social, economic and political communities. Internal divisions, factions, and rivalries could provide conducive conditions for the writing of urban history. John Wood's *Description of Bath* (London, 1742–43), to cite just one notable example, was part of his 'guerrilla warfare' against the obstructive corporation of that city.[14] Before 1700 only twelve urban histories had been published; London, described in Stow's *Survey* of 1598, unsurprisingly, was the first of them. Forty-four more urban histories appeared between 1701 and 1760. Then came the flood. Between 1761 and 1800 no fewer than ninety-six publications of this kind were launched to be received by an obviously appreciative public.[15]

Milner's *Winchester*, therefore, was not an isolated example of its type. Portsmouth, Tewkesbury, Worcester, Tiverton, Leicester, Manchester, Liverpool and Stockton on Tees were other towns which attracted their respective historians in the 1790s. Milner's book, fairly clearly, was symptomatic of a number of general trends. Most fundamentally, its publication expressed (as we have seen) the growth of the urban sector in economy and society and the prevailing eighteenth-century perception of towns as agents of improvement and enlightenment.[16] Publishing town histories catered for a growing, self-conscious, educated 'bourgeoisie' and gratified civic pride; there are examples of corporations helping to defray the cost of publishing individual histories.[17] Second, the appearance of Milner's *Winchester* was related to,

---

13   Sweet, *op. cit.*, 275.
14   *ibid.*, 189.
15   *ibid.*, 9.
16   *ibid.*, 146–81; Corfield, *op.cit.*, *passim*.
17   P. Clark, 'Visions of the Urban Community: Antiquarians and the English City before 1800' in D. Fraser and A. Sutcliffe (eds), *The Pursuit of Urban History* (London, 1983), 117.

and was facilitated by, the growth of antiquarianism at that time. The Elizabethan Society of Antiquaries had been re-founded in 1707. John Milner
was elected one of its Fellows in 1790. Valentine Green who wrote the
History of Worcester that was published in 1796 was another Fellow of the
Society. Milner's book belongs to a severely scholarly genre. Eighteenth-
century urban histories were, in some respects at least, outcrops of a
well-established antiquarian tradition.[18] The third trend is that eighteenth-
century urban historiography was clearly related to the growth of travel and
tourism. Such histories, wrote a contemporary reviewer

> ... fill up the chasms in our topography, are repositories of ancient usages and
> traditions, and record events and transactions which would otherwise be lost
> to history. Besides rendering this public service, they gratify those who are
> connected with the respective places of which they treat and prove very
> convenient to such persons as become temporary residents in those towns or
> districts.[19]

Serious minded travellers like Sir Richard Colt and John Byng always did
preliminary reading before they sallied forth on their tours.[20] Spas and
resorts, very noticeably, never lacked their historians. John Wood's *Description of Bath* (London, 1742–43) is the pre-eminent example of its kind.[21]

Rising standards of literacy and education and the gentrification of towns
also played their part in the rise of urban historiography. The writing of
urban history, like other branches of the subject at this time, was increasingly bound up with the expansion of the professions. More and more
frequently the writers of urban histories (exclusively male, it goes without
saying) were drawn from the ranks of the well-educated 'middling sort'.
Doctors, lawyers, bankers and clergymen were especially conspicuous in
the portrait gallery of authors. Urban historians from more humble backgrounds, such as William Hutton and Henry Bourne, made occasional
appearances, but recognition for them was decidedly an uphill struggle.[22]

We have taken some time to reach the Rev John Milner but, having done
so, we are obviously in a much better position to place him and to see him
not simply as an individual but as a phenomenon. The first point to make
about Milner (1752–1826) is that he was not a native of the city whose
history he documented – and in that respect was fairly typical of the late
eighteenth-century historians. He was born in London, the son of a tailor.
His family, however, had originated in Lancashire, and Milner himself, a

---

18   Sweet, *op. cit.*, 36–73.
19   *ibid.*, 283.
20   *ibid.*, 119.
21   Wood's history and guide went through two editions, each of which was reprinted.
22   Sweet, *op. cit.*, 21.

Roman Catholic, was educated first in Staffordshire and then in Flanders at
the Douai seminary. Ordained priest in 1777 he came to Winchester two
years later and served the Roman Catholic population of the city until 1803.
He was responsible for establishing there a convent for a displaced group of
Belgian nuns who fled Brussels during the Revolutionary Wars.[23] He left
Hampshire to become installed as Vicar Apostolic of the Midland district
and was given the title of Bishop of Castabala. Unquestionably Milner was
first and foremost a Roman Catholic priest, ministering to a maligned and
penalised religious community. He did not live long enough to witness the
Catholic Emancipation Act of 1829.

> Milner was their Moses in their days of bondage [says his biographer, indulg-
> ing the most purple of his prose] It was not indeed permitted to this Moses to
> see the promised land; yet he died in sight of it.[24]

He was a prolific writer, but the principal fields in which he published were
theology and Roman Catholic apologetics. He played an active part in the
early nineteenth-century debate on Catholic Emancipation. Cardinal Newman
later dubbed him 'the English Athanasius'. The only biography of him that
exists, by F.C.Husenbeth, is very much a life of a priest by a priest. Local
history ranked with ecclesiastical architecture as his two chief secondary
interests.[25] He had lived in Winchester for almost twenty years when his
history of the city was first published in 1798.

Why did he write his history and how did he approach his task? The most
immediate part-answer to the first question is that Milner was commissioned to write it by the Winchester printer and bookseller James Robbins.
More fundamentally, however, in the light of his research, Milner was
convinced that a new history of the city was badly needed. All previous
attempts, in his view, were wrong, muddled and unconvincing. Henry Wharton's late seventeenth-century efforts were dismissed as 'vague, jejeune,
unconnected, redundant in many particulars, and deficient in others. Thomas Wharton's account in the mid eighteenth century was undermined by its
many errors and anachronisms. A two-volume history in 1773 had simply
perpetuated these defects through plagiarism. The available guidebooks,
Milner insisted, were almost worthless. Even the bald information contained
in the city tables in the Guildhall was horribly wrong. The tables, he said
dismissively, were 'a public monument that would disgrace the most illiter-
ate village in the kingdom'.[26] By contrast with these worthless 'authorities',

23   On Milner see F.C. Husenbeth, *Life of the Right Reverend John Milner* (Dublin,
1862). The *DNB* article is brief.
24   Husenbeth, *op. cit.*, 2–3.
25   *DNB*
26   J. Milner, *History, Civil and Ecclesiastical and Survey of the Antiquities of Winchester* (3rd ed., Winchester, 1839), I, vii–xvi.

Milner was convinced that he had got it right and that he had much to offer as a result of his 'laborious and patient researches into original documents'.[27] Milner's position as a Roman Catholic priest also prompted him to write. He was determined to set the record straight from the religious point of view as well from the historical. He wanted to offer not simply a local history of Winchester but a Catholic history of the city and cathedral. He distanced himself, therefore, from a prevailing antiquarianism that was chiefly Anglican in its religious associations.[28]

John Milner himself used the term 'local history' in connection with his book and he laid down in his preface the criteria for writing it. What rapidly becomes clear, however, from these criteria is that this author was not chiefly concerned with local history in its own right but with local history as exemplification of national history. Winchester's golden age as a city coincided with its political prime, and its development in all periods was inseparably bound up with religion and with the church. There was no real dividing line in other words, in Milner's judgement, between local and national history, and he had a contemptuously low opinion of those fact-grubbing antiquarians who artificially drew one.

> [The] noble science [of] the study of antiquity [he wrote] is too often disgraced and brought into ridicule by pretended antiquaries who, too dull for any other branch of literature whatever, spend their lives in minute and uninteresting investigations or enumerations, which are incapable of raising any other emotion than that of disgust, or of emitting a single spark of useful information.[29]

Milner's *Winchester* blended two ingredients. It was partly a history of the city from its foundation to the end of the eighteenth century. It also provided a survey of its principal buildings and institutions – cathedral, College, castle, Wolvesey, St Cross, and so on. Most of the second volume is devoted to the survey. The distribution of emphasis in the historical account is significant. Eleven chapters and 239 pages are devoted to Winchester's history up to 1485. Only three chapters are allocated to the following three centuries. It was most definitely the medieval past that Milner – unlike the secular minded philosophical historians of the Enlightenment –venerated, and he was often at odds with the trends of modern times. 'The city furnishes us, he said emphatically, 'but few particulars since the Revolution worth relating'. Modern dress, manners, building styles all alienated him, as did modern recreations, especially the theatre for which he had an undis-

---

27   *ibid.*, II, 275.
28   So much antiquarian interest, after all, was bound up with parish churches and their monuments.
29   Milner, *op. cit.*, I, vii.

guised contempt. He denounced the 'depredations' and 'ravages' committed against the fabric of Winchester's buildings and the ruthless and arrogant way in which the city's medieval walls and defence ditches had been removed and 'meanly replaced with vulgar brick masonry'. The whole concept of 'modernising' buildings was one which repelled him and was based, as he saw it, on 'the presumption of modern builders who have attempted to improve what they did not even understand'. 'Barbarous taste', in Milner's judgement, was now enthroned and was blatantly exhibited in those dreadful bow windows inspired by the 'predominant vice of vanity... a passion to see and be seen'. In this, as in so many other respects, the dedicatedly backward-looking Milner parted company with the progress-loving optimism of most other urban historians writing in the age of Enlightenment and improvement.[30]

The past that Milner venerated and defended was, of course, not simply a chronological past but a Roman Catholic past. The religious changes of the sixteenth century – 'Reformation' was not a term with which he was comfortable – inflicted an immense blow to Winchester and real loss in terms of religion, culture, learning, and social cohesion. 'It is chiefly since the reign of Henry VIII', Milner asserted, 'that Winchester may be said to be no more than a skeleton of its former state'. No words are spared in his account of the second Tudor king, who is denounced as a 'hoary tyrant'. Elizabeth I escapes with scarcely less censure and was branded as 'the second great destroyer of Winchester'. Though he attempted a partial defence of Queen Mary, Milner tended instead to prefer the slightly more oblique strategy of discrediting that classic of sixteenth-century Protestantism, Foxe's *Book of Martyrs*. Milner's verdict was that this celebrated book was nothing more than 'one tissue of falsehood, misrepresentation and absurdity'.[31]

Moving to the seventeenth century Milner's unsurprising conclusion on the Lord Protector was that 'if any name is deserving of execration in this city it is the name of Oliver Cromwell'. The Parliamentarian general was denounced on account of the way he led hordes of 'military barbarians and fanatical sectaries' to wreak havoc in the city and cathedral. Stability returned in 1660 but Charles II's political expediency and religious scepticism prevented him from gaining a high place in Milner's estimation. James II who acted ' a more honourable and conscientious part' received, by contrast, a generous tribute from this Roman Catholic author.[32]

Most of Milner's second volume is devoted to his survey of the buildings of Winchester, and here the author deployed his considerable architectural expertise as well as his historical skills. Milner's account of the cathedral,

30   *ibid.*, II, 43, 48, 81. On the optimism of many other eighteenth-century urban historians see Sweet, *op. cit.*, chapter 4.
31   Milner, *op. cit.*, I, 256, 297, 274.
32   *ibid.*, II, 18, 19, 20, 22, 39.

for example, took great pains to establish very precisely the extent of William of Wykeham's contribution to its building. But his religious bias got the better of him when he launched into a defence of monasticism and its benefits and a denunciation of the insensitivities and atrocities of modern architecture and building methods.[33]

Books in the late eighteenth century could reach publication through different routes. Some urban histories – though not Milner's – were published in parts, both to spread the costs and also to use successive instalments of the books themselves as advertising material.[34] Other histories, such as those on Worcester and Rochester, used a subscription scheme to defray the expenses of publication.[35] Milner's *Winchester* used neither of these well-tried devices. His book was commissioned by James Robbins, the Winchester bookseller and printer, and it was he who bore the cost. Five London booksellers acted as distribution agents in the capital, while for the second edition in 1809 there were four London stockists. The two volumes of Milner's history retailed at £2-12s-6d, putting it only within the reach of the well-to-do. (Even so, urban histories were cheaper and shorter than county histories.)[36] Milner himself received no financial reward for all his labours – only free copies to distribute to friends. The postscript to the second edition mentions opposition to the history coming from two directions, neither of them altogether surprising. The first line of resistance was from the diocese in defence of particular bishops considered to have been disparaged by Milner. The second was from the city, many of whose leading citizens, in Milner's eyes, were 'previously the dupes of fable and absurdity' and deceit. Neither Milner's forthright, uncompromising style nor his Roman Catholicism can have endeared him in some quarters.[37]

Criticism notwithstanding, Milner's history became a considerable success, as its various editions and long shelf life clearly demonstrate. Abridgements, 'intended for the use of strangers and other persons who have not sufficient leisure to read, or else have not the means of procuring' the original, popularised it. Milner's *Winchester* was a blend of antiquarian scholarship and Roman Catholic convictions, and was certainly not a masterpiece in terms of its prose style. Even this author's admiring biographer had to admit that Milner's writing was often clumsy and unpolished.[38]

33   *ibid.*, II, 68, 142–44, 81.
34   Sweet, *op. cit.*, 33.
35   See ibid., 28–31. Though the subscription method was really a form of collective patronage, the role of influential individuals could still be crucial, not least by attracting others to join them.
36   See J. Oldfield, *Printers, Booksellers and Libraries in Hampshire, 1750–1800*, Hampshire Papers (Winchester, 1993).
37   Milner, *op. cit.*, II, 284, 276. Milner's own postscript to the second edition recounts the opposition he faced and his dealings with it.
38   Husenbeth, *op. cit.*, 536.

Milner's history was closely related to the social, economic and religious circumstances which surrounded it at the time of its composition. It is more than a local history. It is a politico-religious statement by a Roman Catholic priest which boldly correlates Winchester's past greatness in the Middle Ages with the ascendancy of the old religion. In that sense it forcibly reclaims Winchester's history for Milner's own co-religionists. Milner's use of the possessive adjective in expressions like 'our venerable cathedral' and 'our city' seems more than merely casual. Milner once wrote a hostile review of the first published instalment of the Catholic *History of England* by John Lingard, one of his former pupils.

> He has not sufficiently refuted the calumnies, nor dissipated the misrepresentations of Protestant or infidel writers; nor has he displayed the beauty of holiness, irradiating the doctrines and heroes of Catholicity... In short the History of England which has lately appeared... is not a Catholic history such as our calumniated and depressed condition calls for.[39]

By so writing, John Milner was, by extension, insisting that no such charge could ever be laid against him. The religious stance of his local history is unmistakable; Winchester's history is seen through the eyes of a Roman Catholic priest and its modern, Protestant, phase receives relatively short shrift. Two centuries after it was first written copies of Milner's book are still readily accessible in libraries in the city, and its author occupies a high-ranking place in local historiography. But, just as significantly, Milner Hall – a Roman Catholic foundation in Winchester – still unambiguously commemorates his distinctive achievement today and claims him for the particular religious group on whose behalf he ministered and campaigned.

---

39   *ibid.*, 394. Milner's oppositon to Lingard's liberal Catholicism was expressed on numerous occasions. See D.F. Shea, *The English Ranke. John Lingard* (New York, 1969), 12, 14, 16, 23, 26, 32, 47, 54, 75–77. Shea describes Milner as Lingard's 'direct opposite, a man congenitally unable to compromise'. (Shea, *op. cit.*, 12).

7

BETWEEN ANTIQUARY AND ACADEMIC: LOCAL HISTORY IN THE NINETEENTH CENTURY

*Alan J. Kidd**

In one of the most influential modern guides to the study of local history, W. B. Stephens expressed his 'prejudice against ... the antiquarian aspects of local studies' which, he warned his readers, meant that in his volume 'no mention will be found of heraldry, brass rubbing, genealogy, campanology and the like'.[1] This particular conjunction of traditional 'antiquarian' activities with certain esoteric leisure pursuits enabled the dismissal of the former as marginal, even eccentric. Thus the field of local history could be clearly distinguished from that of the antiquarian. Equally, however, Stephens went on to exclude academic areas requiring specialist technical knowledge such as archaeology, geology, palaeography and the etymology of place-names.[2] By such means local history could be further defined as a territory appropriate for the *historian*, as opposed to academics in other specialist disciplines. University-based local historians have often felt it necessary to draw such distinctions precisely because of the origins of local history in the work of nineteenth-century antiquaries, archaeologists, historians and others at a time when modern discipline boundaries did not exist and distinctions between amateur and professional were less sharply drawn.

An awareness of their place in history was a characteristic of the culture of the Victorians and a vital intellectual influence throughout the nineteenth century. Despite living in an age which had witnessed unprecedented change in technology and transport, industry and urban growth, social and political institutions and ideas, the Victorians approached the past with a reverence and respect only possible because they no longer felt threatened by it. The social as well as technological processes known as the industrial revolution

---

*   I am grateful for the comments of my colleague Terry Wyke on an earlier draft of this article.

1   W. B. Stephens, *Sources for English Local History* (Manchester, 1973), 1–2.
2   Ibid., 2.

had fractured, though not destroyed, continuity with the past. However, its impact caused concern at the loss of what was coming to be seen as the nation's 'traditional heritage'. This found reflection in a number of ways, from the folklorists' concern to record the decaying customs of popular culture, to the architectural societies which promoted the preservation of the Gothic. What we now call local history arose in this climate. The purpose here is to explore, by means of a case study of the North West, the local history culture which flourished in many parts of England between the 1830s and the 1880s.

The middle decades of the nineteenth century constituted something of a 'golden age' for the serious amateur local historian. The professionals had not yet claimed this territory and the preservation of the past seemed the responsibility of the Victorian propertied classes. Following the formation of the British Archaeological Association in 1844, numerous county archaeological societies were founded. Philippa Levine has described the origins and development of the three overlapping communities of antiquarianism, archaeology, and history and the extent to which these terms were interchangeable for much of the nineteenth century.[3] However, by the 1880s the divisions between

Figure 1. A street scene inside 'Old Manchester and Salford' (1887). The buildings were timber and plaster replicas of long-demolished originals with exterior detail applied in paint. Attendants can be seen attired in various historical costumes.

---

3   P. Levine, *The Amateur and the Professional: Antiquarians, Historians and Archaeologists in Victorian England 1838–1886* (Cambridge, 1986); see also C. Dellheim,

them were becoming solidified by the advent of the university academic disciplines of History and Archaeology, thus marginalising antiquarianism as amateur and implicitly inferior.[4] In this process local history itself became side-tracked by the professionals, only to be taken up by them once again in the generation following the Second World War.

'Local History' was arguably a central feature of nineteenth-century middle-class culture and has been unjustly neglected by historians. Its study not only throws light on the Victorian obsession with the past but also exemplifies the vibrancy of provincial as opposed to metropolitan culture, and highlights the relationship of region to nation in an age when civic pride and local identities were more marked than today. Although generally expressed in the obscurity of the activities and proceedings of relevant learned societies and through the publications of individual local historians, occasionally its public profile was much higher. One such significant moment occurred in the year of Queen Victoria's Golden Jubilee when the city fathers of Manchester chose to include what one can only describe as a heritage theme park, called 'Old Manchester and Salford', in their hugely successful commemoration of fifty years of Victoria's reign, the Manchester Royal Jubilee Exhibition of 1887.[5]

Manchester's pre-industrial 'town' of 1887 was a pattern of narrow streets and open spaces with full-size reconstructions of local buildings from the medieval period to the eighteenth century. It included numerous displays of traditional crafts and was peopled by attendants attired in a variety of historic dress. 'Old Manchester and Salford' was organised by a committee of thirteen men from a variety of manufacturing, mercantile and professional backgrounds. Several were prominent figures in Manchester's literary and intellectual life, including members of the recently formed Lancashire and Cheshire Antiquarian Society (1883), the Historic Society of Lancashire and Cheshire (founded in 1848) and the Manchester Literary Club (1862). If attendance at the committee's 51 meetings is any guide to the relative contribution of its members, then those who were members of these three societies dominated its proceedings. Moreover, the architect commissioned to design 'Old Manchester', Alfred Darbyshire, was a founding member of the Council of the Lancashire and Cheshire Antiquarian Society.

The 1880s offer a vantage point from which to look back at the development of antiquarian and local studies in the nineteenth century. In the

---

The Face of the Past: The Preservation of the Medieval Inheritance in Victorian England (Cambridge, 1982) and S. Piggott, *Ruins in a Landscape: Essays in Antiquarianism* (Edinburgh, 1976).

4   The process took longer in archaeology than in history: see Levine, *The Amateur and the Professional*, 171–2.

5   See A. J. Kidd, 'The Industrial city and it pre-industrial past: the Manchester Royal Jubilee Exhibition of 1887', *Transactions of the Lancashire and Cheshire Antiquarian Society (TLCAS)* 89 (1993), 54–73.

Figure 2. One of the exhibition rooms inside 'Old Manchester and Salford' (1887) with numerous paintings, prints and artefacts loaned by private collectors.

generation or so preceding the Royal Jubilee Exhibition in 1887, a local history community had grown up in the North West based upon the existence of certain key societies. These were broadly of two types. Firstly there were the printing clubs. Members received club publications in return for their annual subscription. Printing clubs such as the Surtees Society, founded in Durham in 1834, and the Camden Society of 1838 established the tradition. The Chetham Society in Manchester followed suit in 1843.[6] The Record Society of Lancashire and Cheshire was founded in 1878 and the Lancashire Parish Register Society in 1898. The Chetham Society, founded for the publication of *Remains Historical and Literary Connected with the Palatine Counties of Lancaster and Cheshire*, shared with the other printing clubs of the 1830s and 1840s the desire to develop the private printing of historical records in the wake of the poor quality and eventual demise of the Record Commission publications and the uncertain future of public records despite

---

6   For the Chetham Society see A. G. Crosby, *'A society with No Equal': The Chetham Society 1843–1993* (Manchester, 1993).

Figure 3. A guide book to the Royal Jubilee Exhibition of 1887 which featured Alfred Darbyshire's imaginative reconstruction of the streets and buildings of 'Old Manchester and Salford'.

the passage of the Public Records Office Act of 1838.[7] Secondly, there were the 'social' societies with their meetings, excursions and events as well as their published transactions. These offered a vastly different experience from the comparative passivity of printing club membership. The two most notable such societies in the North West were the Historic Society of Lancashire and Cheshire, founded in Liverpool, and the Lancashire and Cheshire Antiquarian Society formed in Manchester. Although each was based in a single city, like the Chetham Society they were self-consciously regional in scope. Other county societies in the vicinity included the Chester Architectural, Archaeological and Historic Society of 1849, the Cumberland and Westmorland Antiquarian and Archaeological Society of 1866 and the Derbyshire Archaeological and Natural History Society of 1878. Between 1843 and the 1880s the existence of these and other related organisations encouraged the growth of a 'local history culture' in the North West which was both amateur *and* academic in character. History and antiquarianism had not yet parted company, although the Lancashire and Cheshire Antiquarian Society was formed at the very point when the separation of the paths was being engineered by the emerging class of professional historians in the universities.

The formation of the Lancashire and Cheshire Antiquarian Society marked the culmination of the era of amateur local history in Manchester.[8] In addressing the Society at a conversazione to commemorate its formation, the Society President, the eminent geologist Professor Boyd Dawkins, referred to what he called the 'kindred associations' which had preceded it. He identified not only the Chetham, the Historic and the Chester Archaeological societies but also the Manchester Literary and Philosophical Society, the short-lived Philological and Bibliographical societies and the even more ephemeral Lancashire Antiquarian Society of 1829 which had issued only a single volume of transactions.[9] Dawkins was able to cast the net widely because the realm of antiquarianism and the methods of the antiquaries themselves were broadly conceived. In theory the antiquarian was interested in all aspects of the human past, generally circumscribed only by the passion for collecting, classifying and describing objects. By definition antiquarian objects were objects studied by the antiquarian, from Phoenician vases to flint tools, from Roman coins to ecclesiastical architecture, from literary 'remains' to geological 'remains'.

---

7   F. J. Levy, 'The founding of the Camden Society', *Victorian Studies*, 7(1964), 295–305.

8   Histories of local societies are often worthy but uninspiring catalogues of events and personalities, but the Lancashire and Cheshire Antiquarian Society is fortunate to possess a most able chronicler. I found V. I. Tomlinson, 'The Lancashire and Cheshire Antiquarian Society 1883–1983', *TLCAS*, 83 (1985), 1–39, most useful.

9   *TLCAS*, 2 (1884), 97.

OFFICERS FOR 1883.

President:

PROFESSOR WILLIAM BOYD DAWKINS, F.R.S., F.S.A.

Vice=Presidents:

R. ANGUS SMITH, LL.D., F.R.S.

T. GLAZEBROOK RYLANDS, F.S.A.

Members of the Council:

W. E. A. AXON, F.R.S.L.

SIR THOMAS BAKER.

JAMES CROSTON, F.S.A.

A. DARBYSHIRE, F.R.I.B.A.

LIEUT.-COL. H. FISHWICK, F.S.A.

R. LANGTON, F.R.H.S.

J. HOLME NICHOLSON, M.A.

REV. J. H. STANNING, M.A.

HENRY TAYLOR.

W. THOMPSON WATKIN.

Treasurer:

F. A. WHAITE, F.R.M.S.

Hon. Secretary:

GEO. C. YATES, F.S.A.

Figure 4. The officers of the Lancashire and Cheshire Antiquarian Society in its foundation year.

Electicism remained a hallmark of much in antiquarian studies, as did the desire of 'leisured gentlemen' to possess antiquarian curios which could be displayed at home or at society soirées. However, the day of dilettantism in local studies, so often satirised in the figure of the 'antiquary' from Pope's 'To future ages may thy dulness Last/As thou preserv'st the dulness of the past' and Scott's amiable but gullible Jonathan Oldbuck to the hilarious generalities of the Pickwick Club, was passing.[10] There is good reason to adapt Kargon's analysis of the development of the scientific community in Manchester to that of local history. Kargon argues that the 1840s saw the

---

10   Levine, *The Amateur and the Professional*, 17.

emergence of the class of 'devotees' of science who saw it as their calling, rather than the less committed, more 'gentlemanly' cohort from the previous generation, who often possessed wide-ranging interests. These devotees were still self-trained amateurs, but rather than pursuing science as a form of moral and intellectual elevation or as a means of disseminating knowledge to the lower orders, they were far more concerned with contributions to knowledge as such.[11] Levine argues that the antiquarian, historical and archaeological societies of the Victorian period attracted a similar class of devotee, committed to extending the boundaries of historical knowledge for its own sake.[12]

In practice many antiquarians active in the North West specialised in particular areas and saw themselves as serious scholars contributing to the development of human knowledge. They came from a variety of, mostly professional, occupations. The first Council of the Antiquarian Society included two architects, a librarian, legal clerk, chemist, artist (wood engraver), cleric, university academic, university official and a member of one of Liverpool's merchant families. The undoubted focus of many antiquarians was the locality, whether conceived narrowly to mean the village or town, or more broadly to encompass county or even regional concerns. This was the antiquarianism which gave rise to local history. In reality Dawkins could have cast his net even wider in the search for 'kindred associations', for as well as the printing clubs and archaeological societies of mid-Victorian local history, the activities and interests of the Antiquarian Society had their origins in the work of societies as disparate as the Manchester Literary Club, which had included numerous antiquarian papers in its early sessions plus an annual bibliography of locally published works, and the natural history societies of the Manchester district, especially the Field Naturalists' Society and the Scientific Students' Association.[13]

The contribution of the Field Naturalists' Society and the Scientific Students' Association suggests the attraction of scientific and antiquarian studies to the broader middle class. Each emphasised the sociability of cultivated leisure pursuits conducted in concert with others of like mind and generally of like social status. As well as the self-consciously serious work of the learned devotee, the excursions and soirées of the enthusiastic seeker after leisure and companionship as well as knowledge were part of the appeal of the natural history, antiquarian and similar associational societies. The Field Naturalists' Society, founded in 1860, had as its stated purpose not to make 'recondite scientific inquiries and investigations ...

---

11   R. H. Kargon, *Science in Victorian Manchester: Enterprise and Expertise* (Manchester, 1977), esp. 31–5.

12   Levine, *The Amateur and the Professional*, 7.

13   Tomlinson points to the connection with the natural history societies: 'The Lancashire and Cheshire Antiquarian Society', 6–8.

but to diffuse existing knowledge, to stimulate and assist beginners, and very specially to promote that kindly social companionship which renders the open air study of nature so delightful', hence the emphasis on excursions.[14] The impact of Darwinian evolutionary theory served to undermine the natural history movement of the mid-Victorian era. One of the consequences of this was a move towards other outdoor studies as well as natural history. This was reflected in the renaming of the Society in 1875 as the Manchester Field Naturalists' and Archaeologists' Society. A similar process took place in the Manchester Scientific Students' Association. This society, devoted to a broad range of scientific pursuits including the geological and mechanical sciences, was formed after the meeting of the British Association in Manchester in 1861. By the 1870s the Association's excursions were including those of a clearly antiquarian character, and interest in the collection and display of antiquarian remains is evident in the exhibition by members of objects at the 'Coming of Age' soirée held by the Association in the Free Trade Hall in 1882. These included coins, prehistoric stone implements, arms and armour and antique pottery as well as a selection of fossils, spiders, shells, engineering equipment and working models of steam engines and pumps.[15]

A key member of the Scientific Students' Association (its honorary secretary from 1872) and instrumental in founding the Antiquarian Society in 1883 was George C. Yates, chief clerk of Salford County Court. Yates was the dominant figure in the Antiquarian Society over its first twenty-five years until his death in 1908. Yates combined an interest in scientific and antiquarian studies and amassed a large private collection. He was a Fellow of the Society of Antiquaries and member of the Manchester Literary Club, Chetham Society and the Museums Association. Enthusiastic amateurs like Yates were vital to the organisation of local historical studies, as was the cooperation of university academics like Boyd Dawkins, Professor of Geology at Owens College, friend of leading historians of the day and the Society's first president. Other founding members of the Antiquarian Society included the librarian and bibliographer W. E. A. Axon, and established local historians Henry Fishwick, Henry Taylor and W. Thompson Watkin.

Did the existence of such societies constitute a local history network? It is worth noting the extent to which society memberships overlapped. This is based less on a comparison of general memberships which would draw on a broader base of middle-class supporters of local ventures and elevating pursuits who might not necessarily be local historians as such (this

---

14   *Manchester Field Naturalists' and Archaeologists' Society, Report and Proceedings for 1884*, 1.

15   Special report on the 'Coming of Age' Soirée bound with *Manchester Scientific Students Association, Reports and Proceedings, 1881–3* in Manchester Reference Library.

would be particularly true of the printing societies where nothing more might be required than the payment of an annual subscription) but on the key figures, the members of the respective society councils. Of the 14 members of the Council of the Chetham Society in 1848–9, the year the Historic Society was founded, seven were either founder members of the latter, Liverpool-based, organisation or were to join during its first three years. Three Chetham Society Council members were also elected Council members for the Historic in its first year. This cross-membership between societies, of particular significance at the point of formation, continued over time. When the Record Society was founded in 1878, six of its 13 Council members and officials were members of the Council of the Chetham Society in the same year. Five years later, when the Antiquarian Society was formed, its ten-strong Council included members from the councils of the Chetham Society, the Record Society and the Historic Society. Also represented was the Manchester Literary Club with three members of the Antiquarian Society's first Council.

The overlap in membership with the Manchester Literary Club is interesting, suggesting as it does a broader-based cultural community or the intersection of related branches in Manchester's cultural life. Among the 263 members of the Lancashire and Cheshire Antiquarian Society in its first year the overlap with the Literary Club (31 were members of both societies in 1883) was as significant as the overlap with the Historic Society (32 members of both). By comparison, joint membership of the Antiquarian Society and the nearby county archaeological societies was strikingly low, at four with the Derbyshire society and seven with the Chester society. Both geography and the narrow topographical interests of many in the field limited such inter-society membership. There were, however, notable society enthusiasts such as W. E. A. Axon who, in 1884, was a member of at least seven local societies: the Antiquarian, the Historic, the Field Naturalists, the Scientific Students, the Literary and Philosophical, the Literary Club and the newly-formed Manchester Geographical Society.

What sort of activities did the 'local history' societies generate? The Lancashire and Cheshire Antiquarian Society followed the classic pattern of the nineteenth-century 'social' societies. Papers were read at autumn and winter meetings, excursions were held in the summer and an annual conversazione gathered to hear a guest speaker and to view exhibits from members' collections. However, unlike the Field Naturalists' Society, the Antiquarian Society was not averse to 'recondite scientific enquiries and investigations'. Indeed, from the outset an explicit purpose was to finance appropriate fieldwork. In its first year the Society funded the excavation of a portion of the Roman road at Blackstone Edge, and during its first decade sponsored further archaeological excavations at Chester, Lancaster and Manchester. Such work suggests academic aspirations extending beyond the publication of learned papers. There was also some conception of a public

COUNTY BOROUGH  OF SALFORD.

MUSEUM, LIBRARIES, AND PARKS COMMITTEE.

PEEL PARK

FREE LECTURES

(TWENTY-FIFTH SERIES)

SEASON 1905-6.

THE TENTH LECTURE OF THE SEASON WILL BE GIVEN UNDER THE AUSPICES OF THE ABOVE COMMITTEE ON

Tuesday Evening, Mar. 13th, 1906,

In the GREAT HALL, ROYAL TECHNICAL INSTITUTE,

BY

MR. J. J. PHELPS

(Hon. Director of the "Old Manchester and Salford" Exhibition, 1904).

SUBJECT:

"OLD MANCHESTER & SALFORD"

A BACKWARD GLANCE THROUGH MANY CENTURIES.

SYLLABUS.—*Prehistoric Period.*—Manchester as a British Camp—Local finds of Stone and Bronze Age Implements, Urns, &c.—Traces of Prehistoric Religion—Canoes. *Roman Period.*—Manchester a Fortress—Wall—Hypocaust, Altars, Inscriptions—Worship of Mithras—Samian and Romano-British Pottery—Statuette of *Jupiter Stator*—Coins—Querns—Roads—Neighbouring Camps. *Saxon Period.*—Coins—The "Angel" Stone—Christianity—The People and their Sports. *Norman Period.*—Barons of Manchester—Domesday Survey—Salford Hundred—The Greslets—Seals of Early Landowners in Manchester and Salford. *Mediæval Period.*—The Old Bridge and Chapel—Hanging Bridge—The Old Church—John Huntingdon—Hugh Oldham—Humphrey Chetham—Chetham Hospital—Old Halls—Old Families and their quaint black and white gabled dwellings, &c.

LANTERN ILLUSTRATIONS.

The Lecture will commence at Eight o'clock.

Last Lecture, 27th March, Mr. ALFRED ROGERS,
"Reminiscences of a Cycle-Touring Photographer."

RESERVED SEATS.—A few Seats will be Reserved. TICKETS, price 3d. each, may be had at the Entrance on the night of each Lecture from 7-30 till 8 o'clock.

ADMISSION FREE.

Children under 12 years of age, unaccompanied by responsible personal Guardians, will not be admitted to the Lecture.

ALFRED WORSLEY, Chairman,
MUSEUM, LIBRARIES, AND PARKS COMMITTEE.

Taylor, Garnett, Evans & Co., Ltd., Printing Works, Blackfriars Street, Salford.

Figure 5. Interest in local history may have been encouraged by public lectures such as this advertised in 1906. The list of contents suggests an ambitious chronological survey since prehistoric times with the aid of suitable artefacts and lantern slides.

educative role.[16] The Royal Jubilee Exhibition of 1887 inspired Antiquarian Society members to mount several further public exhibitions of local history over the next 25 years, which suggests a sense of responsibility for the dissemination of knowledge of the local past to the wider public.[17]

The local history culture of the middle decades of the nineteenth century depended upon more than the existence of several relevant societies, although these provided a necessary infra-structure for its survival. It was also sustained by the publications of several local historians; the uncertain existence of a handful of local periodicals devoted to antiquarian, archaeological and historical interests; and the willingness of some newspapers to give column inches to the local interests of journalists and their correspondents. Prolific authors of historical works on Lancashire and Cheshire who were involved in the work of the Antiquarian Society from its inception included J. E. Bailey, J. P. Earwaker, Henry Fishwick and W. Thompson Watkin.

John Eglinton Bailey (1840–88) was in many ways the classic self-taught antiquarian whose life of study and publication was the product of leisure hours away from his work in a Manchester commercial house. Educated at grammar school in Warrington and at Owens College evening classes, Bailey's most enduring work was his life of the seventeenth-century divine Thomas Fuller, published in 1874. Most of his energies were devoted subsequently to a variety of local history and archaeological subjects. He contributed papers to the Literary Club, the Historic, the Field Naturalists and the Antiquarian societies, reflecting the broad church which was Victorian local studies. John Parsons Earwaker (1847–95), in contrast to Bailey, was able to devote much of his adult life to scholarly pursuits. The son of a Manchester merchant, he was educated at Owens College and Merton College, Oxford, graduating in Natural Sciences. Returning to Manchester in 1874, he subsequently retired to North Wales at the age of 34 to devote himself to literary and antiquarian researches. He served on the councils of the Historic and the Record as well as the Antiquarian societies and was often employed by private and public bodies in the investigation of their muniments. For the Manchester Corporation he edited the *Court Leet Records of the Manor of Manchester* (12 vols., 1884–90) and the *Constables Accounts of the Manor of Manchester* (3 vols., 1891–2). Apart from these tasks his most notable work was his two volume *History of East Cheshire* (1877–80). Henry Fishwick (1835–1914) was noted for his *History of Rochdale Parish* (1889) and *History of Lancashire* (1894). This long-serving Rochdale

---

16   Its educational ambitions were considerably more modest than those of the Manchester Geographical Society which, on its foundation in 1884, had envisaged its role to include that of educating society in the value of 'geographical science' to 'commerce and civilisation'. See T. Nigel L. Brown, *The History of the Manchester Geographical Society 1884–1950* (Manchester, 1971), 6.

17   See Tomlinson, 'The Lancashire and Cheshire Antiquarian Society', 27–8.

Lancashire
and Cheshire
Antiquarian
Society.

be Council desire to return you their grateful thanks for your contributions to the "Old Manchester and Salford Exhibition." You will be glad to know that this Exhibition of Pictorial Memoranda and other Relics of the past history of this district has been remarkably successful. In the six weeks during which it has been open the number of visitors is estimated to have exceeded 40,000. The greatest interest has been shown in the Exhibition both by the Public and the Press. At its formal closing on May 11th, the Lord Mayor of Manchester expressed the general hope that the Exhibition may be followed by a permanent collection of illustrations of local history and antiquities. A number of gifts have already been promised, and the Lord Mayor has given an assurance that accommodation shall be provided for the beginning of such a museum. May we hope for your co-operation in carrying out this project either by gifts or loans?

Again thanking you for your generosity which has aided in making the "Old Manchester and Salford Exhibition" so successful and so useful.

We remain,
Yours faithfully,
HENRY TAYLOR, President.
W. BOYD DAWKINS,
C. W. SUTTON,   Past Presidents.
WILLIAM E. A. AXON,
J. J. PHELPS, Hon. Director of the Exhibition.
Manchester,   G. C. YATES, Hon. Secretary (Urmston).
May 17th, 1904.

Figure 6. Antiquarian Society members mounted several public exhibitions of local history consisting chiefly of items donated by private collectors. This letter was sent to those who had loaned 'pictorial memoranda and other relics' for an exhibition held in 1904.

politician was first elected councillor in 1871 and served as Mayor between 1903 and 1905. As well as the Antiquarian Society, of which he became President in 1897, he was a member of the councils of the Chetham, the Record, the Parish Register, the Rochdale Literary and Scientific and other societies. He joined the Volunteer force in 1860, becoming Lieutenant Colonel in 1871, a title he used throughout his life.[18]

18   None of these local historians found their way into the *Dictionary of National Biography*. This information is gleaned from obituaries and the occasional extended article such as W. E. A. Axon, 'In memoriam J. E. Bailey, F.S.A.', *Papers of the Manchester Literary Club*, 14 (1888), 297–306 and that on Earwaker which appeared in *Manchester Faces and Places*, vol.6 no.10 (July, 1895).

An important element in the burgeoning local history culture of the mid-Victorian period was the existence, albeit fitful, of several local history publications and newspaper columns. Local historians and others believed there was a broader market for their work outside the learned societies. Several local newspapers included columns of the 'notes and queries' variety. Most notably J. H. Nodal ran a column with this title in the weekly paper, the *Manchester City News*. Dealing chiefly with antiquarian and historical issues, these columns were published subsequently in half-yearly volumes at an initial subscription of four shillings. Beginning in 1878 the series ran, with different editorships, until the 1920s. Predecessors had been published in both of Manchester's rival daily papers. First was Axon's weekly column of 'Local Notes and Queries' in the *Manchester Guardian*, reprinted each week in a four-page booklet and subsequently in an annual volume. This ran from 1874 until 1877. Similarly, Earwaker had edited a 'Local Gleanings' column in the *Manchester Courier* between 1875 and 1879. It was revised and reprinted each quarter with a print run of 250.[19] Newspapers in other North West towns ran similar features which also led to volume publication, suggesting the fertility and complexity of the local history network. Examples are *Historical and Genealogical Notes* (1878), edited by Josiah Rose and reprinted from the *Leigh Chronicle* 'Scrapbook' and *Local Notes and Gleanings* (1886–8?) edited by Giles Shaw and reprinted from the *Oldham Express*.

Others tried to develop free-standing journals. An early example was the *Cheshire and Lancashire Historical Collector* of 1853–5, edited by T. Worthington Barlow and dedicated to R. E. Egerton Warburton of Arley Hall in Cheshire. Published monthly, it was the editor's stated intention to offer shorter and more frequently published items than could be found in the annual transactions of the Historic Society. In the event it consisted mostly of Cheshire topics in the region of Arley Hall. An interesting feature was the attempt to build up a bibliography of Lancashire and Cheshire history. More substantial publications followed in the late 1870s and the 1880s, although they were no longer lived. In 1879 Earwaker founded his own monthly periodical arising out of his by now discontinued columns for the *Manchester Courier* and under the same title, *Local Gleanings: An Archaeological and Historical Magazine Chiefly Relating to Lancashire and Cheshire*. From a first monthly issue of 40 pages at 1s. 6d. the price was reduced to one shilling by January 1880. By June of the same year the journal was defunct, ostensibly a casualty of the editor's retirement to North Wales but perhaps also of the literary marketplace. The most accomplished of the North West's local history magazines from this period was J. E. Bailey's *Palatine Note Book*, with the subtitle 'for the Intercommunication of Antiquaries,

19   F. Leary, 'History of the Manchester Periodical Press' (unpub. manuscript, n.d., Manchester Reference Library, Local Studies Archives), 359.

Bibliophiles and other Investigators into the History and Literature of the Counties of Lancaster, Chester, etc'. This was published monthly between 1881 and 1885 with a cover price of sixpence for 16 pages rising to 10d. for 36 pages by the time of its closure.[20]

Given the varied local and national historical press, where could a local historian publish? The career of the historian of Roman Britain, W. Thompson Watkin, helps to answer this question. His most notable contributions to local history were *Roman Lancashire* (1883) and *Roman Cheshire* (1886). His articles appeared in a variety of places including national journals such as *Archaeological Journal, Journal of the British Archaeological Association, Academy, Reliquary*; those published in Manchester and Liverpool, including *Transactions of the Historic Society of Lancashire and Cheshire, Transactions of the Lancashire and Cheshire Antiquarian Society, Notes and Queries, Local Gleanings, Palatine Notebook*; and in other county and local societies, such as *Transactions of the Shropshire Archaeological and Natural History Society, Transactions of the Cumberland and Westmoreland Antiquarian and Archaeological Society, Journal of the Derbyshire Archaeological Society, Yorkshire Archaeological and Topographical Journal, Powys Land Club*, and the *Transactions of the London and Middlesex Archaeological Society*.[21]

Although antiquarian studies had come a long way since the easily satirised dilettantism of Scott's Jonathan Oldbuck, the approach to the past it represented was easily marginalised because of its lack of a consistent subject matter, methodology (the break from archaeology with the advent of a more self-consciously scientific methodology in that discipline is instructive) or intellectual purpose beyond recording and recovering. History's claim to university status as a degree subject owed much to its perceived role in the moral and patriotic education of the nation's élite, but its intellectual pretensions were justified on the basis of its documents-based empiricism, a methodology learned from the earlier 'German School' of Ranke, Niebuhr and Mommsen. Thus in the era of Bishop Stubbs, the first historian in England to make a serious contribution to knowledge whilst also holding a post as a university teacher, history became established as a university discipline to be taught, studied and examined.[22] Stubbs' influence also meant that the first generation of English university historians concentrated on constitutional, legal and political history. The combination of wide interests and local focus which antiquarianism represented was thus doubly rejected.

20   Ibid., 392.

21   See T. Formby and E. Axon, 'List of the writings of W. Thompson Watkin', *TLCAS*, 6 (1888), 173–8.

22   G. P. Gooch, *History and Historians in the Nineteenth Century* (London, 1913), ch.18; T. W. Heyck, *The Transformation of Intellectual Life in Victorian England* (London, 1982), ch.5.

Archaeology similarly abandoned the local focus of its pioneers in favour of preponderantly Classical World excavations.

However, the antiquarian and archaeological societies did possess some friends among the leading scholars of the 'Oxford School'. Edward Freeman's imaginative approach to urban history had built on the more piecemeal studies of the antiquarians and led him to observe:

> There is hardly any better historic training for a man than to set him frankly in the streets of a quiet little town like Bury St Edmunds, and let him work out the history of the men who lived and died there ... It is just in the pettiness of its details, in its commonplace incidents, in the want of marked features and striking events that the real lesson of the whole story lies.[23]

When Freeman addressed the Lancashire and Cheshire Antiquarian Society in 1884, he told his audience that 'local researches were of very, very little profit unless they were brought to throw light on the general history of the country' and concluded that:

A local antiquarian society ... should work out the history of every district and spot, not merely, the towns but the smallest villages; should work out every local detail, remembering as they went along that all they were working at locally was part of the history of England, and that the history of England was only part of a greater history – that of the whole of Europe.[24]

---

23   Quoted in J. W. Burrow, *A Liberal Descent: Victorian Historians and the English Past* (Cambridge, 1981), 179–80.
24   *TCLAS*, 2 (1884), 152, 160.

8

THE LOCAL HISTORIAN AND HIS THEME

H. P. R. Finberg

In 1890 a writer in the *Saturday Review* expressed the opinion that 'of all dull books a conscientiously compiled parochial history is the dullest.' More recently an American scholar, engaged in collecting materials for a treatise on the English borough, found it necessary to consult a number of our local histories. He pronounced them to be mostly 'so much dead weight on library shelves: vexatious to the student because of their disorderliness and wordiness; lacking most of what histories should contain, and containing much that histories should omit.'[1]

So, on the threshold of the subject, we are greeted rather peevishly. And, it must be admitted, not without cause. Of the unnumbered books that have been written on the history of our counties, towns, and villages, few, if any, have been heard of by the general reader. There are no classics in this field, no local histories which are esteemed as masterpieces on a level with, say, Macaulay's *History of England*. Except when local piety, or the urgent curiosity of the professed student, blows off the accumulated dust, these folios, quartos, and octavos, fruits of so much devoted toil, are left un-opened. Local history is the Cinderella among historical studies.

Nevertheless in recent years the universities have shown themselves dis-posed to take Cinderella under their protection. This may be just a counsel of despair; but I would rather construe it as an act of faith in the poor creature's possibilities. The first move was made as long ago as 1908, when, thanks mainly to private benefactions, a Research Fellowship in Local History was instituted at Reading. Despite the lustre conferred upon it by its first and only holder, F. M. Stenton, the post was discontinued after four years. In 1921 a Reader in the History of London was appointed at University College, London. Nine years later the University College of Hull set up a committee to promote research in the history of 'the area more particularly served by the College': that is, the East Riding of Yorkshire and north Lincolnshire. Since 1949 there has been at the same college a staff Tutor in Local History; and by

---

1   M. de W. Hemmeon, *Burgage Tenure in Mediaeval England* (Cambridge, Mass., 1914), 9.

establishing, in the following year, a certificate in the subject, Hull again stood forth as one of Cinderella's doughtiest champions. In each case these developments occurred within the framework of existing departments: at London, in the department of history, and at Hull in that of adult education.[2] Only at the University College of Leicester has the subject as yet been accorded a department of it own. For this reason, and also because the department set up here in 1947 is not confined to any one area, but takes the local history of all England for its province, its establishment may be considered as a milestone in the progress of a new academic discipline.

While the younger academic bodies were taking these initiatives, and the senior universities were looking on indifferently, or perhaps averting their gaze in horror, Professor Arnold Toynbee was publishing the first instalments of his great treatise on world-history. That celebrated work might seem at first sight to have little direct bearing on my theme; but the propositions on which its argument is based do in fact constitute an excellent starting-point for a discussion of local history and its relationship with other branches of historical study. Toynbee maintains that historians have been occupying themselves too exclusively with the fortunes of the national state. He shows that the life of England, and still more obviously the lives of France, Germany, Spain, have been profoundly affected at all the crucial points by forces operating from outside the national frontiers. Consequently their history cannot be understood unless we study them as parts of a larger entity. The histories of England, France, and Spain are merely chapters in the history of Western Society as a whole. This greater society is 'an intelligible field of study'; its component nations, taken by themselves, are not. Therefore historians will do well to 'devote a larger share of their energy and acumen' to the study of Western Society and of the other great societies whose actions and interactions make up the sum of world-history.[3]

In urging this plea, Toynbee sometimes uses expressions which could be taken as implying that it is a waste of time to study national history. Nevertheless he would probably admit that it is normal and natural for Englishmen to take a particular interest in the history of England, and even to find it more readily intelligible than the history of other nations. For our part, we may agree with him that it cannot be fully understood in isolation from the supra-national entity of which England has formed a part. Our interest in the story of our own people does not spring only from natural sympathy: it can be fully justified on Toynbee's principles. For, as he himself points out, the national community is an 'articulation' of the larger society to which it belongs; and while urging us 'to think in terms of the whole and not of the parts,' he observes that 'different parts are differently affected by an identi-

---

2   I am indebted to the Registrars of Reading and Hull, and to the Secretary of University College, London, for the particulars given here.

3   Arnold J. Toynbee, *A Study of History* (Oxford, 1934–), I, 17–50.

cal general cause, because they each react, and each contribute, in a different way to the forces which that same cause sets in motion.' We may put it in homelier terms: it takes all sorts to make a world. If every man were just like his neighbours, there would be no employment for the biographer; and it is because nations differ that each of them has a history of its own. Therefore we study the history of Western Christendom in order to grasp the unity of the member-nations, and we study the history of the nations in order to realize their diversity. As one of Stendhal's characters observes, the verisimilitude of a story lies wholly in the details.[4]

Now it seems to me that this argument can be extended and applied with equal force to small communities within the nation. Professor Toynbee, sweeping ecumenical horizons with his telescope, exhorts the student of history to brace himself for 'mental operations on a larger scale.' But the telescope, as others before me have remarked, is not the only instrument that will broaden our minds and enlarge the stock of knowledge: the microscope also has its uses. And within the nation there are smaller communities which have every right to be considered as distinct articulations of the national life. One can think of hundreds of rural and urban communities which have possessed a spiritual and economic vitality of their own, and their own organs of local government. It is true that such communities are not much in evidence today. A man who lived in London all his life might never have the idea of a local community brought home to his consciousness at all. You do not feel that you are crossing a frontier when you pass from the metropolitan borough of Paddington into the royal borough of Kensington. But if you go far enough afield, you can still find local consciousness asserting itself even now at something like its old strength. Last year I spent some time exploring the Forest of Dean. Lying between the Severn and the Wye, this district has well-marked natural limits; and its inhabitants are physically distinguishable from their neighbours. They belong to the county of Gloucester, but if you come from east of the Severn they will say you come from Gloucestershire, and if you come from some other county they will say quite simply that you are a foreigner. Their principal industry, the mining of coal and iron, has been carried on ever since the Roman period. The powers vested in the Coal Commission under the Act of 1938, to grant or refuse a lease of coal entirely at their discretion, operate in all the coalfields of Great Britain with the one exception of the Forest of Dean. Here the powers of the Commission are still subject to the rights and privileges of the Free Miners of the Hundred of St Briavels. The mine-court no longer meets, but the court of verderers still holds occasional sessions at the Speech House, built for the purpose in 1670. One man with

---

4   "Vers le milieu du récit, M. Leuwen commença à faire des questions. 'Plus de détails, plus de détails,' disait-il à son fils, 'il n'y a d'originalité et de vérité que dans les détails.'" – *Lucien Leuwen* (1926), iv, 169.

whom I had some talk began his working life as a miner, then, becoming
partly disabled, opened a garage and started a service of local buses. Pres-
ently one of the big bus companies offered to buy him out. He refused to
sell; so the company tried to oust him by running two buses for every one of
his, with one bus running five minutes ahead and the other five minutes
behind him. But his customers were not going to let a Forest man be done
down by a pack of *foreigners*; and in the end it was the company's buses that
had to be withdrawn.

The commoners and Free Miners of Dean are today what the people of
nearly every English town and rural district were until the day before yester-
day: a self-conscious local community. And though it may be difficult for us
to grasp the fact with our imaginations, it is nevertheless true that for
centuries the local community provided the normal setting in which Tom,
Dick, and Harry lived and worked and played. Their bread was made from
corn grown under a communal system of agriculture in the soil of the parish,
and ground at the local mill. Their other material needs were supplied from
the nearest market town, and their spiritual needs at the parish church or
nowhere. They thought of themselves as Englishmen, certainly; but the
abiding and ever-present reality was that they were inhabitants of Plumstead
or Hogglestock or Barchester.

Each of these rural or urban communities has reacted and contributed in its
own characteristic way to the main currents of English history. And note that
it has done so in its own good time. For its life-span is not necessarily co-
extensive with that of the nation as a whole. A local community may come
into existence at almost any date, lead a more or less vigorous life of its own
for a century or two, or for the better part of a millennium, and then fade out
again, even as the republic of Venice and the empire of Austria have faded
from the map of Western Christendom. Take for example the village of
Whatborough, one of the oldest settlements in Leicestershire, established as
far back perhaps as the sixth century, and so completely blotted out by the
enclosure movement of the 1490s that an estate map drawn in 1586 has a
blank space in the centre, inscribed: 'The Place where the Town of
Whatboroughe stood.'[5] On the urban scale, Cheltenham, transformed in the
second half of the eighteenth century from a rural market-centre into a fashionable spa, and Middlesbrough, down to 1831 a township of fewer than a
hundred souls, now a great manufacturing city and an episcopal see, exem-
plify changes so drastic that we may fairly call them new creations. In our
own lifetime we have seen local communities brought into being *ab ovo* at
Welwyn and elsewhere. Not only in these organisms of recent growth, but in
many a small town and big provincial city there may be found, even at this

5   R. H. Tawney, *The Agrarian Problem in the Sixteenth Century* (London, 1912),
223. 'Town' here signifies a township, or rural community. See also *Studies in Leicestershire Agrarian History*, ed. W. G. Hoskins (Leicester, 1949), 96.

day, a strong civil spirit and a pride in local achievement. But there is not the
old degree of social cohesion. A railwayman or a mill-owner today pretty
certainly feels himself more closely linked in sympathies and interests and
aspirations with his fellow-railwaymen or fellow-manufacturers up and down
the country than with the majority of his fellow-townsmen. Moreover, Levia-
than, as we all know, looks with no friendly eye upon allegiances that are not
centred on its omnicompetent self. It may be that just as the family, once so
powerful a unit, has withered into social impotence, so the local community is
destined to wither in its turn. But while it flourished it yielded only to the
nation, and not always even to the nation, in its hold over men's loyalties.[6]

As soon, however, as we propose to write its history, voices are raised in a
shrill chorus of dissuasion. Dr G. M. Trevelyan makes no secret of the light
in which he views the subject. He writes: 'Ever since the publication of
Tudor Cornwall I have believed that Mr A. L. Rowse had it in him to
become an historian of high rank if he would lay aside lesser activities and
bend himself to the production of history on the grand scale.'[7] So the
dilemma confronts us in all its nakedness: if you write local history badly,
you are the dreariest of bores; and if you write it as well as Mr Rowse, it is a
pity you cannot find something better to do. Then there is Professor Toynbee,
who will argue that if the history of England is not self-explanatory, *a
fortiori* neither is the history of Barchester. And we readily agree that
Barchester, taken by itself, is not a fully intelligible field of study. We know,
for example, that the Latin mass, which had been offered in Barchester
cathedral ever since the cathedral was built, ceased to be offered there in the
sixteenth century for reasons which must be sought ultimately not in
Barchester itself, nor even in London, but at Prague and Wittenberg and
Rome. Even so, the course the Reformation took in Barchester was not that
which it took in Stockholm or Amsterdam; and Barset, though more thoroughly 'reformed' than Lancashire, was perhaps a shade less so than the
eastern counties. Thus Barchester stands out as a distinct articulation, not
only of the national community, but of Western Society as a whole. And if
so, its history is a field of study which deserves to be cultivated for its own
sake.[8] To anyone who thinks it absurd that we should labour day and night

---

6   A leading article has just appeared in *The Times* (27 August 1952) suggesting that
measures should be taken to arrest the decay of our smaller and middle-sized country towns
'in these days when transport by bus has brought about revolutionary changes in country
habits.'

7   *Sunday Times*, reviewing *The England of Elizabeth*, vol. I.

8   As Professor Toynbee implicitly allows, when he declares that history, as a humane study, is properly concerned with the lives of societies in both their internal and their
external aspects. 'The internal aspect is the articulation of the life of any given society into a
series of chapters succeeding one another in time and into a number of communities living
side by side. The external aspect is the relation of particular societies with one another.' –
op. cit., I, 46.

only to 'chronicle small beer,' let Chesterton's parable supply the answer. '"Notting Hill," said the Provost simply, "is a rise or high ground of the common earth, on which men have built houses to live, in which they are born, fall in love, pray, marry, and die. Why should I think it absurd?"'

It may be objected that so many of our English local communities being now either dead or moribund, the historian would do better to concentrate on subjects of living interest. To this the obvious answer is that the Hellenic city-state and the empire of Rome are also dead, but we do not therefore consign them to oblivion. To the historian it may be a positive advantage that he is dealing with something which has finished its course. His ultimate function is to tell a story, and every story is more readable, more shapely, if it has an end as well as a beginning.

The business of the local historian, then, as I see it, is to re-enact in his own mind, and to portray for his readers, the Origin, Growth, Decline, and Fall of a Local Community. If this principle is accepted, it becomes possible to define with something like precision the relationship between his study and other disciplines, whether academic or non-academic. The sources he must consult will be part written, part unwritten. In so far as he deals with unwritten evidences, we may style him an archaeologist. He is also a geographer, since part of his task is to elucidate in detail the process of *défrichement* – we have no English word for it – whereby the soil of his parish has been subdued to human purposes by gradual conquest of the primeval marsh or woodland. He is not a geologist, but he interrogates the geologist on the character of the soil and the structure of the underlying rocks, because without this knowledge he cannot rightly interpret the effects of human action upon the landscape. His contribution to historical geography demands an intensive observation of fields, hedges, roads, and water-courses. Much of his time is thus spent out of doors; but since field-work must be controlled and amplified by documentary research, he is also an assiduous visitor at libraries, record offices, and muniment rooms. He is an economic historian because the greater part of man's life is spent in gaining a livelihood, and a historian of art and education and religion because man does not live by bread alone. Though he never, I hope, utters the fatuous word 'medieval', which has even less meaning for local than for national and ecumenical history, he is perforce a medievalist because the so-called Middle Ages were the formative period in the life of most English towns and villages, and indeed covered something like two-thirds of their whole existence. But he is also a modernist, if that is the right word, because many of them survived as local communities into the age of railways and motor transport. He is thus not a specialist in any one period; nor is his an antiquarian pursuit. Antiquary is a word of fluid meaning, but I take it to mean one who studies the monuments of antiquity – usually a single class of monument – for their own sakes. For the antiquarian the sculptures on the west front of Barchester cathedral, or the cross-legged effigies in the parish churches, are objects to be studied in relation to each other and to similar monuments elsewhere. For the historian they are particular manifestations or expressions of a social life which he is trying to reconstruct in its entirety.

It is sometimes held that local history provides a useful method of approach to national history. And it is true that sometimes a train of momentous happenings is found to have been touched off in some village whose chronicler, by revealing this fact, teaches the national historian something he might not have discovered for himself. It is also true that if the histories of all our parishes were written as they should be written, the history of England would need to be revised at many points. It may be, also, that a teacher who wishes to give his pupils something more than a 'notional apprehension' of English history will find it helpful to illustrate the Wars of the Roses by showing them the tomb of Sir William in the parish church, or the strife of Cavalier and Roundhead by pointing out the ruins of Sir Lionel's mansion. But I am quite sure that to esteem local history only or chiefly for its propaedeutic value is to underestimate it, and that to treat it as an introduction or a contribution to national history is to invert the true relationship between them. We may grant that the history of Meryton or Mellstock will help us to understand the history of England, just as the history of England will help us to understand the history of Western Christendom; but it remains true that a study of the whole will do more to enlighten us about any single part than vice versa. In other words, when we are sufficiently familiar with the European past to read English history intelligently, and when we are thoroughly well grounded in the history of England: then, and not till then, can we begin to think of writing the history of Liverpool or Lydiard Millicent or Saffron Walden. Local history is not an elementary study. It is one to which the amateur or the young student can, and often does, make a valuable contribution; but in its higher reaches it demands mature scholarship and a wide background of general culture.

Another claim that I will venture to make for it is that local history is preeminently a humane discipline. Let me recall here the well-known little rhyme:

The art of biography
Is different from geography.
Geography is about maps,
But biography is about chaps.

History too is 'about chaps,' and local history brings us nearer to the common run of chaps than any other branch of historical study. It gives us, in the language of the films, a close-up of them on their farms and in their workshops and behind their counters. It studies them as social beings, as members of a rural or urban community; but by seeking them at their home address it enables us to see them as flesh and blood, and not just as pawns on the

national chessboard. The national historian, dealing with some vast agglom-
eration which he labels villeins, Puritans, the lower middle-class, or what
you will, tends to lose sight of the human person.[9] In the preface to *The
Reign of Elizabeth*, one of the earliest published volumes of the Oxford
History of England, the author, Professor J. B. Black, says: 'In the present
volume we have been compelled to observe events predominantly through
English eyes, or, to be more correct, through the eyes of the English government.' He goes on to remark that other points of view have an equally good
claim to be considered, and says he has tried to bear this in mind, 'but *the
paramount necessity of placing the reader at the standpoint of the queen
and her ministers* has prevented a rigorous following out of the principle.'[10]
We naturally wonder who laid this necessity upon him: was it the editor, or
the delegates of the Clarendon Press? But no explanation is vouchsafed. If
the reign of Elizabeth II had to be dealt with on this plan, I suppose one
would begin to write its history from the standpoint of Mr Churchill, and if a
general election should bring Mr Attlee into power, keep the printer working
overtime to bring out a revised edition. For let us remember that the phrase
'Her Majesty's Opposition' dates only from 1826; in the time of the first
Elizabeth opposition was just a short cut to the scaffold. The standpoint of
an angel, gazing with pity and comprehension at the antics of mortal men, is
of course beyond our reach, but one can think of several purely human
standpoints from which national history could be studied more intelligently
than from that of the group which has contrived to make itself, at a given
moment, master of the state. Local history brings us face to face with the
Englishman at home, and reminds us that it is he who foots the bill his rulers
have run up for him. By so doing, it restrains the propensity to worship mere
power and success, a propensity which loses none of its baseness from
being carried back into our study of the past.

From time to time we seem to detect, in the making of national history, an
element of downright imposture. Take for example the case of Richard
Strode. Strode came of a Devonshire family seated at Newnham, in Plympton
St Mary; and he represented the borough of Plympton in the parliament of
1512. He was also an owner or part-owner of tinworks. It appears that two
partners, William Rede and Elis Elforde, started digging for tin on Strode's
land. These two were jurors for Plympton at a Great Court of the Devon
Stannaries which had just reaffirmed the right, guaranteed to all tinners by
immemorial custom and by charter of Edward I, 'to dig tin in every place

---

9   'Even in the study of history a kind of acquired simplicity is needed just to see
things as they really are, just to see things naked, instead of envisaging them in the
categories which historians have created to fit them into – attributing thing to the Renaissance when the Renaissance is a mere label that historian have chosen to apply to a
generation of people.' – H. Butterfield, *Christianity and History* (London, 1949), 115.
10   The italics are mine.

within the county of Devonshire whereas tin may be found'; and the Great
Court had decreed that any one obstructing this right should be liable to a
fine of forty pounds. In order to rid himself of his unbidden guests without
incurring the penalty appointed, Strode introduced a bill into the parliament
of Westminster to restrain mining operations in the vicinity of seaports,
alleging that the harbours of Devon were being choked with refuse from the
mines. The bill, though it did not become law, aroused great indignation
among the tinners; and at the next law-day the under-steward caused Strode
to be presented at all four stannary courts for conduct subversive of the
miners' liberties. The culprit was fined forty pounds in each court; but
refusing to pay, was arrested 'and imprysoned in a dongeon and a deepe
pitte under the ground in the castel of Lidford ... the which prison,' as he
afterwards feelingly declared, 'is one of the most annoious, contagious, and
detestable places wythin this realme.' After languishing there for some three
weeks, he was released by a writ of privilege from the Exchequer, not as a
member of parliament, but as a collector of the subsidy that had just been
voted to the Crown. Before releasing him, the deputy warden required him
to give bail for one hundred pounds. To secure himself against forfeiture of
bail and further pursuit, Strode now complained to parliament, and persuaded it to pass a statute not only annulling his condemnation in the
stannary courts, but granting immunity to him and his associates for anything done or to be done by them in that or future parliaments.[11] It is
important to note that the provisions of the act are limited to Strode himself
'and every other of the person or persons afore specifyed': that is, those
'other of this house' who had joined him in promoting a bill against the
tinners. It was thus a particular, not a general statute; and the only question
of principle involved was whether the legislative competence of parliament
should or should not override that of a self-governing local body like the
Stannaries. Neither the parliament which enacted it, nor Henry VIII who
gave it his assent, had the least intention of making it a corner-stone of
privilege. Both before and after the passing of Strode's act the sovereign
claimed and sometimes exercised the right to punish members of the house
of commons when they overstepped their constitutional function as voters
of supply. But under the Stuarts this right became the subject of hot debate.
The upholders of parliamentary immunity never shrank from using bad law
and bogus history to support their claims;[12] and as one of the five members
whom Charles I tried but failed to arrest was a lineal descendant of Richard

11   4 Hen. VIII, c. 8. A schedule annexed to the act enables us to follow the affair in
detail.
12   Hence the interesting design of the Lord Keeper Francis North to print and
publish "all the records of state and parliament,' because he was convinced that such
publication would help the monarchy against its adversaries. – *Lives of the Norths*, ed. A.
Jessopp (1890), I, 355.

Strode, the precedent of 1512 was not likely to be overlooked. Finally, in 1667, Lords and Commons, evidently persuaded that two and two make five if parliament will have it so, passed a joint resolution affirming the 'Act concerning Richard Strode' to be 'a general Law ... declaratory ... of the ancient and necessary Rights and Privileges of Parliament.'[13] After this, it is not surprising to find even so eminent an authority as Halsbury censuring the Tudor and Stuart monarchs because they 'chose to regard it' in a different light.[14]

It was said of the Leicester antiquary Thomas Staveley that 'having passed the latter part of his life in the study of English history, he acquired a melancholy habit.'[15] And when we consider the spirit in which our national history has all too frequently been written, we can understand the poor man's feelings. We may liken English history to a dish cooked in a vast kitchen, where the smoking fat of nineteenth-century liberalism mingles with the stale cabbage of Elizabethan no-popery propaganda and with a hundred other odours, new and old. But with local history we can escape, if we choose, into the fresh air. One cannot hope to establish a thesis of general application by writing the history of a parish, as Macaulay, for example, nearly succeeded in establishing the Whig thesis by writing a history of England. Therefore there is the less temptation to indulge in generalized passions for or against the various 'isms – feudalism, Protestantism, capitalism, and the rest. By setting us face to face with flesh and blood, local history puts a curb on those abstract hatreds which can so easily turn the heart to stone. For instance, you may hold that popery deserves the worst that has ever been said of it, and yet find it comparatively easy to acknowledge that the priest whom Burghley's police caught saying mass up at the manor-house, and who paid for it with his blood at Tyburn, was a not wholly despicable character. You may execrate the landed gentry and everything they stand for, and yet freely recognize that the present squire's grandfather was adored by his tenants and reared the finest herd of Ayrshires in the county. I am far from contending that local history will furnish us with any automatically effective antidote against partisanship. The local historian, like other men, will have his personal preferences and prepossessions. But if the milk of human kindness is not dried up within him, some fellow-feeling with 'Hodge and his masters' will arise, even when he deems their conduct most perverse. You cannot paint a miniature with great splashes of blood-red.

---

13   *Journals of the House of Lords*, XII, 166. The Commons admitted that the statute was made "upon a private and particular Occasion"; but in the teeth of history, and by a plain misreading of the text, they asserted that it was meant to cover "all Members that then were, or ever should be."

14   *The Laws of England* (London, 1907–17), XXI, 782.

15   John Nichols, *History and Antiquities of the County of Leicester* (1795–1815), II, 677.

The reasons why so many of the older local histories fail to satisfy us are now clear. The writers were content to heap up all the facts they could discover, without order, art, or method, and with no criterion for distinguishing the trivial from the significant. Their theme, if they can be said to have had a theme, was not the rise and fall of a local community, but the fortunes of one or two armigerous families. In this respect they had a perfect, if unconscious, spokesman in the late Sir George Sitwell. Mr Evelyn Waugh tells us that he was standing one evening, with other guests, on the terrace of Sir George's mansion at Renishaw. 'In the valley at our feet ... lay farms, cottages, villas, the railway, the colliery, and the densely teeming streets of the men who worked there ... Sir George turned and spoke in the wistful, nostalgic tones of a castaway, yet of a castaway who was reconciled to his solitude. "You see," he said, 'there is *no one* between us and the Locker-Lampsons."'[16] Many of the older local histories were written by country gentlemen of scholarly tastes like Sir George Sitwell, or by the parsons whom they had presented to their livings; and they reflect the interests of that class. Page after page is filled with details concerning the successive families who have been lords of the manor. Few subjects are more tedious, yet to this day the descent of the manor occupies a quite inordinate amount of space in the Victoria County Histories; and at the end one is left with the impression that nobody ever lived in the parish but the squire and his relations. In this particular, and in some others, the Victoria County Histories, planned as they were over half a century ago, must be said to embody a conception of local history which is now largely obsolete.[17] I do not mean to imply that the squire either can or should be left out of the picture. On the contrary, one of the most important questions the historian should try to answer is how far the element of lordship is fundamental in the make-up of the local community. But though genealogy, family history, is a perfectly legitimate branch of study, it is but one of many which the local historian will lay under contribution if he has taken the full measure of his task.

History, as we all know, is a Greek word meaning enquiry. Multifarious are the questions the local historian will put to himself as he tramps the fieldpaths or scrutinizes antique parchments. Of what condition were the men who founded his community? Were they veterans of an Anglo-Saxon war-band, maintaining themselves chiefly by the labour of the conquered Britons, or free peasants brought over to fill homesteads from which the defeated race had fled? What nucleus of cultivation did they find awaiting them? By what stages did their descendants enlarge their holdings at the

---

16   Osbert Sitwell, *Laughter in the Next Room* (London, 1949), 349.
17   A welcome announcement by Mr R. B. Pugh, editor-in-chief of the *Victoria County Histories*, has just appeared (see *The Amateur Historian*, I, 1952, 4). It foreshadows changes of emphasis and treatment which will go far to obviate the criticism levelled at the older volumes.

expense of the surrounding marsh or woodland? What considerations guided the marking out of the manor and parish boundaries? When was the borough carved out of the manor, and for what purpose? At what date was the communal system of agriculture superseded by enclosures, and why not earlier or later? How successfully has the community withstood, from century to century, the vicissitudes of population and trade? In what degree have religious differences contributed since the sixteenth century to its disruption? Has the acceleration of transport in the last hundred years prolonged its life or hastened its decay?

Some of these questions may prove to be unanswerable. When the historian has done his best with the remainder, and with the hundred others that arise, let him muster every ounce of narrative and expository skill that he possesses, and begin to tell his tale. He may be confident that an audience will not be lacking. For as the older 'glories of our blood and state' begins to wane, and the social revolution of the twentieth century brings in a new order which not all men find congenial, many of our fellow-countrymen are filled with a deeper curiosity than ever before concerning the old market towns of England: Stamford, Ludlow, Chipping Campden – the very names are music; and the beloved villages: Castle Combe, Colly Weston, Finchingfield: all those places which embody, in varying degrees of perfection, a social life that is fast vanishing, if it has not already gone; and they are eager to hear what the historian can tell them about that life, if only he can set forth an intelligible tale.

The local historian today starts out with one great advantage over his predecessors. With all their zeal and erudition, the writers of the old school lacked a central unifying theme. At their best they produced fine works of reference, but rarely a book that could be read from cover to cover with pleasure as well as profit. Today, with a much vaster and more accessible range of materials to draw upon, the scholar who sets out to trace the history of a rural or urban community has but to keep this theme steadily in view, and every fact that he uncovers will fall into place. His narrative will take shape as a block of marble takes shape under the sculptor's chisel.

If the ideas I have tried to develop here meet with approval, they may fitly serve as guiding principles for the conduct of the department which the University College of Leicester has entrusted to my care. Indeed, they may be said to have shaped its course already under my predecessor. The 'new school' – as Mr Rowse termed it in a recent broadcast – has produced no historian more widely and justly admired than W. G. Hoskins. His books and lectures are at once learned, graphic, and humane. As first Reader in English Local History he set an example which may well inspire a feeling of diffidence in his successor, particularly a successor who has spent much of his working life in other fields. But his writings, and the discussions I have had with him at various times, lead me to believe that Dr Hoskins takes a view of local history which differs only in detail from mine. It is good to know also that the department which occupies itself with national and international history has, in Professor Simmons, a head keenly alive to the value of local history. Finally, I take some courage from a backward glance at three great amateurs in whose performance there was nothing amateurish. First, John Nichols (1746–1826), to whose enthusiasm we are mainly indebted for that grandest of record-publications, the folio edition of Domesday Book (1783), and who, after publishing five volumes on *The History and Antiquities of the County of Leicester* at a loss of as many thousand pounds, went on undismayed and completed one of the finest of the older county histories by publishing three more. Then his son, John Bowyer Nichols (1779–1863), who superintended the publication of Ormerod's *Cheshire*, Baker's *Northamptonshire*, Hoare's *Wiltshire*, and a long list of other topographical master-works; and his grandson, John Gough Nichols (1806–73), who helped to found the Camden Society and edited many of its publications. Few, if any, families have done more to advance historical knowledge; and I find it inspiriting to recollect that they accomplished so much while carrying on their day-to-day business as printers and publishers: trades which it has been my fortune also to ply.

The primary aim of the department, then, will be to foster, in our own minds and in the minds of any who look to us for guidance, a reasoned conception of local history, such as will set a standard of performance by which our work and the work of others may be judged. That conception will oblige us to demand, from ourselves and others, exact scholarship, wide sympathies, and a style of writing at once precise and vivid. We must persuade scholars that no perfection of attainment is out of place in local history; that there is room here for a Maitland's brilliantly directed curiosity, for a command of documentary materials equal to that of Stubbs or Round, and for a narrative art comparable with the art of Green or Froude. And we must convince the public at large, not that local history is a fascinating subject, for the public is aware of that already, but that scholars have at last taught themselves how to unfold its true significance. If we can do this, the coming generation will be measurably nearer to producing the classic histories of our English towns and villages that are waiting to be written.

It is with these resolves, and with a feeling of deep gratitude to the College for giving me the opportunity to act upon them, that I take up my appointed task.

9

ENGLISH LOCAL HISTORY: THE PAST AND THE FUTURE*

W. G. Hoskins

The inaugural lecture is one of the most difficult of art-forms, with many pitfalls for the complacent and the unwary. When Sir Thomas Smith was appointed to the new and highly-paid Regius Professorship of Civil Law in the University of Cambridge in the year 1540, he confessed afterwards that he had been overwhelmed at the thought of the responsibilities involved. He had, he said, prayed for death in the utter desolation which swept over him on hearing of his appointment. Nevertheless, his inaugural lectures – for he gave two eventually – were, says his recent biographer, 'one long hymn of self-praise.' Even for an inaugural lecture, continues his biographer, who must have been permanently marked by some academic experience, 'even for an inaugural lecture, the self-satisfaction was remarkable.'

I hope to steer my own course tonight somewhere between the Scylla of sudden death and the Charybdis of self-congratulation. There seems ample room for a middle course.

Though the study and the writing of local history in England is now some 400 years old, and has produced an immense literature, the University of Leicester is still the only university to recognize the subject as one worthy of serious academic pursuit. Founded now nearly twenty years ago as the Department of English Local History, it was from the first designed to take the whole of England within its purview. It is therefore not merely local history confined to Leicestershire or even to the Midlands. It is not a School of Regional Studies such as one or two other universities now tentatively possess. It takes all England, the most diverse and complex country in the world in relation to its area, within its province.

Like some other now academically respectable subjects, as for example botany and zoology, local history in England was mostly if not entirely the creation of generations of amateurs, in this instance of squires and parsons, and later of doctors, lawyers, and school-masters. But unlike botany and

---

*   Hoskins's inaugural lecture was delivered on 3 March 1966 at the University of Leicester and was published (without footnotes) in the same year.

zoology, it has largely remained the domain of the amateur right down to the present day; and this, in my view, has been fatal to the growth of the subject in stature, for its failure to achieve a tough discipline and to define a clear objective. Somehow it failed to take the path that botany took in the second half of the seventeenth century in the hands of John Ray and Robert Morison, or that zoology took about the same time. Scientific zoology began, like local history, in the sixteenth century with the amateur collectors of curious facts, but made the profound jump into systematizing and classification, without which no science is possible, some 300 years ago. Local history is still, by and large, in the fact-collecting stage. Even the great enterprise of the *Victoria History of the Counties of England* – now totalling some 120 volumes – is still, in its topographical volumes at least, basically fossilized at this stage.

When I say that local history in England is still fossilized in the fact-collecting stage – and too often of merely curious facts at that – I am not forgetting the best work of the past twenty years, some of it achieved in the Department of English Local History under the aegis and direction of my predecessor, Professor Finberg. His work on Anglo-Saxon land charters, above all, and that of pupils in the same field, ranks high in the scholarly development of local history in this country. And there have been books written outside the universities, by distinguished amateurs, which can stand beside any work of scholarship in other fields, notably the work of Sir Francis Hill on *Medieval Lincoln*, published in 1948 and recognized at once as a classic study of the history of an English city.

As in so many other fields of human endeavour, the best amateur can equal – perhaps surpass – the achievement of the professional; but this does not alter the fact that over these fields as a whole – the analogy of cricket comes to mind here – the average standard of professional achievement is likely to be considerably higher than that of amateurs as a whole.

We must look at the origins of local history for our failure to advance. These we can pin-point fairly precisely round about the year 1570. In that year William Lambarde wrote the first book that is recognizable as a local history (though it was more strictly a survey as its title implies: *A Perambulation of Kent*) and in the same year Christopher Saxton began work on his county maps which culminated in 1579 in the first national atlas to be produced here or in any country. William Lambarde was a Kentish gentleman, and his book was, as Professor Simmons has pointed out elsewhere, 'essentially a book produced by a gentleman for gentlemen.' Lambarde's book inspired gentlemen in other countries to do likewise for their own territory – Sampson Erdeswicke in Staffordshire, Richard Carew in Cornwall, and then William Burton, the squire of Lindley, who published his *Description of Leicestershire* in the year 1622.

I have written about the development of local historiography elsewhere and do not wish to traverse that ground again. Suffice it to say that throughout the seventeenth and eighteenth centuries the flow of county histories, good, bad, and indifferent, grew in volume. They varied in their emphasis and treatment, but basically they had one thing in common and that was that they continued to be written by gentlemen for gentlemen, with all the limitations of subject that that implies. They were interested mainly in one social class – the land-owning class – its pedigrees, heraldry, possessions, and appendages like the parson and the church; though occasionally a more imaginative writer would devote a page or two to the working conditions of the labouring class.

Histories of towns were naturally different in their authors and subject-matter. The first town history we can recognize as such as John Stow's *Survey of London*, published in 1598, and a few others were written before the end of the seventeenth century. They were written mainly by the official class – town clerks, chamberlains, and such-like – and suffered from the same narrow preoccupations as the works of the gentry. They ignored the live of the great mass of the human race, and wrote only about the very small governing class in the towns, less than five per cent of the total population. And parish histories, when they began to flow in the eighteenth century, tended to be written by parsons and to be mostly concerned with the squire and his relations. There were of course notable exceptions to these generalizations, but they stand out because they are so rare, like John Lucas's *History of Warton* in Lancashire, which was compiled between 1710 and 1740 but not published until 1931. Lucas was a schoolmaster and therefore had a wider range of sympathies and interests than the squires and the parsons.

The most remarkable exception to the general run of local histories, and it still remains unique in its plan and treatment, deserves some special attention. Indeed, I must resist the temptation to devote to it the rest of my lecture. Both the author and the place he writes about are unknown to fame. It is Gough's *History of Myddle*, a parish in Shropshire. Written in 1700–01, it was not published in full until 1875. A few imperfect copies were privately printed in 1834 by Sir Thomas Phillipps, himself a remarkable character, under the inviting title of *Human Nature Displayed in the History of Middle*, a very appropriate title for such a book. Richard Gough was not a squire or a gentleman – I use these terms in their precise seventeenth-century connotation – but a yeoman-freeholder who lived on his own small estate in the parish of Myddle. Born in 1634, he died at the age of 89 in 1723. His book was written when he was sixty-six or -seven, at an age when he might have felt he was nearing death and could safely write down – as I too sometimes feel nowadays – the scandalous inner history of his native place.

After describing the topography of the parish and the principal features in it – the church, the castle, the parks and commons and roads, the lords of the manor, all of this more or less inevitable – he then does something which

had never been done before. He gives an account of the different families in
the parish, the ordinary people who make up most of the human race. For
this purpose he introduces the plan of the parish church and, taking each
pew in turn, he gossips about the occupants as he had known them all his
life. I do not know any other book which gives such a detailed human
picture of seventeenth-century England. The historian's greatest problem is
to make the men and women of the past really come alive, for you who are
listening tonight must admit that even our great-grandparents are often but
shadowy figures to us and that before them the generations blur into one
grey mass, unbelievable, unrealizable, as though they had never lived.

Richard Gough's book is a masterpiece in bringing alive the essential
England of 300 years ago. He was eight years old when the Civil War broke
out in 1642 and heard many stories of the war then and afterwards. He tells
us for example of the men who enlisted: no fewer than twenty went from his
parish, 'of which number thirteen were killed in the warrs.' And he deals
with them on by one. Thus he says of one Nathaniel Owen, the son of John
Owen of Myddle:

> the father was hang'd before the warrs, and the son deserved it in the warrs...
> His common practice was to come by night with a party of horse to some
> neighbour's house and breake open the doores, take what they pleased, and if
> the man of the house was found, they carryed him to prison, from whence he
> could not bee released without a Ransome in money; so that noe man here
> about was safe from him in his bed; and many did forsoke their owne houses.
> This Nat. Owen was mortally wounded by some of his owne party, in an
> alehouse quarrell, neare Bridgenorth, and was carryed in a cart to Bridgenorth
> to bee healed, but in the meane time the parliament party had laid seidge to
> Bridgenorth and the Garrison soldiers within the towne sett the towne on fire,
> and fledd into the Castle, in which fire this Owen (being unable to helpe
> himselfe) was burnt to death.

Let me take one more vignette out of many hundreds of this parish, and
one I choose for a reason that will be plain, though I am not descended from
the gentleman in question. Richard Gough is discoursing upon the occupants of the fifth pew on the north side of the south aisle, about the Hayward
family.

> Thomas Hayward ... was a handsome, gentile man, a good country scholler
> and a pretty clarke. He was a person well reputed in his country and of a
> general acquaintance ... Hee married with Alice, the daughter of Mr Wihen,
> High Schoolmaster in Shrewsbury. Hee had a good fortune with her in money,
> besides houses in towne of considerable yearly value. Shee was a comely
> woman, but highly bredde and unfit for a country life, besides shee was
> shrewed with tongue, soe that they lived unquietly and uncomfortably, and
> their estate consumed insensibly. Hee had little quietness att home which
> caused him to frequent publick houses merely for his naturall sustenance, and

there meeting with company and beeing generally well beloved hee stayed often too long. His intimate friend was Mr Hoskins of Webscott, and indeed there seemed to bee a naturall sympathy betweene them for they were both of them very just honest persons and well beloved – but theire deportment when they were in drinke was very different, for Mr Hoskins could goe butt not speake, and Mr Hayward could speake as well and seemed to be more acute and witty in his drinke than att other times, but hee could not goe.

Another Hayward, we are told, married the eldest daughter of Mr Edward Muckleston. Of her Richard Gough says briefly

Shee was short sighted and of noe comendable Beauty butt shee was a vertuouse and religiouse woman.

But I must leave this entrancing secret history of a Shropshire parish in the seventeenth century. Rather small beer you may think, a sardonic old man's gossip. But real life at any time is mostly very small beer (only some historians contrive to inflate it); and as for gossip it is one of the most important sources for the historian who has any imaginative insight into the past. Gossip can be serious historical evidence: to be tested of course, wherever possible, like any other kind of evidence. The truth is not necessarily to be found in records, however authoritative, in the Public Record Office or in the British Museum. Certainly it does not repose necessarily in diplomatic despatches, in legal records, or even in tax assessments, or whatever class of written record you may believe is impeccable.

Gossip to be useful to the historian must pass two tests. It must be consistent within itself, making a pattern of its own however varied the informants; and it must be consistent with the known facts derived from other kinds of evidence. Given this consistency, the historian who disdains gossip, imagining that the truth lies rather in some official record, is too naive to be called an historian. There are many occasions when informed gossip is nearer the truth than any written document. In local government, for example, we hardly ever discover from the printed or written records how and when a momentous decision was actually arrived at.

The local historian should use the reminiscences of the elderly as one of his sources, and he should encourage the best of them to record their recollections.

Richard Gough, to return to him for a moment, wrote a book of great originality. His book is a series of vignettes, of character sketches, of minor comedies and tragedies. But when one has read it all, one has a total view of seventeenth-century England such as no professional historian could possibly have achieved. For my present purpose he showed that all classes of human beings were of profound interest to the historian. The unimaginative have often said that the poor have no annals. On the contrary, the annals of the poor are interminable.

Few later local historians emulated Gough even distantly in treating of all classes of human beings, though some have tried. Lord Hylton's *History of Kilmersdon* in Somerset, published in 1910, made a considerable effort in this direction; but on the whole local history remained largely weighted with the history of the manorial class and its appendages until recent years. As I have remarked elsewhere: 'The dead hand of the seventeenth-century squire still guided, until recently, the hand of the living antiquary.' And here we have, in my view, the fundamental reason why English local history never made the jump from the amateur collection of facts to the status of botany or zoology. There are no social classes among plants and animals. When one looks back upon the narrow preoccupations of the local historian for so many generations, it is as though the botanist had decided centuries ago that orchids and lilies were the only plants of any scientific interest and had limited his studies accordingly. A hundred years ago rickets was known as 'the English disease.' Today I am inclined to think it is a secret preoccupation – not with sex which is now openly discussed in all its aspects – but with social class. However hidden this preoccupation may be, it remains as powerful and crippling as ever in some academic fields. It is a sort of mental rickets, keeping people intellectually deformed, mentally bandy. Historians are very prone to it. I believe, as Flaubert once said, that class distinctions belong to the domain of archaeology.

In recent years there has been an enormous growth of serious interest in local history all over England – not least in extra-mural classes which are doing much original work. Hence much of this narrow preoccupation with the history and fortunes of one social class has been diluted and weakened beyond recovery.

The other major criticism one could make about local history writing arises directly from the first: that it has been preoccupied with facts and not with problems. It has been well said that antiquarians collect facts; historians discuss problems. Too many local historians are still stuck at the antiquarian stage, and even those who are trying to move beyond it may not always be sure what are the fundamental problems they should be tackling. So, with all the good work that has been done over the past twenty years by devoted amateurs, local historians have still not made the massive contribution to general history that they might have done.

The local historian's basic tool is the microscope. More and more, historians working on a larger canvas have come to realize that for many important questions in their own fields the answers will have to be sought in microscopic studies of particular regions and particular places before we know how historical changes actually take place.

The study of population and of all the factors affecting its growth throughout history has recently leapt into fashion under the title of historical demography; and it is here that the serious local historian, using his micro-scopic technique and asking the right questions of an enormous mass of confused and often imperfect data, can make one of the most rewarding contributions to history at large.

Recently I visited the church of Burnham Thorpe in the north of Norfolk, a church more redolent of Lord Nelson (who was born in the parish) than of the Almighty, but none the less interesting. Here I purchased a History of the parish written by a recent rector, a fair example of local history as it has usually been envisaged. It describes in its early pages a raid by the Danes on this exposed coast, and what followed '... a group of long-limbed red-haired Danes rushes along that road [a prehistoric road in the parish] cursing the warning column of smoke beginning to show from Beacon Hill ... later, returning with captives, laden with spoils, the wing-helmeted marauders face the maddened Saxon fathers and husbands ...' One resists the tempta-tion to ask what the maddened Saxon husbands and fathers had been doing all this time, and what they were mad about: but as a contribution to population-history we must regard this episode as wholly imaginary.

There is a vast amount of scientific work to be done in this field of research, at first sight duller in its approach than that of the rector of Burnham Thorpe: but the truth, however dull, is more fascinating than any fiction. For this reason I find I cannot bear to read even the best of historical novels.

In the field of population history the fundamental record is the parish register of baptisms, marriages, and burials, in theory a complete record since the autumn of 1538. This is not the place to discuss its imperfections and shortcomings. There are some nine or ten thousand ancient parishes, and among this vast number we can find enough complete, or substantially complete, registers to work upon in the necessary microscopic detail.

Every region of England and Wales has a different population-history. In this field the generalizations of the historian working on a national canvas are more than ordinarily useless and misleading. Let us take the simplest record first, that of burials, for baptisms and marriages both present special difficulties of interpretation. It is relatively easy to produce a static picture of mortality in a given place over a period of some 400 years. By studying the numbers of burials in every year, and in particular the years in which burials rise well above the local average, one can trace the epidemic-history of the place, or better still of the region. One can see an epidemic starting in a particular household, and trace its incidence from house to house, and follow it week by week. Not all past epidemics were plague, much too simple a word for a very complicated subject. There were, for example, massive epidemics of influenza at various times during the sixteenth cen-tury, and other outbreaks and widespread deaths from causes which have yet to be identified. Disease is a reaction to a particular environment: hence the pattern of disease changes from time to time in history.

The study of mortality figures in this way is the most elementary exercise one can undertake, yet it can produce none the less a picture of the history of public health over a long period of time. A somewhat more dynamic picture is produced if one goes on to study the baptism figures over the same period, and then their relationship to the burial figures. If burials exceed births, as they often do at different periods of time in different places, why should this be? When deaths rise in a given place, the reasons may not be far to seek. But when births, as reflected in baptisms, rise, or more complicated still, fluctuate over a long period, this raises much more difficult questions. What is happening when baptisms rise not just in one year, as at Plymouth the year after the Armada – a predictable result when all the men had come home, but over a period of some decades? In answering such questions as these the local historian applies his microscope not merely to the statistics drawn from the parish register but to all the local social and economic conditions which might have a bearing on the figures. Only he with his background knowledge can profitably do this.

If births are rising over a considerable period of time, there may be various explanations, all of which will require close analysis. Is a change taking place in the average fertility of marriages, and if so, why? Is it because there is a fall in the average age at which marriages take place, above all of course in the average age at which a woman marries? Clearly, under natural conditions with no artificial methods of limiting families, a woman marrying three or four years younger than her mother is likely to produce two or three more children during her child-bearing period. And if the average age of marriage is going down, as it did in England in the closing decades of the sixteenth century, why should this be happening? Is it due to local opportunities for employment, or to boom conditions in the national economy, or perhaps both? Why do people get married at a younger age than their parents?

A rise in the birth-rate can also come about if there is a considerable immigration of younger people into a given district, so altering the age-composition of the community? There are no statistics for internal immigration in England before the nineteenth century. The local historian testing this theory must therefore have recourse to the parish register, to wills, to all the contemporary records that give surnames, to see whether there is a notable influx of new surnames into the parish or the town which would suggest perhaps a younger population of men and women looking for and finding employment in a locally prosperous area. One of the primary objectives of the Surnames Survey which has recently been initiated in the Department of English Local History is to trace local movements of this kind, for they may well have a bearing on population-history, as well as other aspects of social history.

Conversely, when the number of births fall in a given community, what is really happening? It may be due to women getting married at a higher age (which can be demonstrated statistically from the parish register) or to a longer average interval between births, which can also be demonstrated statistically. If births are being spaced out at longer intervals, why is this so and how is it being achieved? What changes in social customs and attitudes lie behind such decisions? And equally difficult to answer, how is this result achieved under natural conditions?

To pose an elementary question, yet one which so far baffles historians interested in population-changes, how is it that women marrying at an average age of say 25 and theoretically capable of producing about twenty children by the end of the reproductive period at 45, rarely did so, even in the sixteenth to eighteenth centuries when artificial methods of family limitation were allegedly unknown?

There is on the wall of York Minster a small mural tablet to a good lady which records that she died at the age of 38, in the course of her twenty-fourth labour. Her husband solemnly adds that 'she fell like a sentinel in the course of duty.' Passing over this bland masculine remark without comment, one can only say that it shows what was theoretically possible and – mercifully – very rarely realized.

But one cannot discuss the birth-rates of the past from exceptional cases alone. Again a microscopic counting of baptisms at different periods reveals averages, from a large number of examples, which reflect the truth of the matter more closely. One of the popular myths about the past in so far as population is concerned is that our ancestors had large numbers of children, of whom the great majority died in infancy, leaving only two or three to grow up and reproduce the following generation. I myself was led to question this myth, which sounds so plausible, by the discovery in my own family that an ancestor begat five sons and five daughters between 1584 and 1603, all of whom survived infancy, grew up and married in turn. Perhaps this was an exceptional case, too. But it led me to examine the whole question of birth-rates and death-rates in the sixteenth and seventeenth centuries more critically. Even ten children was a large number in Elizabethan England, but it represents only half the theoretical total in a normal marriage.

It is difficult to speak of average families at any time. It depends on social class to some extent, and on the precise period in history. But one thing is quite clear and that is that women in the sixteenth and seventeenth centuries – and I can only speak with special knowledge of those centuries – in fact produced far fewer children than one would have expected under natural conditions. Theoretically one should find a baptism every eleven or twelve months under these conditions. In practice one finds an interval between baptisms of something between two and three years. I am not going into the difficulties presented by stillbirths and miscarriages which would not be recorded anywhere. The fact remains that by this kind of microscopic examination of particular families or particular parishes one finds there is a question to be answered.

The answer is, I believe, that while women were breast-feeding their children they were unlikely to conceive again. I am well aware that modern doctors regard this as a pernicious doctrine and warn young mothers not to trust in its efficacy. But what I am saying as an historian, dealing with large numbers and with statistical probabilities, is not the same as a doctor talking to an individual patient. The doctor is right to warn of the considerable degree of risk in particular cases; but the fact remains that historically speaking this is how families in preindustrial societies limited their numbers and prevented the total population from exceeding the available food supplies within a generation or two. How far they also employed abortion and infanticide is not known in England, though I am told that the figures for infanticide in eighteenth-century France can be ascertained.

There are other important questions which the local historian can answer affecting the total population, and also its age-composition. We all know that the expectation of life in modern times has lengthened greatly, with the result that we now have a population with a high proportion of elderly and aged, and that this proportion is going to grow throughout the forseeable future. The proportion of a population within the age-group of economic productivity, in relation to the non-productive burden of young and old which it has to carry, is one of the cardinal factors for economic growth, particularly for a preindustrial society in which technical changes are slow at best.

In other words, one of the things we need to know more about in the past is the expectation of life. This again will vary between social classes and at different periods of time. Generalizations are useless. There are considerable variations between different regions at the same date, and no doubt between different social classes. Thus in the middle-class Shakespeare family, living in a small Midland town in the second half of the sixteenth century, we have the following demographic picture. Four sons and four daughters were born to John Shakespeare, of whom William was one. Two of these children died in infancy, representing an infant mortality rate of 250 per 1,000 – about the average for the time, though one cannot generalize from the vital statistics of one family. Another child (Anne) died at the age of eight. Of those who survived childhood, Edmund died at 28, Richard at 39, Gilbert at 46, and William at 52. The average age at death of the four Shakespeare brothers was 41, again a fairly typical figure as far as we yet know. Of the females, two died in infancy, one at eight years, and Joan – the only one to survive the perils of a Tudor childhood – at 77. But the average age of the female at death was still only 42. The expectation of life for a child born to Shakespeare's parents was only 31.4 years at birth; but if we ignore the first year of life, always the most perilous, the expectation of life at the age of one was just about 42 years.

This is a picture for only one family for whom we possess every genealogical detail, but I think it is probably not untypical for bourgeois families in Midland England at this date. We need a good deal more research on this interesting subject, and I commend it to those local historians whose tastes lie in this fascinating field. On the other hand, in the Lincolnshire marshland parish of Wrangle between the middle of the seventeenth century and the middle of the eighteenth it has been calculated that the expectation of life at birth was only 14 years, and at the age of one it was still only 24 years. Clearly there are very considerable regional differences; and perhaps equally wide differences between the social classes.

I have spent some time over the contribution that the local historian can make to historical demography because I regard changes in the level, and rate of growth, of population as one of the fundamental fields of economic and social history. All manner of consequences flow from such changes.

But now it is time to say something about the study of topography. Every place anywhere involves a multitude of topographical facts. When we reach a place as large as an industrial city like Leicester the multitude of facts about its appearance and growth becomes overwhelming. This of course is true of any field of knowledge, unless one learns what questions to ask which will reduce this primeval chaos to order.

The start of topography as a study is akin to that of genealogy before the great J. H. Round began asking the right questions. For here, too, we have millions of facts about scores of thousands of families over a period of many centuries. Unless one is a pure genealogist, interested only in collecting all the known facts about a particular family and its kindred, one must define certain fundamental questions to which the answers are required as Round did some seventy or more years ago. In this way, he gave a new value to genealogical studies, to quote the *Dictionary of National Biography*, and he opened up a large new field of enquiry which such scholars in our own time as Sir John Neale have used with immense profit in the realm of political history above all. What is needed in the study of English topography is another John Horace Round to survey the whole confused scene and to reduce it to order by asking the right questions.

Let me illustrate what I mean by suggesting the kind of questions one should ask in looking at an English town from a purely topographical standpoint, for although the town has been studied extensively by historians it has nearly always been considered as a legal institution – a borough – rather than as a physical structure. Indeed, historians have seemed unaware of this side of a town's history, and better work has been done by the historical geographers; though even they have not got to the bottom of the subject.

I always bear in mind the aphorism: '*Cities do not grow, they are built.*' This keeps one's feet firmly on the ground. Geographers are apt to talk loosely about the growth of a town and relate it to more or less geographical factors, but like historians they should really ask who *built* the town, what determined the creation of certain street patterns, who financed such building from time to time, and why so often growth took place in one direction and not in some other.

In looking at a town which has produced an exceedingly complicated pattern on the large-scale map, a few basic questions help one to start looking. The questions are: How old is it? Secondly, where precisely did it have its origin, and why at that point and not some other? And thirdly, having ascertained the precise point at which a town started, the question arises: how did it grow from this point and what has influenced its subsequent shape?

In answering questions like these we are compelled to use a wide range of evidence, not only the earliest documents, which frequently did not come into existence until the town was some centuries old, but also the evidence of place-names, of coins, of literary sources in some cases, and finally, but most important of all, the evidence of the large-scale map, which is the most important single record that we possess for the study of local topography.

In working out the early growth of a town, we find ourselves involved inevitably in scrutinizing urban parish boundaries, in studying street-names in the older parts of the town – taking care that the existing names are the original ones – and, if the information is available, the location of the churches of the town, as recorded in Domesday Book and as revealed in early structures. In other words, we use not only written evidence and material evidence of all kinds, but also the visual evidence, which is often the oldest that we have.

In the countryside, fieldwork – that is to say, the examination of visual evidence – is of even greater importance and value. I can only indicate briefly two examples of what I mean. The first is concerned with boundaries all over England. There are historic boundaries still to be tracked down on the ground, and someone one day will write a pioneer book on English Boundaries. Generally speaking, county boundaries were marked out in the ninth and tenth centuries, and to anyone with any historical imagination and curiosity the way they run on the map presents question after question, making one go out and see what they look like on the ground. The boundaries of hundreds date from the early tenth century and they too are worth study on the ground; and even more so are the boundaries of parishes and manors. What do they look like and why are they here? Some of these boundaries may well go back to those of Romano-British estates which were taken over by some later arrangement and still survive in the deep countryside. The English landscape is a palimpsest, written upon again and again.

Related to the subject of boundaries is that of hedge-banks. Where a hedge-bank forms a boundary of an English parish, or of a farmstead which is recorded in the Domesday Book, and therefore dates from at least Saxon times, such a boundary may have remained unaltered for 800 to 1,000 years or more. Many of these hedge-banks can be located with certainty on the Ordnance map. Years ago I felt certain that where one had hedge-banks of this great antiquity, they ought to show significant differences in their flora from hedge-banks or hedges constructed, say, a the time of the parliamentary enclosures in the latter part of the eighteenth and early nineteenth century. These were the obvious extremes of date; but I also felt sure that if one could identify, as one can, hedges and hedge-banks constructed in Tudor times, they also might be significantly different in their botany from early hedge-banks or later ones.

But I knew no botany beyond the fact that, even to my untutored eye, the massive medieval hedge-banks of my native county of Devon were very different in their botanical appearance from those that I have now become accustomed to in Leicestershire. And now many years on, in conjunction with a botanist on the staff of the Nature Conservancy, we have between us arrived at a hypothesis, and it is no more than that at present, that for every hundred years of its life in an unmanaged condition a hedge-bank will have added one more species of shrub to its flora. In other words, a hedge-bank constructed in the tenth century should show ten different species of shrub; and earlier and later hedge-banks can be approximately dated from their flora even when we have no documents.

It is obvious that this simple hypothesis, which on the face of it sounds almost too good to be true, will need a great deal of further work upon it. The flora of hedge-banks and hedges will vary not only with age, but also with types of soils, the degree of management, local climate and so on. But at any rate, here is a field in which the local historian with the necessary botanical knowledge can probably hope to add greatly to the secret history of his chosen study. I call it secret history because what is revealed in our hedge-banks and hedges more often than not is a kind of history that has never been written down in any document. Sir George Stapledon once said, 'Vegetation accurately read is a remorseless and wholly objective historian.'

This saying could be applied with equal truth to the evidence to be derived from buildings of all kinds. One of the special fields of English topography is the study of what has come to be termed Vernacular Building; that is to say, buildings of all kinds, built in a provincial style and speaking as it were a local dialect. Thus a farmhouse in Yorkshire is different not only in appearance but also in its plan and in its general lay-out from the farmhouses of the east Midlands, or those of southwest England. They are adapted to their particular environment. Vernacular building includes every kind of building from barns and cow-houses, cottages, churches and farmhouses, and houses in towns, up to the level, which cannot be precisely defined, where building merges into true architecture with a national style.

One of the most important tasks of the local historian in any part of England is to make a thorough survey of all such buildings in his chosen area, recording them in photographs and drawings and by means of plans and elevations. Not only this, but he must couple his structural evidence with that of the documents wherever they are available. Buildings speak to an historian as a musical score speaks to a musician. They speak objectively and do not lie.

I have ranged over a fairly wide field in considering what local historians ought to concern themselves with, but this is only a small part of the ground. I should like to touch upon one more possibility before gathering up the threads of this discourse. In talking about the humblest of all records – the parish register – I tried to show the immense amount of serious scientific work one can devote to it, far beyond the simple genealogical uses to which it has hitherto been put. The same record can be put to other uses than the study of demography.

The distinguished American sociologist Lewis Mumford has said: 'Men are attached to places as they are attached to families and friends. When these loyalties come together, one has the most tenacious cement possible for human society,' and he goes on to say that 'in the restless movings about of the last two centuries, this essential relation between the human spirit and its background was derided, under-estimated, sometimes overlooked … Where men shifted so easily no cultural humus formed, no human tradition thickened.'

So the local historian must learn to ask sociological questions. Would that the sociologist for his part would learn to ask some historical questions. He must study the longevity of families in his chosen area and their interrelationships, and how much families move about at different times. The great strength of a rural community above all lay in this interrelationship and longevity. All this will emerge from the parish register as the basic record, and from numerous other local and central records, not forgetting headstones in churchyards which often tell one in a moment what might have taken days to find out from a blind search in the written records.

To the true local historian no human record, whatever its form – a hedgebank, a wall, a street, a headstone, a farmhouse, an old man's gossip, wills and tax assessments and the thousands of other written things, a memorial tablet on a church wall – a multitude of evidences in every shape or form – no human record fails to tell him something about the past. All these evidences, whatever form they take, are interrelated. The local historian needs to be a little of everything – a physical geographer, a geologist, a climatologist, a botanist, a medical man, a builder, as well as an historian. And as he cannot be all these things, he must enlist the aid of all these colleagues. For what he is doing in the last resort is trying to restore the fundamental unity of human history which the ever-increasing mountain of available records has caused to be fragmented into a score of specialisms. In the course of these academic developments, inevitable at the national level, we have lost sight of Man as a single being and treat him in compartments rather as the human body is treated, so I understand, in American medicine: so that the whole man is overlooked and suffers accordingly as he passes from one specialist to another. The local historian is in a way like the old-fashioned G.P. of English medical history, now a fading memory confined to the more elderly among us, who treated Man as a whole.

This unity which the local historian is better qualified to restore than any specialist may well be termed Human Ecology. I had considered whether one might call it Micro-History following well-known precedents for setting up new branches of knowledge, but I have a temperamental allergy to such inventions. One realizes fully, towards the close of an academic life, how important it is to invent a new term like this; and then to invent a vocabulary of esoteric jargon rather than try to write plain English. (I once wrote a book with a simple title of *The Making of the English Landscape* but I ought to have called it *The Morphogenesis of the Cultural Environment* to make the fullest impact.) And finally one must make use of a computer: a new title for one's subject, a glossary of jargon, and a computer, and one has the most lethal combination for academic advancement conceivable. One would then qualify to work in some shiny academic palace. But scholarship thrives in small quiet rooms; and the scholar and the library are the real foundations of a university.

Haeckel coined the term Ecology in the year 1869. Ecology is that branch of science which treats of plants and animals in relation to the environment in which they live. Human beings ought to be studied in this way. We have forgotten they are part of the animal kingdom. The local historian, provided he is properly trained – and this we propose to do in the Department of English Local History – is best qualified to make this study. As historians we must study man as revealed in his infinite responses to the stimuli of his environment. Here is the link between the various fields of local history that I have touched upon in this lecture, fields that might have seemed at first sight to be a rather haphazard collection of disparate subjects. But they have an underlying unity, a relationship to each other.

We should be studying living human communities and their reaction to their environment, and to changes in that environment, over the past 2,000 years. Among animals and plants, a high mortality in Nature serves to maintain a working balance of population and food supply. How did the human race adapt itself to the limitations of its local environment? Can one define an *ecosystem* for human beings at some historical period? What are the criteria?

Men construct houses, farm-buildings, warehouses, factories, all manner of structures in response to a particular environment. House-shapes change

– houses grow or contract – rooms multiply or diminish, all for good reasons and not by accident. Walls are made or pulled down – hedges made or pulled down – boundaries defined and obliterated – all in response to the material environment. Towns are built laboriously and then destroyed. It has been said that Man has become the cancer of the natural world, proliferating and destroying wherever he now goes, not always destroying wantonly or wittingly, but simply by upsetting the long-established ecosystems of Nature through pure ignorance. He has forgotten that he is a part of the living landscape. His relationship to his physical background is now, as Mumford said, derided or forgotten. Many people hardly know what I am talking about when I say this. I believe then that local history, properly conceived and practised by professionally-trained workers, is not a miscellaneous collection of skills and disciplines – borrowing here and borrowing there – but a science of Human Ecology. And yet I hope amid all the scientific method and vocabulary we shall remember that, being History, it is about People – the kind of people that Richard Gough described in such human detail for his Shropshire parish nearly 300 years ago. Behind the graphs and statistics of the scientific method we must always be able to hear men and women talking.

10

NEW AVENUES IN ENGLISH LOCAL HISTORY

Alan Everitt

We read of one of our early local historians, William Somner, that he was so well pleased 'with his lot of breathing first in this fair ground [of Canterbury], that neither mind nor body could be moved to any distance from it: he took pleasure to call it the place of his birth, education, and abode: and here, in studious content, he took up his cradle, his mansion, and his grave.'[1] I cannot emulate these distinguished connections of the first historian of Canterbury. Neither can I claim the advantage of his fellow-countryman R. H. Barham, the author of *The Ingoldsby Legends*, whose biographer tells us that he 'mitigated the prejudices of his education by the innate candour of his disposition.'[2] All I can say is that it was the mere accident of having been born in the same country as these two worthies that first awakened my own interest in the subject of English Local History.

The local historian has generally been regarded by the world at large with a certain well-meaning condescension, not unmingled with a little kindly amusement. I am not sure whether it was kindly amusement, or whether it was merely condescension, that explained the arrangement of a recent publisher's catalogue, in which all works of local history were listed, not under the section headed 'History', still less in a category of their own, but under the section headed 'Juvenile Literature'. In the nineteenth century there was a valley in the Lake District frequented in the summer months by wandering scholars, amongst them local historians, and these visitors, we are told, 'were generally looked upon by the dalesfolk as harmless individuals, though as lacking something mentally.' For the benefit of scientific colleagues, it must be added that the botanists and geologists who visited the valley were bracketed in the public mind with the local historians. On one occasion, when the great Adam Sedgwick was staying there, a local gentleman pre-

---

1   Quoted in *Excursions in the County of Kent ...* (1822), 36–7, from White Kennett's biographical sketch prefixed to Somner's *Treatise of the Roman Ports and Forts in Kent* (1693).
2   *Dictionary of National Biography*, s.v. R. H. Barham.

sented him with a shilling, being as he expressed it, such an 'exceedingly intelligent old man.'[3] A compliment, and a piece of good fortune which in my experience have not often fallen to the lot of local historians.

This reputation for a certain oddity goes back beyond the nineteenth century. Appearing for the first time, I believe, in English literature in the year 1628, the local historian was then described as 'one that hath that unnatural disease to be enamoured of old age, and wrinkles, and loves all things (as Dutchmen do cheese) the better for being mouldy and worm-eaten ... He loves no library, but where there are more spiders' volumes than authors, and looks with great admiration on the antique work of cobwebs.'[4] I suppose it must be confessed that we owe something of our reputation to genuine peculiarities of habit and temperament. As a rule the great local historians of the past – and there have been such, men like John Nichols and Edward Hasted – have been more remarkable for their monumental scholarship and their provincial patriotism than for a sense of humour or of art. Certainly there is a delightful, deadpan kind of wit occasionally to be found in the 7,000 pages of an Edward Hasted; but it is rather like finding a bottle of very dry cider in the middle of the Arizona desert.

Over the past 10 or 20 years, however, a gradual but widespread change in the local historian's image has begun to take place. One of the reasons for the change has been the remarkable growth of interest in the subject. Though we in Leicester still have the only independent department devoted to it, departments of history or economic history in many universities, and schools of education like our own here, have developed a flourishing interest in it. As a proof of this fact, it may be mentioned that half of all postgraduate theses in English history in this country are now devoted to some kind of localized study.[5]

By no means all the recent growth of interest in local history has taken place within the universities, however. There can be no doubt that most of it has occurred amongst amateurs. Some of the best of this amateur work has been stimulated by departments of adult education; but much has also grown up, almost as if by spontaneous generation, in colleges of education and schools, in county and city record offices, and in scores of local history societies all over the country, many of them only founded within the last ten years. In 1968 an exhibition by one of these societies on the history of the little Kentish town of Edenbridge attracted more than 2,000 visitors in one week, or nearly a third of the population of the town.

---

3   *The Annals of a Quiet Valley*, by a Country Parson, ed. John Watson (1894). The passage specifically refers to botanists and geologists, but other allusions in this book suggest that antiquaries were also amongst these visitors.

4   John Earle, *Microcosmography* (1920 edn) [first published in 1628], 57, describing 'An Antiquary'.

5   This remark is based on an analysis of the *Theses Supplement* for 1968 of *The Bulletin of the Institute of Historical Research*. The exact figure is 51 per cent.

In the midst of all this expansion, our place here in the Local History Department at Leicester may seem a comparatively modest one. But it has been clearly marked out by my two distinguished predecessors, and I am sure I speak for my colleagues in the Department in saying that we hope we shall not depart, and shall not have to depart, from the basic functions of the Department developed by Professor Finberg and Professor Hoskins. With a still youthful discipline, academically speaking, the first function must be to continue to discover and elucidate by research, and to propagate by publication, the general historical principles and patterns that appear to govern, in varying guises and degrees, the story of the local community and the local landscape in England. This is essential because so much local historiography, though undertaken from the most praiseworthy motives, is still amateurish as well as amateur, and because many local historians look to us to provide them, if we can, with some kind of guidance on these basic ideas. The second, and equally important, function of the Department is the teaching and training of postgraduate students, in research topics, and in the ever-growing techniques and materials of the local historian and topographer. Not all our teaching is at postgraduate level, however. The teaching of specialist courses for undergraduates in kindred departments is one that has led to happy links over the past few years, and has ultimately brought us some of our best postgraduate students.

What exactly is English Local History? Over the centuries very different answers have been given to this question, and today we seem as far from achieving unanimity as ever. A recent television programme from Tavistock was introduced with the remark: 'The history of Tavistock is surely the history of Sir Francis Drake.' In the Local History Department, it need scarcely be said, we do not believe that the town of Tavistock commenced its life in 1540, and expired in the year 1596. Neither do we believe that local history consists in brass-rubbing or in editing cookery-brooks, both of which are still widespread popular delusions about the purpose of our subject. In a phrase now well known Professor Finberg defined the task of the local historian in a very different sense. It involved, he said, the re-enactment in the historian's own mind, and the portrayal for his readers, of the Origin, Growth, Decline, and (where appropriate) the Fall of the Local Community.[6] For the purposes of what we try to do at Leicester, this seems to me, generously interpreted, to be still the best definition.

What exactly does it involve? It means in the first place that, so far as possible, we should study the *whole* local community, and not merely a single class or industry or section of it. Secondly, it means that we study the *structure* of the local community, as an organism, so to speak, with a more or less distinct and continuous life of its own. Among the topics we study,

---

6   See H. P. R. Finberg, *The Local Historian and his Theme* (1954), 115 above; and *Local History in the University* (1964), 7–8.

for example, are the changing pattern of the community's topography, the construction and form of its buildings, the structure of its population, the pattern of landownership in the community, the changing structure of its occupations, its society, its family life, its religious life, and its cultural life. Finally, and equally important, it is also our task to trace the *connections* between these different aspects of the local community: for example, the effect of population changes on the occupational structure, the influence of the occupational structure upon religious life, of family life upon cultural activity, and of economic life upon local buildings and the local landscape.

Another of the tasks of local history, as we endeavour to pursue it at Leicester, is the *comparative study* of local communities. Over the past generation or so historians have come to recognize increasingly not only the diversity of local societies in England, but also the fact that there are a number of distinct types or species of rural and urban community.[7] Though every place is essentially unique in its development, there are often marked resemblances of society and topography between, for example, marshland settlements in Kent and Lincolnshire, or woodland settlements in the Weald and the Forest of Arden.

Even within any one county, such as Yorkshire, Somerset, or Kent, there are often striking differences in rural economy. To an urban age like our own these may seem relatively trivial matters: there are villages, and there are towns, and there is no more to be said. Until the nineteenth century, however, England was fundamentally a farming country, and for the vast majority of her inhabitants these differences formed the basic facts of life. As between a typical marshland village in Hanoverian Kent and a typical downland village in the same county they might be quite literally vital. The parish of Murston, near Faversham, we are told, was so afflicted with marsh agues or malaria at this time that the inhabitants' 'complexions from those distempers become of a dingy yellow colour' and 'seldom any, though born here, continuing in it, have lived to the age of twenty-one years.'[8] There can be no doubt that this was a major reason for the sparse population of most of the marshland parishes in Kent.

Not many miles away, however, on the breezy, healthy downlands, we find a striking contrast. By common repute the two healthiest parishes in the whole county were Coldred and Barfreston, remote little windswept settlements between Canterbury and Dover. If we can believe a story of Edward

7   See, for example, J. M. Martin, 'The Parliamentary Enclosure Movement and Rural Society in Warwickshire', *The Agricultural History Review*, xv, i (1967); Joan Thirsk, (ed.), *The Agrarian History of England and Wales*, IV, 1500–1640 (1967), Chapter I, 'The Farming Regions of England'; Dennis Mills, 'English Villages in the Eighteenth and Nineteenth Centuries: a Sociological Approach', *The Amateur Historian*, VI (1963–5).

8   Edward Hasted, *The History and Topographical Survey of the County of Kent*, 2nd edn, VI (1798), 144.

Hasted's they must have taken some beating. When the parson of Barfreston died in 1700 at the age of 96, his funeral sermon was preached by a minister aged 82, whilst the reader of the service was 87, the parish clerk was 87, the sexton was 86, his wife was about 80, and several people from Coldred who attended the service were 'above 100 years old'.[9] Yet despite the alleged longevity of their inhabitants, downland parishes like these were as a rule relatively poor and thinly populated, so that there must have been considerable emigration of their people. How far, one is led to ask, was the growth of Kentish towns in the eighteenth and nineteenth centuries due to migration of this kind from the downland?

I need not weary my audience with a list of the many species and sub-species of local society in England. They are rather too numerous to catalogue, and many of them in any case we are only now beginning to identify. But I should like to select one type of local community of particular interest, as an illustration, and discuss its features in more detail. The kind of places I refer to are the market towns of England, and more particularly the lost market towns.

The English landscape is scattered, all over the country, with scores and indeed hundreds of places which at one time in their history acquired the right, usually by a grant from the Crown, to hold markets and fairs. By the acquisition of these trading functions they became distinguished, in some degree, from the purely agricultural villages around them, although most of them still remained for many generations centres of farming as well as of trade. In some cases the commercial functions ultimately ousted agriculture completely, and this is how the majority of our modern English towns have originated, great cities like Birmingham, for example, as much as little towns like Market Harborough. But in very many cases, after a life-span varying from less than a century to as much as 600 years, the market eventually died out and the trading activities came to an end. And yet, in spite of their decline, most of these lost markets of England retained certain peculiarities in their topography and their social structure, marking them off in some sense from purely farming villages, and continuing to shape their destinies until the nineteenth century and even today.

Nobody knows exactly how many of these market towns, surviving and decayed, there are in England. At the peak period, in the early fourteenth century, there were certainly more than 1,200, and there may well have been nearly 2,000 of them.[10] If we also include grants subsequent to the four-

---

9   *Ibid.*, X (1800), 71; cp. VIII (1799), 95–6, for Elham, another downland parish, where the age of 40 was "esteemed that of a young person."

10   The *Royal Commission on Market Rights and Tolls* (1889), I, 108–31, lists 2,713 grants between 1199 and 1483; but some of these were to places overseas, some were for the translation of the market to a new site, many were re-grants to places already possessed of market rights, and many were for fairs only. On the other hand the *Royal Commission*

teenth century, possibly one in five or six of the 10,000 medieval parishes of England have at one time or another contained within their boundaries some kind of regular trading centre. For a number of counties more precise figures can be worked out. In Gloucestershire there were at least 52 medieval market centres, of which about 20 survive today, so that Gloucestershire now has more than 30 lost towns within its borders.[11] In Leicestershire and Northamptonshire (if we may mention them in the same breath), there were at least 61 medieval markets, of which 16 or 17 may still be said to exist as towns; so that in these two counties there are quite 44 vanished trading centres, and probably a number of others I have not been able to trade.[12] In the two much larger counties of Kent and Suffolk the decline in numbers is still more remarkable. In medieval Kent as many as 96 places obtained the right to hold a weekly market, whilst in Suffolk the comparable figure was 102.[13] Yet in each county only about 20 of these places have managed to survive as trading centres into our own time. In each of these two shires there are, therefore, somewhere about 80 lost market towns scattered up and down the countryside. I use the word 'town', of course, very much in the old-fashioned sense, simply as a settlement of some kind. Most of these places we should not nowadays recognize as truly urban at any stage of their history. My point is merely that they were not farming villages pure and simple; they were centres of trade, for buying, selling, or exchanging the goods of their region, rather than only producing it.

The case of Kent is a particularly interesting one. Kent is often thought of today as a county of picturesque villages; yet in fact probably none of these picture-postcard places in the county originated as villages. It is doubtful if

---

does not include 'prescriptive' or traditional markets. Dr Bryan E. Coates has calculated that there were grants of market rights to more than 1,200 places in England and Wales between 1227 and 1350 alone ('The Origin and Distribution of Markets and Fairs in Medieval Derbyshire', *Derbyshire Archaeological Journal*, LXXXV (1965), 96). His figures are based on grants recorded in the *Calendar of Charter Rolls*, I–V, covering 1226–1417.

11   H. P. R. Finberg, 'The Genesis of the Gloucestershire Towns', *Gloucestershire Studies* (1957), 52–88, records 45 markets in the county in existence by 1465. By the sixteenth century seven further places had come to be recognized as markets: Bisley, Blockley, Falfield, Great Witcombe, Horton, Leonard Stanley, and Stroud.

12   On topographical grounds a number of other villages in both counties bear a close resemblance to former market centres, but I have not been able to trace definite evidence of a market and have excluded them from the figures in the text.

13   For a list of Suffolk markets I am much indebted to Miss Gwenyth Dyke, who generously placed her manuscript list at my disposal. For Kent I have relied on the grants recorded in Hasted, *op. cit.*, I–X, *passim*, and individual parish articles and histories. A number of Kentish markets were prescriptive and have never had a grant. This must be the origin of the two or perhaps three Chipsteads in the county (in Chevening, Penshurst, and possibly also West Kingsdown parishes). But I have only included prescriptive or traditional centres when, as in the case of Sevenoaks, there is undoubted evidence of continuous market activity. Hasted is in general remarkably thorough in recording grants, but he does not always mention the prescriptive markets.

there is a single truly nucleated village, in the Midland sense of the word, in the county. Places like Lenham, Goudhurst, Chilham, Elham, Groombridge–and there are scores of others–so beloved of the trigger-happy tourist, are all, as we know them today, really decayed towns, vanished centres of trade, not true villages. Gradually, over the centuries the trade of the county of Kent has become more and more concentrated in fewer and larger towns. This development has also occurred, in varying degrees, in nearly every English county: in Leicestershire, Northamptonshire, Gloucestershire, Suffolk, and Yorkshire, as well as in Kent.

When exactly did these markets, of which so many have now vanished originate? In most counties a few existed at the time of Domesday Book, though as a rule these Domesday markets can be numbered on the fingers of one hand. A few more were founded in the eleventh and twelfth centuries; but the golden age of the new market towns does not begin till about 1200 and from then it continues at a rapid pace till about 1330 or 1340. The period varies somewhat from county to county; but three-quarters of the 102 markets of Suffolk, for instance, were founded between 1200 and 1330, and nearly 60 per cent of those in Kent. Sometimes, as in Kent, a second more limited phase of foundation occurs in the late fourteenth and fifteenth centuries; and occasionally, as in Lancashire, as late as the sixteenth.[14] By and large, however, the great period of market foundation in England was the period of about 130 years from 1200 to 1330. It is to this period that the humble urban origins of perhaps two towns in three in England today may still be traced.

Though most places did not acquire market rights before the thirteenth century, it is noteworthy, in Kent at least and perhaps elsewhere, how many of the earliest centres of primary settlement in the county acquired market charters at some time during the medieval period. It is possible that many of these earlier communities had in fact always existed in some sense as local trading centres and were now merely seeking to safeguard their position at law. Places like Elham, Chilham, Wingham, Yalding, Reculver, Eastry, Milton Regis, and Minister-in-Thanet had probably all originated during the earliest phases of settlement in the county, and they all subsequently acquired market grants. A long line of similar settlements, stretching across the

---

14   It is interesting to note that the phasing of grants was appreciably later in Kent than in Suffolk. By 1300 there were 76 markets in Suffolk, but only 46 in Kent. The difference is partly due to the fact that some of the grants recorded by Hasted were in reality re-grants. Possibly, too, in the very large parishes of the Weald, with their weak manorial control, more places existed as traditional markets before acquiring a grant. There are other grounds, however, for supposing a relatively late date for urban settlements in much of Kent, particularly in the chartlands and the Weald. The numerous markets on the northern side of the county tend to be earlier in origin; but it appears that Sittingbourne only acquired a market in the sixteenth century, Deal in the seventeenth, and Whitstable in the eighteenth. See Table I (p. 159 below).

county beneath the scarp of the downs, were significantly sited close to the
Pilgrims' Way, though few of them were directly on it. Amongst these were
markets like Maidstone, Lenham, Charing, Wye, and Folkestone. Quite
possibly these places had always retained a measure of control over the
economy of their neighbouring daughter settlements. Certainly Wye had
been the regional centre of one of the original lathes of the county, and it
must have also acted as some kind of economic centre from the earliest days
of Jutish Kent.

When and why did so many of the market towns of England decay? It is a
frequent experience of the historian that the death of an institution or settlement is more difficult to track down than its birth, and we can rarely date
with precision the death of these markets. What we do know is that, by
about 1640, the 1,500 or 2,000 medieval markets of England had shrunk to
fewer than 800. In Leicestershire they had dropped from at least 30 to a
mere 13; in Northamptonshire from 31 to 14; in Gloucestershire from 52 to
34; and in Kent and Suffolk from about 100 to 33 or 34. There can be little
doubt that many, perhaps most, of these places had died out as a result of the
Black Death in the middle of the fourteenth century. Many of them must
always have been small, and the drastic fall of population due to the Black
Death must have spelt their total extinction as centres of trade.[15]

With the seventeenth and eighteenth centuries another factor operated to
the detriment of the smaller markets. This was the rapid increase of travel
and the gradual improvement of roads and transport. The turnpiking of
scores of major roads in the eighteenth century tended to channel the growing volume of trade and traffic through the major towns on these routes, and
hence away from the smaller places situated merely on country lanes. Whilst
the larger towns, like Leicester and Northampton, thus became ever more
frequented, because they offered greater variety of trade, better facilities,
and more competition, the smaller towns slowly but surely began to die out
as market centres. There can be no doubt that this was the reason for the
decay of numerous little towns like Hallaton in Leicestershire, for example,
King's Cliffe in Northamptonshire, and Appledore in Kent, which had managed to survive into the seventeenth century, but by the 1830s were extinct
as markets.[16]

The coming of the railways carried the same process a stage further. It
was the completion of the London to Dover line through Ashford in 1844,
for example, that led to the rise of Ashford as one of the largest livestock
markets in southern England. A great new market place was laid out along-

15   Alan Everitt, 'The Marketing of Agricultural Produce', in Joan Thirsk (ed.), *The Agrarian History of England and Wales*, IV, 1500–1640 (1967), 467–76.
16   Samuel Lewis, *A Topographical Dictionary of England* (1833 edn), indicates that the markets of Hallaton and King's Cliffe had by then been extinct for some time. That at Appledore had probably come to an end earlier and is not referred to at all by Lewis.

side the railway itself, outside the old town centre, and several little neigh-bouring towns, which had hitherto shared the expanding cattle and sheep trade of Kent, rapidly died out as agricultural markets. By 1870, after five or six centuries of life as centres of the livestock trade, we find that Elham, Marden, Charing, Lenham, Smarden, and Wye had all declined to the status of mere villages.[17] They had not, of course, died out as human settlements; but if you visit them today, you will not expect to find their streets thronged with the sheep and cattle of Romney Marsh or the Weald, as you would have found them in the eighteenth century. The cattle and sheep are still being raised and fattened, but they are now sent to Ashford market instead.

In what kind of situation may one expect to discover these lost medieval markets of England? In most cases the original grant was obtained through the initiative of some powerful local landowner or ecclesiastic, and for this reason one may find them in almost any kind of countryside. Nevertheless they tended to proliferate on some particular sites and terrains more than others. On certain main routes, for example, they became especially numer-ous. Along what we call the A6 in Leicestershire and Northamptonshire there were as many as 12 market centres within little more than 50 miles, including several, like Kegworth, Kibworth, and Great Glen with little or no urban character today, though each of these settlements still has its old market place.[18] On a 50-mile stretch of the road from London to Canterbury there were 11 market towns if you went by way of Watling Street, and 13 if you took the alternative route at that time by way of Gravesend.[19] Amongst them was the tiny settlement of Singlewell, in the parish of Ifield, with a mere 40 inhabitants today.

One particularly interesting and numerous group of markets were what may be called the frontier markets: those that sprang up at the boundaries of counties, of parishes, or of manors. Many of these places, though not all, originated after the Conquest, in the twelfth or thirteenth centuries, on hitherto uninhabited sites. Stony Stratford in Buckinghamshire, a well-known example, originated on the parish boundary of Wolverton and Calverton: one side of the High Street was in one parish, and the other side was in the other. When Stratford acquired two medieval churches of its own, the High Street – the great Roman road which gave its name to the little town –

---

17   By 1870 there was no longer a market at any of these places, though there were still two annual fairs in the spring and autumn at Wye and Charing and one at Marden in October. J. M. Wilson, *The Imperial Gazetteer of England and Wales* (1870).

18   The 12 were: Kegworth, Loughborough, Mountsorrel, Leicester, Great Glen, Kibworth, Market Harborough, Rothwell, Kettering, Finedon, Irthlingborough, and Higham Ferrers.

19   The 13 were: Canterbury, Faversham, Teynham, Sittingbourne, Milton Regis, Newington, Gillingham, Rochester, Gravesend, Milton-by-Gravesend, Northfleet, Dartford, Crayford, Gillingham, Milton Regis, and Faversham were strictly a short distance off this road.

remained the boundary between the two tiny urban chapelries of St Mary Magdalene and St Giles. When these became independent parishes in the eighteenth century, by private Act of Parliament, they comprised only 153 acres between them, carved out of the edges of Wolverton and Calverton parishes on either side of the street.[20] In Leicestershire the town of Mountsorrel developed in a somewhat similar way at the parish boundary of Rothley and Barrow-on-Soar. At the end of the nineteenth century, though it had several hundred years as a busy little market town behind it, Mountsorrel was still divided between its two parent parishes, for it had never acquired its own independence. Although the town has one of the finest Georgian parsonages in Leicestershire, the church itself was technically only a chapel-of-ease to Barrow-on-Soar, and the patron of the living was the vicar of Barrow himself.[21]

There are, indeed, many curious and amusing examples of these boundary markets. The little Kentish town of West Malling was founded at the junction of two jurisdictions, the manor of Malling in the hands of the abbess, and the liberty of Malling in the hands of the Bishop of Rochester.[22] Quite why this occurred is something of a mystery, though there are parallels elsewhere. The fact that in the thirteenth century there were two weekly market days, on Wednesday and Saturday, may suggest that there were originally two distinct grants, to the bishop and the abbess.[23] At any rate, the consequence was that the boundary between manor and liberty actually ran down the middle of the market place, and a row of posts was erected to mark the division. If your market stall was on one side of the posts you paid your rent and your tolls to the bishop; if it was on the other side, you paid them to the abbess. In the seventeenth century, when the manor had come into lay hands, this situation led to angry disputes with the tenants of the bishop, and

20   Maurice Beresford, *New Towns of the Middle Ages* (1967), 398. The date of Stony Stratford's market grant is not known. Churches dedicated to St Giles are often associated with fairs; that at Stratford was the focus of the July fair and is typically sited next to the market place. Fenny Stratford had a similar origin to Stony Stratford, on either side of Watling Street. – *ibid.*, 397–8.

21   Wilson, *op. cit.*, *sub* Mountsorrel; John Nichols, *The History and Antiquities of the County of Leicester*, III, i (1800), 85. The boundary ran along Barn Lane, at the end of which stood the old market cross, on the site of the present market house built in 1793.

22   According to Hasted (*op. cit.*, IV, 523–4) the site of West Malling, which before the abbey was founded and the market granted 'was plain fields, and almost without an inhabitant, became ... exceedingly populous from the numbers who flocked to it from all parts, who building themselves houses here, increased the village to a large size, well suited for trade, to the no small emolument of the nuns'. Its original name of Malling Parva was in consequence gradually superseded by Town Malling or West Malling.

23   Public Record Office, E. 134, 15 Car. I, E. 13; Hasted *op. cit.*, IV, 523. The right to both market days was, however, claimed by the abbess in 1278. The abbey had been founded by Bishop Gundulf of Rochester in 1090, in his manor of West Malling, and it remained subject to the see of Rochester throughout its history. The abbess claimed a grant of a market dating from Henry III's reign.

even before the dissolution of the abbey it can scarcely have been conducive to ecumenical relations.[24]

At Gravesend, the situation was even more curious. Like a number of other towns Gravesend is in fact a double settlement. Its real name, as it was incorporated by Queen Elizabeth in the 1560s, was 'the borough of Gravesend and Milton'; and it had evidently originated on the boundary between these two ancient parishes. The original grant of the market, in 1268, had in fact been to Milton, not to Gravesend itself, though it is possible that Gravesend then already existed as a traditional market centre, without any formal charter. At any rate, the curious result was that East Street and the eastern part of Gravesend High Street were in the parish of Milton, whilst only West Street and the western side of the High Street were in Gravesend itself. Indeed, the whole of the Market Place, together with the town hall, the free school, and the famous Gravesend ferry across the Thames were actually not in Gravesend at all, but in Milton. Needless to say, this was a state of affairs intolerable to the mind of a corporation in which, whatever the charter might say, Gravesend was much the more important partner. In 1695, accordingly, they succeeded in purchasing the manor of Parrocks in Milton, in which the ferry, the free school, the market place, and half the High Streets were situated. In those happy days, however, even the might of a municipality or of parliament itself found it difficult to annul the eternal facts of a parish boundary. The market place, it seems, was still in Milton.[25]

There cannot be many parishes that have succeeded in creating two quite separate market towns within their borders; but there is one at least, and this is the parish of Speldhurst, also in Kent. For good measure both these places appeared not only on the parish boundary, but on the county boundary with Sussex too. The study of settlements and place-names along the borders of Kent forms a curious and entertaining pastime. It is remarkable how many of them are in some way connected with the Devil, who seems to have a peculiar predilection for boundaries of all kinds.

The first of these two markets in Speldhurst that I refer to is Groombridge. In all probability Groombridge had originated before the Conquest as a military post or frontier station between the two independent territories of Kent and Sussex, for its name appears to mean 'guard's bridge' or 'watchman's bridge'. Its existence as a market, however, does not begin till the year 1286, when it was founded by charter of Edward I. One used to be told

---

24   Public Record Office, E. 134, 15 Car. I, E. 13. When the posts were erected is not stated, but they seem to have been an old-fashioned feature of the market place at the time of this commission.

25   Hasted, *op. cit.*, III, 319–20, 339–41. As at West Malling, there were two market days at Gravesend, on Wednesday and Saturday, and these may possibly have originated in different grants to the two parishes. Hasted does not record a market charter for Gravesend as distinct from Milton, but the two fairs were granted in 30 Edward III (*ibid.*, 324).

in Kent that if you sent a letter to Groombridge you had to address it to
'Groombridge, Sussex'; but this story was only a picturesque fiction invented, one suspects, to raise the hackles of Kentish nationalists. It is certainly
true, however, that the railway station and the upstart settlement around it
actually are in Sussex. They may well remain there, in their ugliness, and
leave the enchanting old village itself, round its grass-grown market place,
in Kent. At the foot of the market hill is the bridge whose predecessor gave
its name to the settlement and which still marks the boundary with the
county of Sussex. Groombridge, like Mountsorrel, did not become an independent parish. It is still in Speldhurst, and its life as a market was probably
relatively short: almost certainly it was over before the year 1500. But it has
its own remarkable little chapel, first erected in the thirteenth century and
dedicated to St John, and then rebuilt by the local squire in 1625, and re-
dedicated to St Charles, as a thank offering for the safe return of Charles I
from Spain *without* having married the Spanish Infanta.[26]

The second market to be founded in Speldhurst, at the other end of the
parish, could scarcely be more different, and indeed one would not normally
think of it as a market town at all. This is Tunbridge Wells, founded in the
early seventeenth century at the junction of two counties and three parishes,
on the uninhabited manorial waste of Speldhurst, Tonbridge, and Frant. The
origins of this town, as a watering-place, are of course more complex than
this; yet as a boundary market it is a curious example of history repeating
itself in very different circumstances. The charm of The Wells, as it was for
long simply called, to those who first frequented it for the waters was its
remoteness. Situated as it then was several miles from any other settlement,
it was blessedly free from the prying eyes of parish constables, country
justices, and Cromwellian army officers. Like so many boundary communities it developed, as a consequence, a remarkably free, and indeed permissive,
society. It began as a sort of squatters' settlement for jaded Carolean courtiers,
who camped in tents on the common; it then developed as a sort of plotters'
settlement, composed of both Cavalier and Republican daredevils, during
the days of the Cromwellian Protectorate; and it continued its life, in the
days of Charles II, as a curious mixture of extreme Nonconformity, high-
flying Anglicanism, and a rake's paradise.[27]

---

26   J. K. Wallenberg, *The Place-Names of Kent* (1934), 96; Hasted, *op. cit.*, III, 288,
292. Like many decayed markets, Groombridge still retained its fairs till the late nineteenth
century, though its population in 1851 was only 180. – Wilson, *op. cit.*, *sub* Groombridge.

27   Hasted, *op. cit.*, III, 276 sqq.; Alan Everitt, *The Community of Kent and the Great
Rebellion, 1640–60*, 1967, 268, 287, 304–5; W. Jerrold, *Highways and Byways in Kent*,
1907, 309 sqq.; Wilson, *op. cit.*, *sub* Tunbridge Wells. The fullest account of the social
history of Tunbridge Wells is to be found in Margaret Barton, *Tunbridge Wells* (1937). For a
valuable contemporary account see T. B. Burre, *The History of Tunbridge Wells* (1766),
chapters VI–VIII.

Each of these three last features is still reflected in the intriguing topography of Tunbridge Wells. The town really arose with the gradual fusion of the four or five original villages with which its existence began: Mount Sion, Mount Ephraim, Mount Pleasant, Bishop's Down, and The Wells. These were situated in the valley of the springs itself and on the hills surrounding it, and each village developed its own distinctive character. Mount Ephraim, in Speldhurst parish, was the original Nonconformist village, both Baptists and Presbyterians having their earliest meeting-houses there. In George I's reign the Presbyterians, a wealthy section of the community, moved their chapel to the rival village of Mount Sion, on the opposite side of the valley in Tonbridge parish. By the third quarter of the eighteenth century there was also an Independent meeting-house near The Wells, and there were chapels for the followers of John Wesley and the Countess of Huntingdon. With an almost symbolic gesture, the Anglicans had built their chapel (in the year 1684) in the middle of the valley between the other settlements, next to the springs themselves, and on the exact spot where the two counties and three parishes met. The pulpit was in Speldhurst parish, the altar was in Tonbridge, and the vestry was in Frant. With a fine flourish of defiance to the Dissenters, moreover, the new chapel was dedicated to King Charles the Martyr. Almost adjoining King Charles's chapel was the famous Pantiles, the wide tree-lined promenade we still know today: and it was these walks that formed at once the rake's paradise and the market place. Like the chapel, the market and promenade were situated in two counties and two if not three parishes. They are now entirely in Kent, but you may still see the evidence of the old division in the name of the Royal Sussex Assembly Rooms, on the Frant side of The Pantiles, and once actually in Sussex.[28]

Though Tunbridge Wells is obviously in many ways unrepresentative of the market towns of England, its history does point up a number of features characteristic of these places generally, both of those that survive and of those that have decayed. In the first place, like Tunbridge Wells, most of these places have tended to remain throughout their history relatively *free communities*. By that I mean that, as a rule, they rarely came to be dominated, it seems, by a single local squire or a few large landowners. Through all their vicissitudes of fortune, the landed property within them tended instead to remain much split up, among many small freeholders, instead of, as in so many purely agricultural villages, becoming gradually engrossed by one or two landed magnates. In those that have remained urban centres

---

28   *The National Gazetteer of Great Britain and Ireland* (1868), *sub* Tonbridge Wells; Hasted, *op. cit.*, III, 276 sqq.; Burre, *op. cit.*, 104; *Pelton's Illustrated Guide to Tunbridge Wells* (1879), 104–5 and n. The present Congregational church on Mount Pleasant was not built till 1848, but the origins of the congregation go back to 1830, when it took over the then disused Presbyterian chapel, and it was evidently a revival or re-formation of an earlier Independent group.

throughout their long history, this freedom is no doubt to be expected; but it is remarkable how many of these that have reverted to village status yet managed to retain their freedom from aristocratic domination. This is not invariably true, but in many counties the tendency seems to be striking.

If I may descend into technicalities for a moment, I hope I may illustrate my point. In the year 1860, an enquiry was held into the distribution of landed property in England, and from the resultant Returns we can deduce, in a rough and ready way, the structure of landownership in each county and parish. Simplifying a very complex situation, we find that in many parishes all the land was in one hand or a few hands; whilst in others it was subdivided or 'much subdivided' amongst many small proprietors. For convenience' sake we may christen the former 'estate parishes', since they appear to have been dominated by a single landed magnate or a few large proprietors; whilst the latter we may denominate 'freeholders' parishes', since their society seems to have been composed of a large number of small independent freeholders.[29]

Now it is remarkable, in most counties, how many of these freeholders' communities turn out, on examination, to be not simply agricultural villages in origin, but decayed market towns. This is not the only origin of the freeholders' settlements, but it is the origin of a remarkable number. Though in 1860 many of them had ceased to be markets for several centuries, they still retained a certain freedom in their society, a certain independence of the landed aristocracy around them. This might not have been very apparent to the casual traveller passing through them; but we may rest assured that for the small freeholders themselves, who composed the community, it was the essential fact of their livelihood.

In Suffolk, for example, nearly 70 per cent of the 95 markets for which information regarding landownership is available were still 'freeholders' communities' in the 1860s. In Gloucestershire, the figure was more than 70 per cent, and in Kent and Leicestershire it was almost 80 per cent.[30] In each of these four counties, and particularly in Suffolk, there were some former markets that had decayed so completely that all the property in them had been engrossed by one or two landowners. But in all four shires, and especially in Leicestershire and Kent, the vast majority of former market

29   See Wilson, *op. cit.*, where brief details of landownership based on the Returns of 1860 are given under each parish entry. The following paragraphs are based on an analysis of this information for all known markets or former markets in the counties of Gloucestershire, Kent, Leicestershire, Northamptonshire, and Suffolk. A few places in each county (21 in each) for which details are inadequate have had to be excluded. The analysis is given in tabular form on p. 26. It is obvious that a survey of this kind can only give a summary guide to landownership patterns in the 290 market centres covered. Each place really calls for minute local examination. I have not examined forms of landownership in other counties, except Lincolnshire, where the same pattern as that described in the text seems to obtain.
30   See Table 2 (p. 160 below).

towns had managed to survive as fairly populous communities, composed principally of small freeholders, and still retaining a certain independence.

There was one county, however, in which it is interesting to find that this rule does not entirely hold good, and this was Northamptonshire. There may well have been others, of course, which I have not myself examined in detail. In Northamptonshire nearly half the medieval market towns of the county had not only ceased to be markets by 1860, but either had become very small, exclusive estate villages, entirely owned and controlled by some local magnate, or else in a few cases had virtually disappeared as settlements. One that had vanished completely was Fawsley, a few miles from Daventry. Nobody would guess, who did not already know it, that the grass-grown fields of Fawsley Park, sloping down to the lakes in the valley beneath the Hall – itself now derelict and half-ruinous – conceal the market place and the streets of a medieval town.[31] Yet so it is; and although there are few market centres quite so decayed as Fawsley, there are many in Northamptonshire in which, by the nineteenth century, all the little freeholds appear to have been bought up by a single magnate or a few large landowners. Naseby, Culworth, Brington, Aynho, Rockingham, Fotheringhay, Helpston, and Grafton Regis: all these and other former towns in Northamptonshire had become mere estate villages by the nineteenth century. Their decay as freeholders' communities as well as towns bears witness to the quite exceptional power of the landed aristocracy in Northamptonshire, and there was nothing quite parallel to it, on this scale, in the other four counties. By the eighteenth century there were said to be more resident peers in Northamptonshire than in any other shire of similar size and there are still, of course, more grandiose country mansions than in any comparable county.

But in this respect the lost markets of Northamptonshire seem, as I say, to be something of an exception. The typical decayed market town appears to have remained throughout its history a community of small freeholders. In Leicestershire we have a classic example of one of these places in the village of Bottesford, at the far north-eastern tip of the county, in the lush centre of the Vale of Belvoir. I call it a village, and probably everyone does who knows it; but in fact it is a decayed market town, and it still has a market place and a market cross, though it has had no market since at least the seventeenth century. Bottesford is in an area of Leicestershire which was much dominated by great landowners in the nineteenth century, of whom the greatest of course were the dukes of Rutland at Belvoir Castle. In 1860 nearly all the villages around Bottesford were simple estate villages, where all the property was in the hands of a single owner or a few large proprietors. Eaton and Eastwell, Plungar and Barkestone, Muston and Redmile:

---

31   The grant is said to have been in 8 Henry III in John Bridges, *The History and Antiquities of Northamptonshire* (1791), I, 64. The original grant was for a market on Sunday; it was subsequently changed to Thursday.

these and others all come within this category. But Bottesford was different. Though at the heart of the Rutland estates, its beautiful church almost overwhelmed by the superb tombs of the ducal family, it yet remained, in its own right, a community of small freeholders. Though no doubt its economic fortunes were in some sense dependent on aristocratic favour, yet its people were not entirely dependent in the same sense as those of the neighbouring villages of Eastwell, or Plungar, or Redmile. They could not be turned out of their freeholds if they chose to snap their fingers at the Castle.

There was one way in which a very large number of the inhabitants of these decayed markets like Bottesford did choose to snap their fingers at the Establishment. For one of the most remarkable features about them was the extraordinary vigour of their Nonconformity. There can be little doubt, I think, that this vigour stemmed directly from the relative freedom of their society. They were not tied, like the estate villages, to the squirearchy and the Church. They were not the only places in country districts where Nonconformity flourished, it is true; but from the seventeenth century to the end of the nineteenth they were among the most prominent. In Leicestershire, for example, the two lost markets of Arnesby and Kibworth were noted centres of Nonconformist influence, certainly of more than local importance, at the beginning of the eighteenth century.[32] In Northamptonshire the former town of Long Buckby is still dominated in its centre by the two great Dissenting chapels of the Baptists and the Congregationalists, each in it own large churchyard; while the parish church lies tucked away on the edge of the village, looking over the fields.

By the year 1851, when we get the first and last complete census of religious allegiance ever taken in England, it is clear that the great majority of these decayed markets, in all parts of the country, have become centres of Nonconformity. There were few without at least one Dissenting chapel, and in many places there were two, three, four or even more.[33] The Leicestershire village of Bottesford itself was not untypical in 1851 in having four Dissenting chapels within it, as well as the large parish church, for a population of less than 1,500 souls. Perhaps the most extraordinary example of all in the nineteenth century was the decayed market town of Haxey, in Lincolnshire. Here, to serve about 2,000 inhabitants, there were in 1851 no fewer than 12 Methodist churches. I forbear to describe the many subtle gradations and subdivisions of Methodism, and the absorbing varieties of religious experience, which must have been represented in these 12 Dissenting bodies.

---

32   The Church Book of the Arnesby Baptist church (1699–1757) in Leicestershire County Record Office shows members living in Coventry, Northampton, Leicester, Rothwell, Fridaybridge (Cambs.), and Ramsey (Hunts.). These were evidently subsidiary churches of Arnesby; the Coventry members at least later established their own church (1710).
33   See Table 3 (p. 161 below) for details of the distribution of chapels in market centres.

Another interesting characteristic of many of these former market towns was their development, during the nineteenth century, as small industrial centres. Once again I have little doubt that this was often in some way connected with the relative freedom of their society. The industrial village was, of course, one of the most characteristic forms of local community in England at this time, far more so than it is today. Even in southern counties like Kent, which are commonly thought of as agricultural in the nineteenth century, there was a fair sprinkling of semi-industrial villages.[34] In Leicestershire and Northamptonshire one scarcely needs to emphasize their importance in the local landscape; for many of them are still so obviously, and some so painfully, with us. Yet there were once certainly many more industrial villages in both these Midland counties than there are today: places like Somerby and Billesdon in the heart of east Leicestershire, for example, or Walton and Gilmorton near Lutterworth, or Brixworth and King's Cliffe in Northamptonshire: a century ago all these, and many other places now wholly rural or residential, were industrial as well as farming centres.

Though certainly not all of these industrial villages had once been market towns, it is remarkable how many, on close inspection, turn out to have been so. In Leicestershire a typical example is Kegworth, a few miles from Loughborough, where in the 1860s the inhabitants were employed not in farming but in framework-knitting, basket-making, embroidery-work, malting, and brewing. In Northamptonshire, a typical decayed market which developed into an industrial village, and still remains one, is Irthlingborough. Here in the 1860s the inhabitants were engaged in lace-making, parchment-making, and the manufacture of boots and shoes.[35] In fact much of the Northamptonshire shoe industry and Leicestershire hosiery industry was at this time concentrated in little decayed markets like Irthlingborough and Kegworth.

It is unfortunate that at present we know very little about the economy of most of these settlements between their decay as market towns, usually before the seventeenth century, and their emergence as small industrial communities in the nineteenth. This is one of the many fields of study in which work is being done by local historians, but an enormous amount still remains to be discovered. What exactly did their inhabitants do for a living during this long hiatus in their history? Were they all engaged in farming, or was there throughout these centuries a variety of small crafts and local trades to occupy them? The answer to these questions must doubtless vary a good deal from place to place and county to county.

---

34   For example, in the obscure Wealden parish of High Halden there were in the 1830s 'many manufactories' of 'common earthenware', and a hone-making industry, whilst marble and 'crownstone' were also worked. – Lewis, *op. cit.*, *sub* Halden, High.

35   Wilson, *op. cit.*, *sub* Kegworth and Irthlingborough.

Quite possibly, I suspect, a fair number of them may have borne some resemblance to the little decayed town of Hanslope, a centre of both farming and local industry in north Buckinghamshire.[36] Hanslope had disappeared as a market certainly by the late seventeenth century, and by the end of the eighteenth perhaps much of its ancient market place had been filled in with shops and houses. With probably more than 1,000 inhabitants, however, it was still, in the 1790s, much the largest settlement in the area. At that time two-thirds of its menfolk seem to have been principally engaged in farming; but the remaining third consisted of a wide variety of retailers and craftsmen, a few professional people, and a group of lace-dealers. It was no doubt these lace-dealers who organized the local industry of Hanslope. The making of lace was probably done chiefly by the women, in their cottages; but it was also undertaken by the boys and girls of the villages, and possibly by the menfolk at certain seasons. The Hanslope children were sent to the lace-schools to learn the craft at the age of five years, and by the time they were 11 or 12 they were said to be sufficiently skilled to be able to support themselves. In eighteenth- and early nineteenth-century Hanslope, then, we find a former market town transforming itself into a kind of industrial centre, and yet still retaining a good deal of its agrarian character.

These, then, are a few of the features one might expect to find in the old market towns of England before about 1870, and more particularly in the decayed ones. Such places were only one of many different types of community in the English countryside. The features I have described, moreover, were not their only characteristics, and I have perforce discussed in detail the markets of four or five counties only. Yet it does seem that these places tended to form cells of a particular kind of life, with a fairly distinct form of social organization, and often of topography, and sometimes a surprisingly fierce kind of existence. By and large they were freer communities than many of the purely agricultural villages around them; dominated rather by small freeholders than by powerful landlords; more varied in their society than mere farming villages, more diverse in their occupations, often more industrial during their later years, usually much more. Nonconformist, and frequently, perhaps, more given to lawless pursuits. The tendency to lawlessness I have not touched on, and it was not everywhere apparent amongst them. But it was sometimes a pronounced feature, particularly of the boundary markets, and of a number of

<hr>

36   The following account is based on an analysis of the entries for Hanslope and neighbouring parishes in the Buckinghamshire Posse Comitatus of 1798, in the Buckinghamshire County Record Office, Aylesbury; and on Lewis, *op. cit.*, *sub* Hanslope. The Posse Comitatus lists the names and occupations of male inhabitants liable for service in the county militia. Lace-making was said to be still 'extensively carried on' in Hanslope in the 1860s, as it probably was in many similar places in north Buckinghamshire and west Northamptonshire. – Wilson, *op. cit.*, *sub* Hanslope; cp. the entries for Moulton (Northants.), Towcester, Brixworth.

the later towns, such as Deal and Whitstable in Kent, that originated on extra-parochial tracts or stretches of manorial waste.[37]

The comparative study of communities in different areas may be said, then, to be one of the basic tasks of English local history as we study it at Leicester. Much of the work of all of us in the Department necessitates classification of this kind: whether of local building-types, for example, of local surname patterns, of local topographical features, of local demographic patterns, or of local forms of community. Yet I must not suggest that comparison and classification are the local historian's only task, or his ultimate object. For of course the buildings and the topographical development of no two places are identical, and the genius of every local society is individual and unique. It is precisely at the point where divergence from the mere type begins that the fascination of the subject so often lies. In the words of G. K. Chesterton's poem, we may look upon this country as 'an island like a little book, full of a thousand tales.' For the local historian every one of these thousand tales will be different, and every one will be worthy of study.

Or are they indeed worthy of study? Are we not perhaps wasting our time, and burying our heads, in examining the ordinary inhabitants of insignificant places like Hanslope and Bottesford and Groombridge? The possibility that we may be is an idea with a lengthy and respectable lineage behind it. It is one to which forceful expression was once given by John Ruskin. It is true he was referring specifically to a novel, not a formal work of local history. But since it was a novel of George Eliot's it was also a remarkable historical re-creation of life in an early nineteenth-century provincial town, in this case Gainsborough: and it was really to this that Ruskin objected. *'The Mill on the Floss'*, said Ruskin, 'is perhaps the most striking instance extant of this study of cutaneous disease. There is not a single person in the book of the smallest importance to anybody in the world, but themselves, or whose qualities deserve so much as a line of printer's type in their description. There is no girl alive, fairly clever, half-educated, and unluckily related, whose life has not at least as much in it as Maggie [Tulliver's], to be

---

37   This topic would repay further investigation. As a town Whitstable was a later boundary settlement and did not emerge till the eighteenth century. It developed along the shore, nearly a mile from the original centre, and was for long called 'Whitstable Street' in contradistinction to 'Church Street', the original settlement inland. Much of Whitstable Street was in fact not in Whitstable parish but in Seasalter, and was not under the jurisdiction of the local constables and J.P.s, but under the borough of Harwich in Essex. This peculiarity enabled a kind of 'free trade' community to develop, based on fishing, the coal trade, and smuggling. In Hasted's time most of the 80 houses in the Street had been built within living memory and Whitstable was rapidly expanding. The inhabitants were 'thriving, though of an inferior condition in life, and coarse trades, consisting mostly of those employed in the fishery and oyster dredging, the coal trade, the passage-hoys to and from London, and in the shops which supply the whole of them with the necessities of life, and above all the illicit trade of smuggling.' – *op. cit.*, VIII, 506–7, 513–14.

described and to be pitied ... while the rest of the characters are simply the sweepings out of a Pentonville omnibus.'[38]

At the other end of the spectrum of opinion we have Arnold Bennett. He too was describing the life of a nineteenth-century provincial town, in this case one of his Five Towns in the Potteries. Samuel Povey, said Bennett, in *The Old Wives' Tale*, of his character the draper of Bursley, 'could not impose himself on the burgesses. He lacked individuality. He was little. I have often laughed at Samuel Povey. But I liked and respected him. He was a very honest man. I have always been glad to think that, at the end of his life, destiny took hold of him and displayed, to the observant, the vein of greatness which runs through every soul without exception.'[39] Well, I am not sure that I should go quite so far as Bennett. There are a few of one's acquaintance in whom it is at times hard to perceive any very striking vein of greatness. Yet it was he and George Eliot – concerned as they were with the ordinary people of provincial places – who spoke for the local historian. And of the two attitudes, theirs and Ruskin's, it was surely theirs that was the more percipient and creative, the more hopeful, and the more humane.

---

38   Quoted from *Fiction, Fair and Foul* in Joan Bennett, *George Eliot: her Mind and her Art* (1962), 116n.
39   Arnold Bennett, *The Old Wives' Tale*, Pan edn, 250.

APPENDIX

Table 1. *Market origins in Kent and Suffolk*

	Kent	Suffolk	Total
Before 1086	6	10	16
12th century	1	2	3
13th century	39	64	103
1300–1348	21	14	35
1349–1400	9	3	12
15th century	6	–	6
16th century	2[2]	1	3
Date not known[1]	14	8	22
Total	98	102	200

[1] Medieval or earlier; in several cases prescriptive.
[2] Sittingbourne and Newington-next-Sittingbourne. These two places are not included in the discussion in the text, where a total of 96 medieval markets is mentioned for Kent. Both were late-sixteenth-century grants.

ALAN EVERITT

Table 2. *Markets and property patterns, 1860*[1]

		Gloucester-shire	Kent	Leicester-shire	Northampton-shire	Suffolk	Total
I	Property in one hand	–	–	2	2	2	6
II	Property in few hands	13	19	4	10	28	74
III	Property subdivided	13	20	8	7	21	69
IV	Property much subdivided	20	54	14	9	44	141
	Inadequate information	6	3	2	3	7	21
	Total of III & IV	33	74	22	16	65	210
	Grand total	52	96	30	31	102	311

[1] The table is based on information derived from the Property Returns of 1860 as summarized, under each parish, in J. M. Wilson, *The Imperial Gazetteer of England and Wales* (6 vols., 1870). All known medieval markets, whether surviving or extinct in 1860, are included. In each county there are a number of places for which information about property is not conclusive, and which can only be categorized provisionally. For most of the sizable towns still existing in 1860, for example, no information is given; but it seems safe to assume that property was 'much subdivided' in places of this kind. For 21 places, however, I have not felt justified in making any categorization.

Table 3. *Markets and Nonconformity, 1851*[1]

	Gloucester-shire	Kent	Leicester-shire	Northampton-shire	Suffolk	Total
No chapel	11	22	3	6	40	82
One chapel	9	33	7	6	29	84
Two chapels	6	10	3	9	9	37
Three or more chapels	20	21	16	10	17	84
Inadequate information	6	10	1	–	7	24
Total	52	96	30	31	102	311

[1] The table is based on the 1851 census. All medieval market towns, whether surviving or extinct in 1851, are included. Of the 82 markets where there was no Nonconformist chapel, 56 (68 per cent) had become 'estate villages' by this date, with their land in the hands of a few large proprietors or a single proprietor. Of the 79 former market towns in the five counties which had become 'estate villages' by this time, 56 (71 per cent) had no organized Dissent of any kind.

11

A NEW HISTORY FROM BELOW: COMPUTERS AND THE MATURING OF LOCAL AND REGIONAL HISTORY

Pat Hudson

This article considers the growing impact of computer use on the nature and importance of regional and local history. The first significant expansion of computer-aided historical research in Britain occurred in the 1960s. It was mainly associated with the development and use of statistical packages applied to data easily available in national archives or in published form. In economic history these studies were encouraged by a preoccupation with the nature and causes of national economic growth. Quantification linked to econometrics was, for a time, seen as the great panacea of the discipline of economic history, opening up the possibility of confident judgements about economic choices and economic efficiency in the past.[1] And a similar enthusiasm was afoot in political and social history where, by the 1970s, the rush to quantify and computerise was being felt in all sorts of studies from voting behaviour and the composition of Parliaments to strikes in nineteenth-century France and the relationship between political violence and family interaction.[2]

Not surprisingly, these first waves of computer applications in history had as many critics as advocates. Judt, writing in 1979, spoke of the profession succumbing to 'the delirium of statistical series',[3] arguing that historical

---

1   As an introduction to the claims, emergence, achievements and pitfalls of econometric history see: R. W. Fogel and S. L. Engerman (eds.), *The reinterpretation of American economic history* (London, 1971); C. H. Lee, *The quantitative approach to economic history* (London, 1977); D. N. McCloskey, *Econometric History* (London, 1987).

2   W. O. Aydelotte, *Quantification in History* (New York, 1971), ch. 5; C. Tilly, 'The changing place of collective violence', in C. L. and R. Tilly (eds.), *The rebellious century* (Harvard, 1975); M. Matossian and W. D. Schafer, 'Family, fertility and political violence', *Journal of Social History* XI, 2 (1977). For the most condemnatory survey of this trend in social history see T. Judt, 'A clown in regal purple: social history and the historians', *History Workshop* 7 (1979).

3   Judt, *op. cit.*, 74, partly quoting from M. Perrot, 'The strengths and weaknesses of French social history', *Journal of Social History* 10, 2 (1976).

data were rarely sufficiently robust for the sort of rigorous statistical manipulation which was being encouraged by computer software.[4] The obsession with numbers and their uses was too often a substitute for properly conceived historical questions. There was also a strong tendency to exclude the unquantifiable from historical work and hence a reduction of interest in anything before 1750. Other voices warned of the computer as the harbinger of mindless empiricism. Richard Cobb's essay in caricature, 'Historians in White Coats' written in 1971, derided a specific piece of research:

> the computerisation of 516 urban riots ... in France for the whole period 1815–1914. The end product will no doubt reveal some highly interesting patterns: that, for instance, market riots occurred on market days, on or near the market, that marriage riots take place after weddings, that funeral riots take place either outside the church or near the cemetery, that Saturday riots take place on Saturday evenings after the wineshops and bals have closed ... that rent riots occur on rent days ... the religious riots, especially in towns or bourgs in which there exist two or more religious communities, favour Sundays, Catholic feast days, St. Bartholomew's Day or the Passover. Perhaps we thought we knew already; but now we *really* know.[5]

Charles Tilly, whose work was the object of Cobb's derision, felt forced to admit in an ensuing discussion that the scale and complexity of historical computer projects produce periods when researchers are so preoccupied with problems of coding, file construction, statistical procedure, computer techniques and coordination of the whole effort that they practically lose contact with the people, events, places, and times they are studying.[6]

An unhelpful bifurcation emerged in the profession. There were those who talked in huddled groups at conferences of nothing but their latest hardware and software acquisitions, excitedly using the new jargon of computer-speak. And there were those who rejected the use of computers entirely. Disenchanted by their colleagues, encouraged by the methodological shortcomings of much computer-aided quantitative analysis but sometimes just deeply conservative, many historians suggested that the relationship between computing and history was not quite respectable. This slowed down the rate of acceptance of computer use in historical research.

Thanks largely to developments in computer software and hardware, which have occurred independently of historians' needs, the last decade has seen innovations in, and a new acceptance of, computers in historical work. The use of a range of social science and historical statistical packages, particularly for simple numerical manipulation and display, is now wide-

4   Judt, *op. cit.*, 66.
5   R. Cobb, 'Historians in white coats' (1971), quoted in C. Tilly, *As sociology meets history* (New York, 1981), 72.
6   Tilly, *Sociology meets history*, 82.

spread.[7] And the traditional lonely encounter of one person with one document, which Cobb in 1971 feared was being undermined by the new technology, is currently being promoted and reinvigorated by the use of laptops and new types of software which allows qualitative as well quantitative computer-aided research.[8] Those who were critics of computer use in the 1970s and 1980s are being converted to the computer as an indispensable tool of research. Most undergraduate degree courses and taught M.A. programmes in history, economic and social history and the humanities and social science more generally include elements of computer training, a fact reflected in increasing numbers of student projects and dissertations which employ a wide range of computer-aided techniques. Where computers once dealt mainly with the study of easily available, mostly national, statistical series and the formation and testing of econometric models, their historical use is now growing fastest in relation to very different sorts of empirical investigations. In particular, they are being used in rigorous interrogation, evaluation and analysis of masses of previously unused primary source materials generated at local and regional level. This revolution in computer use is freeing local and regional history from its antiquarian roots, enlarging the scope of enquiry and creating a new role for research at these levels.

This article considers the effects of computing on local and regional research, drawing on examples from recent work, under three main heads: first, the greater accessibility of local sources which is occurring through computer indexing, listing and transcribing; secondly, the new intensity and variety of interrogations of local data made possible by new data storage, retrieval and display techniques; and finally, the possibility of rescuing the lives of families, communities and ordinary people from the silence of the historical record.

It used to be the case that one practically had to live in an archive and rely on the memory and length of service of archivists to gain knowledge of, or access to, required source material. Or was it sometimes that archivists felt the need to establish a rapport or trust before remembering that extra box of possibly-relevant material which turns out to be the crucial source hidden away in an unlisted collection. This happened to me more than once in research on the Yorkshire textile industry during the early 1970s. In those

---

7   For an indication of the more commonly-used packages see Daniel I. Greenstein, *A historian's guide to computing* (Oxford, 1994), especially chapter 4.
8   For recent introductory texts indicating the current rage of computer-aided research see Greenstein *op. cit.*; and E. Mawdsley and T. Munck, *Computing for historians: an introductory guide* (Manchester, 1993).

days, before the formation of the West Yorkshire Archive Service, archive keepers included branch librarians, churchwardens and council caretakers. They were more likely to have an open fire, a pet dog or a plate of pie and chips in their search room than a computer terminal or even a good hand-written catalogue and index of holdings. This was not just a function of the cosy chaos of West Riding (and other) repositories in the early 1970s but also of the early stage of development, and expense, of computerised index-ing systems. But how much more useful the catalogue of business records which I assembled in 1975 (560 pages covering more than 120 collections) would have been if it had been possible to form it as a computer index capable of sorting by name, precise record type and subject matter of document.[9]

There are signs of the beginning of a revolution in cataloguing and cross referencing of archival material in local repositories which will open up many collections to thorough investigation for the first time. Although it is not yet well advanced, the development of machine-readable listings in many repositories is resulting in the frequent publication of both disc- and hard-copy updated information about holdings. Most record office systems are now using flexible and accessible databases with keyword updates and dynamic (changeable) indexing.[10] Various forms of word searching (free text and key word) and hypertext are also widely used as methods of information retrieval from archive listings or transcripts.[11] Expert systems (with flexible data structures, eliminating the need for known algorithms) are also being explored for the specific purposes of archive control and evaluation.[12] Some repositories and county record offices have also embarked upon projects of transcription of archival material into machine-readable copy as an aid to preservation in addition to greater accessibility.[13] Such

---

9   P. Hudson, *The West Riding wool textile industry. A catalogue of business records from the sixteenth to the twentieth century* (Edington, 1975).

10   For a survey of some of the database technology used in this way see Greenstein, *A historian's guide*, ch. 3. Such methods have been even longer established for bibliographi-cal indexing relevant to local historical research, as with the East Yorkshire bibliography at the University of Hull. See B. English, 'Electronic bibliography: an example from East Yorkshire', *The Local Historian* 19, 3 (1989), 117–19.

11   See for example E. Stazicker, 'The local record office and the computer today', AHC 1990; M. Moss 'Jubilant and joyful or distraught and disillusioned – computer appli-cations in the search rooms: the experience of Glasgow University Archives' in E. Mawdsley, N. Morgan, L. Richmond and R. Trainor (eds.), *Historians, computers and data: applica-tions in research and training* (Manchester, 1990).

12   M. O'Sullivan, 'Expert systems and archive finding aids', AHC 1990. For more on expert systems and their application to historical research see P. Denley, S. Fogelvik and C. Harvey (eds.), *History and Computing II* (Manchester, 1989), 90–102.

13   See M. Moss, 'Computer applications in the search rooms' and A. Wilson, 'Liber-ating the historical record' in Mawdsley, Morgan et al. (eds.), *Historians, computers and data*.

transcription, in the case of suitably printed or written documents, and the conversion of transcribed documents into database, spreadsheet, cartographical or graphics format, has been revolutionised by the development and increasing sophistication of scanners during the last decade or so. Scanners can now be used in conjunction with graphics and other visual processing software to produce high resolution pictures and plans especially useful in projects dealing with architectural or technological history.

These developments will proceed slowly in the public sector in this era of retrenchment but access to local data is being expedited by various private, educational and research initiatives which are building up collections of local and regional datasets on different subjects and creating wider access to them. Notable examples include the regional labour markets database at Queen Mary and Westfield College; parish register data at Cambridge, Liverpool and Southampton universities and elsewhere; population census material at universities including Edinburgh, Belfast and Southampton; small towns data at Leicester; Scottish history and business history databases at Glasgow; Irish history at Belfast; various history of medicine databases, notably those associated with Wellcome research units; and the ESRC data archive at the University of Essex. The entry of key sources into databases, both flat file and relational, with text encoding, hypertext or similar, facilitates their use for multiple research purposes. The Irish Ordnance Survey Memoirs database at the Queen's University of Belfast has developed the use of QUILL (Queen's University Interrogation of Legal Literature) to index and retrieve information from this unique source providing a detailed description of Ireland and Irish society before the famine. The database can now be interrogated to produce material on a variety of separate specialist subjects such as architecture, employment, topography and genealogies.[14] Similarly the Gloucester port books project at Wolverhampton comprises a mass of machine-readable information on traded goods, ships and cargoes derived from 160 ledgers covering trade during the period 1581–1765. The database is being used to study the pivotal role of Bristol, trade patterns in raw materials and finished products, innovations in manufacturing, the changing domestic and industrial uses of commodities, marketing techniques and consumer attitudes. The information will also be valuable for researchers working on the history of particular manufacturing or trading enterprises or particular industries.[15] One of the most sophisticated examples of database construction designed to encourage multiple-purpose research is the Domes-

---

14   A. Day, 'The Irish Ordnance Survey Memoirs database and publication project', AHC 1990.

15   Contributions by P. Wakelin, A. Brown and D. Hussey, AHC 1990. Also P. Wakelin, 'Comprehensive computerisation of a very large documentary source: the portbooks project at Wolverhampton Polytechnic', in P. Denley and D. Hopkin (eds.), *History and Computing* (Manchester, 1987).

day Book mapping project at the University of Hull. This has involved embedded coding of the entire Domesday text (a million words) including coding of place names (incorporating a hierarchy by size and importance), search and spreadsheet software and the incorporation of grid references to enable automatic mapping of all vills, manors, estates, landowners, and 'commodities' such as pigs, cattle or slaves on estates.[16]

Some national, local and university storage and retrieval systems may be accessed more widely using INTERNET via SUPERJANET or W3 (World Wide Web), but progress in making archival information available on-line was at first very slow in Britain because of a prolonged debate about the adoption of uniform standards for archival description and the control of entries into databases.[17] In North America these necessary standards were adopted by most repositories in the 1980s and it quickly became common to enter archival descriptions on to on-line databases so that the content of record collections was publicly available across the continent. Some progress along these lines has now been made in this country by the National Register of Archives and the wider adoption of MAD2 is bringing the possibilities for a fuller exchange of archival information into focus.[18] At the same time the massive storage potential of CD ROM is facilitating the transfer of archival listings and transcriptions in disc form enabling fast access to large datasets. Multi-media developments are further extending the richness and variety of visual and oral as well as documentary sources which can be stored, manipulated and transferred.

Once access is gained, the computer is also revolutionising the use to which particular sorts of local and regional data can be put. This is best illustrated with reference to one or two specific sorts of local records. It is no accident that large-scale studies of collections of probate inventories have appeared only with the use of database systems. Before this, these documents were employed mainly to fill in detail in biographical studies or at best they were sampled to illustrate the possessions of particular small communities. Now, once inputted in ways amenable to manipulation and interrogation, these

---

16   J. Palmer, 'Mapping Domesday', AHC 1990. See also G. Slater, 'The Hull Domesday textbase: a programmers view', *University Computing* (1988), 2–8.

17   By contrast, the Association for Industrial Archaeology early adopted a successful standardised system for recording industrial sites: IRIS.

18   M. Cook, 'Data exchange and archival information', AHC 1990. MAD2 is the acronym for the *Manual of archival description*, 2nd edition (London, 1990). For early computer cataloguing developments at the National Register of Archives see J. Parker, 'Computerisation of the National Register of Archives: designing a system for staff and public use', in Mawdsley et al. (eds.), *Historians, computers and data*, 29–36.

documents are proving a major source in the study of agricultural change in different regions of the country over the seventeenth and eighteenth centuries and can be used effectively to consider the changing mix of agricultural and manufacturing assets found in proto-industrial communities. Once in a database, such documents can be employed to pick out the profile, in terms of possessions, of particular occupational groups or they can be used to study the diffusion of new consumer goods: textiles, furniture, clocks, crockery, cutlery and cooking utensils. This fills the gaps in our knowledge about the otherwise elusive home market for manufactured products of different sectors of industry in the seventeenth and eighteenth centuries.[19] Thus probate inventories, as a source, have moved from being used almost solely for limited and discrete pieces of research to being engaged in work, mostly at the regional and local level, on some of the major issues in economic and social history.

The same is also true, of course, of parish registers. Twenty years ago these were used largely for either the study of local trends in the three vital series of baptisms, marriages and burials or for biographical/genealogical research. Whilst no archivist can claim that genealogical enquiries are not still the major demand placed upon parish registers, their use has been revolutionised in demographic research and in social and economic history more generally by the advent of the computer and of increasingly specialised software in this field. Although the idea and methods of family reconstitution predate the computer, it is only the new technology which makes reconstitution feasible for anywhere but the smallest parish. And it is only the new technology which may enable standard criteria and algorithms to be used so that reconstitution results can be compared one with another. Thus the local variation underlying national trends in population growth and change can be identified, free from the distortions created by different reconstitution conventions.[20] And this can be incorporated into the analysis

---

19   M. Overton, 'Computer analysis of probate inventories: from portable micro to mainframe', in Denley and Hopkin, *History and Computing*; idem., 'The diffusion of agricultural innovations in early modern England: turnips and clover in Norfolk and Suffolk, 1580–1740', *Transactions of the Institute of British Geographers*, 10 (1984), L. Weatherill, *Consumer behaviour and material culture in Britain, 1660–1760* (London, 1988). J. Spavold, The Church Gresley inventories project – computerising personal and household data', AHC 1990.

20   The use of shell files can assist with uniform formatting and information storage as well as direct comparability of linkage criteria and greater accuracy of formatted data. Shell files are expert systems with an editor (where schemas and rules are entered) and a development engine (which permits the processing of rules and reasoning and can thus extend the knowledge base, detecting missing or inconsistent rules and allowing corrections and completions). There is also a trace command which can test the accuracy of the database by applying the rules listed in the editor. See, for example, Caroline Bourlet and Jean Luc Minel, 'From an historian's know how to a knowledge base: using a shell' in Mawdsley et al., *Historians, computers and data*, 55–66.

of long-run demographic change at national level. Computers enable greater cross-checking of reconstitution results with other sources. Parish records can thus be integrated with taxation documents, census enumerators' books and civil registration records not just for back projection but for verification of a range of detailed demographic research at local and regional level including migration, occupation- and age-specific mortality and fertility, endogamy, family size and structure, illegitimacy and the demographic effect of poverty and income variants.[21]

Taxation and rating documents such as the late-seventeenth-century hearth tax returns and eighteenth- and nineteenth-century poor rate assessments can be pressed into new uses, once they are in machine-readable form. They can be made to reveal much about the social structure of localities and regions on a comparative basis. Similarly the eighteenth-century land tax in database format can be sorted by owner, by occupier and by property to provide longitudinal as well as cross-sectional data on the size of landholdings, their transfer and their lineage within families. Often such records are best used alongside databases containing complementary information from other sources, such as parish registers and land surveys. For example, the land tax with other earlier records is being put to good use in the Winchester property project, which employs a relational database to analyse property transfers over 1,000 years.[22] This research is not undertaken just for narrow antiquarian ends but to address broader historical issues about long term urban development. For this type of enquiry the use of machine-readable versions of urban rate books is also invaluable. Urban rate books can be interrogated to provide cross-sectional and dynamic views of the movement of urban rents and the distribution of property values between economic sectors. Interesting computer-aided analysis of the early-nineteenth-century Manchester rate books by Lloyd Jones and Lewis has shown that there was more capital sunk in inns and public houses in 'cottonopolis' in 1812 than in factory premises![23] This indicates the need to further address the relative importance and distribution of merchant and industrial capital

21   A good example of this is S. A. King, 'The nature and causes of demographic change in an industrialising township', unpublished Ph.D. (University of Liverpool, 1994). This is part of a wider project jointly with P. Hudson on 'Demography, material culture and everyday life in West Yorkshire manufacturing townships' due to be completed in 1996 with the aid of funding from the ESRC and the British Academy. This project, together with others using relational database techniques, is described in S. W. Baskerville, P. Hudson and R. J. Morris (eds.), *History and Computing special issue: Record Linkage*, 4, 1 (1992).

22   M. Doughty, 'Relational databases and urban history – the Winchester project', AHC 1990.

23   R. Lloyd Jones and M. J. Lewis, 'A database for historical reconstruction: Manchester in the industrial revolution', in Mawdsley, Morgan, et al. (eds.), *Historians, computers and data*. See also idem, *Manchester in the age of the factory: the business structure of cottonopolis in the industrial revolution* (London, 1988).

during the industrial revolution. Once again a central issue in debates about the economic history of Britain can be illuminated in new ways by computer-aided research using local sources.

Once documents such as the land tax and urban rate books are made machine-readable they (like parish registers) can be compared across localities and regions to answer interesting questions about local variations and to provide a foundation for more reliable aggregate data. Similarly, highway accounts are no longer confined in their use to the study of particular and local road building projects over short periods but can be milked in such quantity as to provide reliable indices of manual wages and price series for building materials at regional and national levels. The accounts of overseers and churchwardens can be linked to parish registers to reveal life cycle and other factors in the receipt of poor relief and to study the labour supply policy of parish élites in the payment of relief, in the billeting of pauper apprentices and in the execution of settlement policy.[24]

Later nineteenth- and twentieth-century material at local level survives in such quantity that computers have an even bigger role to play in expediting a level and range of information extraction which was previously impossible. Computer application has enabled entirely new levels of analysis of the census enumerators' books. There are currently several large databases derived from these records, notably the 10 per cent sample of the 1851 census collected under the direction of Michael Anderson at the University of Edinburgh. Such data can now be used to consider local variations in household size and structure, occupational and migration patterns and can be linked to other local sources to consider poverty and the context of hospitalisation or criminality, for example.[25]

Oral history is also entering a new computer-oriented phase where transcripts of interviews are inputted and tagged by keyword or using a full hypertext system.[26] Oral accounts can thus be used, providing care is exercised, for a multiplicity of purposes aside and beyond the original project for which the interviews were arranged. Diaries, autobiographies, novels

24   Work in progress, University of Liverpool (see note 21). B. Stapleton, 'Inherited poverty and life cycle poverty: Odiham, Hampshire, 1650–1850', *Social History* 18, 3 (1993). Work concentrating on poor relief and the elderly is also in progress directed by R. M. Smith at the Cambridge Group for the History of Population and Social Structure.

25   See for example, S. J. Page, 'Researching local history: methodological issues and computer assisted analysis', *The Local Historian* 23, 1 (1993), 20–30; H. Rhodri Davies, 'Automated record linkage of census enumerators' books and registration data: obstacles, challenges, solutions', *History and Computing* 4, 1 (1992), 16–26; Edward Higgs, 'Structuring the past: the occupational and household classification of nineteenth century Census data' in Mawdsley et al. (eds.), *Historians, computers and data*, 67–73.

26   P. Teibenbacher, 'The computer, oral history and regional studies', in Denley, Fogelvik and Harvey (eds.), *History and Computing II*; L. Ritter, 'Oral history and the use of a database: a case history', *History and Computing* 2, 1 (1990).

and advice books can also be used in new ways to form sources for collective biography and wider research. A project at the University of Edinburgh is using tailor-made software on MS DOS to study social networks by analysing the text and language of personal diaries dating from the eighteenth and nineteenth centuries.[27] So once again computers are moving the use of a wide range of primary sources away from limited, very specific projects to more representative and general use where broader and more important questions can be asked of the material.

Computers can, of course, also aid the interrogation of national bodies of data for local and regional research. The example which springs most readily to mind here is the use to which the various national databases of insurance records have been put in local and regional research on industrial capital formation and on urban growth and development in particular.[28]

Before leaving the subject of the interrogation of documents at a local level, mention should also be made of the sorts of software which enable information to be presented in a variety of ways. Especially interesting and important here are spreadsheets, graphics and cartography packages.[29] For local and regional research new mapping possibilities are particularly exciting. Cartographic facilities are promoting renewed consideration of data already analysed by more conventional means. The current work by Lord and Kissock on the Midland peasant involves computer analysis and mapping of the same sources which W. G. Hoskins used.[30] The rapid development of Geographical Information Systems (GIS) since the mid-1980s has the greatest potential importance. These systems enable the integration of multiple sets of data on the basis of geographical coordinates, and have major implications for the development of regional databases in economic and social history.[31] Important

27   S. Nenadic, 'Identifying social networks with a computer-aided analysis of personal diaries', in Mawdsley, Morgan et al. (eds.), *Historians, computers and data*; L. Bernard, 'Primary to secondary: using the computer as a tool for textual analysis in historical research', in Denley and Hopkin (eds.), *History and Computing*.

28   Machine-readable listings of Sun Fire Office policies are available in the ESRC data archive at the University of Essex, having been assembled for a number of ESRC-financed projects. They are being used for various pieces of local and regional research. Their potential is explored in L. D. Schwarz and L. J. Jones, 'Wealth, occupations and income in the late eighteenth century: the policy registers of the Sun Fire Office', *Economic History Review*, 36, 3 (1983) 365–73.

29   Developments of software in these areas are covered in the annual review of information technology in *Economic History Review*, May issue. That by R. Middleton and P. Wardley in XLIV, 2 (1991) is particularly useful on spreadsheets. On graphics see also D. Speath, 'Graphics', *History and Computing* 2, 2 (1990).

30   E. Lord and J. Kissock, 'Approaches to the history of the midland peasant', AHC 1990. See also R. A. Faugeres, 'Automatic cartography in historical research' in Denley and Hopkin (eds.), *History and Computing*, 211–15.

31   M. Overton, 'An introduction to geographical information systems', AHC 1990; H. Southall and E. Oliver, 'Drawing maps with a computer or without', *History and Computing* 2, 2 (1990), 146–54. The GENIE project at the Department of Computing,

geographical concepts like central place or growth pole theories can now be demonstrably put to the test using sources such as sales and purchase ledgers, whose volume and complexity had confined their use largely to the narrower sphere of individual company histories without the help of the computer.

The current proliferation of parallel projects on different localities and regions creates the possibility of comparing and merging machine-readable material so that new perspectives can emerge regarding the functioning of the economy and society as a national whole. Something of the possibilities of merging local and regional databases can be seen in Southall and Gilbert's work on English labour markets, wages and labour organisation.[32] Other similarly new series of wages and prices have emerged from research under the same ESRC initiative on prices and incomes.[33] These developments expose divergent trends and experiences in different regions and localities and demand their explanation in comparative terms, whilst also giving a more sophisticated understanding of the broader national experience. Such research also encourages comparative work between British and overseas localities, regions and nations.

As, if not more, important than this comparative work is the prospect that regional and local research can for the first time be deployed to produce fresh evidence of the movement of major variables at the aggregate national level. One good example is the small towns project at Leicester University which is contributing to new indices of national rates of urbanisation.[34] Perhaps the best illustration of the need for such developments is found in the shortcomings of current work on indices of the pace and nature of industrialisation in Britain in the late eighteenth and early nineteenth centuries. A few years ago, Joel Mokyr, commenting on the continued analysis of macro-variables produced by Crafts and others for the industrial revolution period, stated that this research had run into the diminishing returns of analysing the same body of data over and over again. The best strategy for the future was a return to the archives to gather new, fuller and more reliable series of sectoral inputs and outputs, wage and price movements, the distribution of the labour force and the growth of productivity.[35] Only by a new attack on archival sources at local and regional level can deficiencies in the national series have some chance of rectification. Intermediate and semi-processed output, for example (at present directly excluded from the macro-estimates), must be calculated on the basis

---

University of Loughborough, is linking a range of data sets and mapping packages under the direction of Dr I. A. Newman.

32   H. Southall and D. Gilbert, 'The British nineteenth century labour markets database at Queen Mary and Westfield College', AHC 1990.

33   For example see J. Boulton, 'Living standards in seventeenth century London', AHC 1990.

34   A. Wilson, 'The English small towns project, 1550–1851', AHC 1990.

35   J. Mokyr, 'Has the industrial revolution been crowded out? Some reflections on Crafts and Williamson', *Explorations in Economic History* 24, 3 (1987), 306.

of transfers of goods within and between firms. Local archives are our only source of pinning down such transfers and for examining the large areas of economic activity which have left no easy source of quantitative data at all: the small firm sector, penny capitalism, multiple sources of income, reciprocity, householding, and much of women's work. All of these went on outside the boundaries of the formal economy which confines the national accounting estimates. Getting the various national series right also requires guesstimates about sectoral weights and their change over time, which can be sophisticated by further work on local and regional archives. It is also through research at this level that we are going to uncover the range and variety of regional and local growth experiences and of innovativeness which characterised the industrial revolution period and went on under the surface of the slow-moving national economic indicators.[36]

It is very likely that regional and local understanding of the process of industrialisation and its social and political corollaries will have much to offer in the next few years to studies of the national economy as a whole. New regional building blocks, using sources which can only fully be interrogated with the aid of computers, will form the basis of a new understanding of the national picture and of comparative work transnationally.[37]

New developments in the power and sophistication of database software in particular make real the prospect of a much fuller economic and social history from below, where the lives of masses of ordinary people can be rescued from local archives. This is achieved by data linkage across a large number of nominal files assembled from a range of different sources relating to a parish or locality. The increasing sophistication of relational database software is vital here.[38] The analysis of social structure and social and

---

36   For more of the author's idea on this issue see P. Hudson (ed.), *Regions and industries: a perspective on the industrial revolution in Britain* (Cambridge, 1989), 5–38; ibid., *The industrial revolution* (London, 1992), 37–50, 101–32.

37   For further discussions of these points see P. Hudson, 'The regional perspective' in *Regions and Industries*, 5–38.

38   On relational database developments, nominal record linkage and file merging for historical applications of this kind, see Denley and Fogelvik et al. (eds.), in *History and Computing* II, 44–102; M. Thaller, 'Methods and techniques of historical computation' and C. Bourlet and J. L. Minel, 'A declarative system for setting up a prosopographical database' in Denley and Hopkin, *History and Computing*, D. I. Greenstein, 'Multi-sourced and integrated databases for the prosopographer', in Mawdsley, Morgan et al. (eds.), *Historians, computers and data*; C. Harvey, 'Record linkage and the relational model', AHC 1990; Baskerville, Hudson and Morris (eds.), *History and Computing*.

economic relations in the parish of Stiffkey in the late sixteenth century is a good example. The research of Morgan, Hassel Smith and others at the University of East Anglia has shown that the lives of a significant proportion of the most humble parishioners can be brought under the spotlight.[39] This sort of approach mirrors the research pioneered by historians working since the early 1980s at the Max Plank Institüt für Geschichte in Göttingen. Kreidte, Medick and Schlumbohn have been reconstructing the social and economic history of three central European proto-industrial localities since the early 1980s using relational database software specially developed by Manfred Thaller.[40] Their CLIO system was one of the first to integrate statistical software with relational database facilities for historical research and has been adapted by other similar projects in Europe, including a detailed reconstruction of the Languedoc.[41]

My own work involves the reconstruction of families, individuals and social and economic relationships in two manufacturing townships of West Yorkshire (Sowerby near Halifax and Calverley between Leeds and Bradford) during the period c.1680–1820.[42] The project benefited in its early stages from the close interchange of ideas and a 10-week visit to Göttingen.[43] Working outward from primary files derived from the parish registers and nonconformist material, other secondary files from the hearth tax, poor rates, religious censuses, the land tax, probate inventories and wills, poor

---

39   V. Morgan, 'Differentiating the humble – an aspect of the Stiffkey project on the late sixteenth century', AHC 1990.

40   For the ideas behind CLIO see M. Thaller, 'Methods and techniques of historical computation', in Denley and Hopkin (eds.), *History and Computing*, 147–56. For published research using CLIO on studies of industrialising communities see P. Kriedte, *Eine stadt am seidenen faden. Haushalt, hausindustrie und soziale Bewegung in Krefeld in der mitte des 19. jahrhunderts* (Göttingen, 1991); J. Schlumbohm, *Lebenslaufe, familien, Hofe. Die bauern und heuerleute des Osnabruckischen Kirchspiels Belm in Proto-industrieller zeit, 1650–1860* (Göttingen, 1994).

41   J. Smets, 'South French society and the French Revolution: the creation of a large database with CLIO' in Denley and Hopkin, *History and Computing*.

42   For more on the background to this project and some preliminary results see P. Hudson, 'Landholding and the organisation of textile manufacture in Yorkshire rural townships', in M. Berg (ed.), *Markets and manufacturers in early Industrial Europe* (London, 1990) and P. Hudson and S. A. King 'A sense of place: industrialising townships in eighteenth century Yorkshire' in R. Leboutte (ed.), *Festschrift in honour of Franklin Mendels* (Geneva, 1995).

43   Starting in 1986, the Yorkshire project initially used the relational database SQL/DS with a REX interface on the IBM mainframe at Liverpool. The mainframe was then changed to the Sun System so the project has switched to MS/DOS and now uses Ingres. These days it would be possible to contemplate using a PC and PC software such as MS Works or Lotus 123 for such a project, although the storage and manipulation capacity required for a project using the full range of local sources should not be underestimated. See S. A. King, 'Record linkage in a proto-industrial community', *History and Computing* 4, 1 (1992), 27–33.

relief disbursements, settlement certificates and examinations, bastardy papers, apprenticeship indentures, enclosure awards, property surveys and early census returns have been added. Deeds, court cases and business records are also included. The database itself has many manipulative facilities for retrieving data, but the addition of new software has expedited a semi-automated approach to nominal record linkage. It is now possible to relate landholdings to occupational groups, to discover the social and economic origins of vestry officials, to look at how élites managed vestry affairs, to study the movement of a whole array of demographic variable and to discuss in depth the links between familial, social and economic ties.

It is also possible to assemble case study material on the lives of people who would otherwise never figure in historical research. The possibility of a detailed retrospective ethnography is emerging. I do not wish to exaggerate the 'hit rate' for record linkage, but to give an example derived from an enquiry about the social mobility of pauper apprentices, we were able to link over 200 of the 551 pauper apprenticeship indentures for eighteenth-century Sowerby to at least two other records, and reasonably detailed life histories are available for 46 people who were pauper apprentices as children. Twenty-one of these are female. We can see why they became paupers, who their parents were, where they lived at different points in their life, who they married, what occupation they took, whether they became landholders in the township and whether they became involved with the law or poor relief later in life.

In case studies of the poorest groups of landless cottages, we can now see how often and at what points in the life cycle they received poor relief; discover from whom they rented accommodation or land; identify the ways in which their occupation changed over time; and study the constant short distance movement which appears to have been characteristic of weavers and labourers in the townships. We can see who they married, how many children they had, how many died in childhood or became pauper apprentices, to whom they were indentured and on what terms. We can occasionally analyse the size and composition of poor households, where the poor lived in relation to their wider kin or others of the same social group, and we can sometimes learn details of their employment history in settlement examination or the records of putting-out employers. Other details revealed by the database include brushes with the law for illegal coining, horse stealing, or other offences, and if they left a will or acted as a witness to a document, we can find out if they were able to sign their name. We can see when they died, sometimes the cause of death and occasionally a list of their possessions at death or whether they had a pauper's funeral. For small employers, landowners and yeomen whose lives have left no specific archive collections, we can derive similar information to add to insurance records, trade directories and other documents where they might be mentioned. We learn about the role of tied housing, attitudes to illegitimacy, the scope of occupational and

Fields	Function	Length
Refno	Unique ID Number	6
Bd	Birth Day	2
Bm	Birth Month	2
Byear	Birth Year	4
Sx	Sex	1
Fname	Forename	15
Sname	Surname	20
Status I	Birth Date	10
Status II	Status	10
Residence	Residence	30
Ffname	Father forename	15
Fsname	Father Surname	20
Focc	Father Occupation	20
Fstatus	Father Status	10
Fres	Father Residence	30
Mfname	Mother Forename	15
Msname	Mother Surname	20
Mocc	Mother Occupation	20
Mstatus	Mother Status	10
Gppat	Paternal grandparent	35
Gpmat	Maternal grandparent	35
Psnamecode	Surname code of child	4
Fsnamecode	Surname code of father	4
Msnamecode	Surname code of mother	4
Tscoremdb	Refno of parent marriage	8
Tscoremds	Refno of own marriage(s)	8
Tsoremdg	Refno of kinship linked marriages	20
Wbfamily	Social Status indicator	1
Mfamily	Landholding indicator	1
Tscore	Confidence flag	2

An example of file structure from the Yorkshire database, including linkage fields: Anglican baptisms, Calverley.

geographical mobility and the lineage of social and family groups in long-established neighbourhoods which partly underpinned the networks and expansion of proto-industries. All these potential lines of research have become possible by using the computer to squeeze every available detail out of a record and to store such details so that they can be retrieved, reordered and linked in a variety of different ways to create new files on the life histories of individuals and business ventures. Although one still has to listen carefully to the silence as well as to the historical record relating to these people, with this computer-aided method the record is fuller than ever before.

Such multiple record linkage enables ideas derived from anthropology, psychology and sociology to be applied to local and regional history, so broadening the conceptual basis of historical research. It is real local history, dependent on familiarity with person and place. But it is not antiquarian in its concern because the level and breadth of detail made possible by the employment of a relational database opens up the possibility of large scale comparative projects and multiple use of the source material. Thus the potential of local research is enlarged and the conditions are created for a broader range of theoretical issues to be addressed.

For many periods and especially for the eighteenth and nineteenth centuries we are badly in need of new data and new sorts of analysis in considering major questions of social, economic and political history. The use of computers, especially with the newer generation of relational database and hypertext software, together with portable machines, has revolutionised the prospects for local and regional history and the role which research at these levels may play in the future broader development of the discipline of economic and social history.

Before this, the hard high-status edge of research in economic and social history was in macro or national level studies using econometric or sociological models and statistical testing which the first generation of computers had encouraged. Local level research was (sometimes justifiably) subject to the charge of unrepresentativeness, antiquarianism and particularism. Today, however, the use of the computer in local and regional history is increasing the accessibility of archival material; enabling new levels of interrogation of data; opening up the prospect of new comparative and aggregative approaches and making possible the creation of a new 'history from below'. In economic history these developments will enable more realistic assessments to be made of the movement of major economic variables by region and sector as well as at the aggregate level. In both social and economic history local level reconstruction of communities and families and collective biographical research open the way to new levels of understanding of the lives of ordinary people previously hidden from history. The detailed knowledge generated by such computer-aided projects both facilitates and necessitates a wide range of new ethnographical and anthropological approaches. Together these developments amount to a maturing of regional and local history so that it becomes an important source of new data and new analytical ideas when considering major questions about economic and social change. And the status and importance of enquiry at these disaggregated levels can only increase alongside future innovation, and extension, of computer use.

ACKNOWLEDGEMENTS

This article started life as a keynote address to the Annual Conference of the Association for History and Computing at Wolverhampton Polytechnic in April 1990. Some references relate to papers presented at that conference, reproduced in summary form in the Conference booklet and referred to below by name of author, title of the original paper and AHC 1990. The essay has subsequently been updated to take account of more recent developments and to enable fuller reference to progress with the Yorkshire research which has been financed by the British Academy and the ESRC. My thanks go to Dr Margaret Bonney and to two anonymous referees for helpful advice in preparing the present article for the journal.

12

THE FUTURE FOR LOCAL HISTORY: BOOM OR RECESSION?

Kevin Schurer

To the average 'man in the street', if such a person exists, it might appear that the desire to explore the history of 'local' places has never been so strong. Driving up and down the countryside, for example, it would appear that the last few years has seen a proliferation of roadside signs, often in a distinctive sludge brown and accompanied by a Tudor rose, directing the motorist to heritage centres, museums, collections of various kinds, and other places of local interest. Of course, not all of these places are of historical interest, yet many are. As a result of increased leisure time and a shift in the pattern of recreational activities, what has become known as the 'heritage trade' has recently entered the world of business.

The growing commercial aspect of local history is not the only development. Perhaps most encouraging is the fact that, after being a 'non-subject' for so many years, the study of local history has now invaded the territory of the classroom. With educationalists and teachers being concerned with the ways in which children are taught, and with the teachers' apparent continuous quest to find more interesting, less boring ways to instill the bare bones of history into children, local history has crept into the classroom more and more over recent years. The traditional history of kings and queens, statesmen and acts of parliament, battlefields and foreign treaties has to some extent been elbowed out to make room for local history. It is not unusual for school trips to be organised to places or sites of local historical interest. Indeed, some may even visit the local record office or alternatively a local collection in the public library with the aim of compiling information for a classroom project detailing some aspect of local life. These are all relatively recent innovations, however. The extent to which the introduction of the 'core curriculum', GCSEs and other examinations will herald a return to 'traditional' methods of teaching history remains to be seen.[1]

---

1   An interesting review of the position of local history in the classroom is given in

Outside the classroom it would also appear that the situation is reasonably healthy. Despite financial troubles and the threat of introducing charges,[2] record offices are as crowded now as they ever have been. Admittedly many present-day users would be best classed as genealogists and family historians rather than local historians, yet it is true that in a large number of cases an interest in the history of one's own family creates an initial point of departure which later branches out into the more general and broader area of local history. The fact that the last decade has witnessed a substantial increase in the number and range of local history courses being taught, as well as a parallel increase in the activities of local history societies would in general tend to support this trend.

Yet is this all for the good? Although the study of local history is increasing, does this necessarily mean that the study of local history is actually progressing? Like it or not, it is the case that there is and always has been a gap between the study of local history and the study of what might be termed 'history proper', with the former always being looked upon as the poor relation to the latter. With this in mind, it would seem that the last few years has seen the gap between the two widen rather than narrow, despite the increase in the practice of local history. Indeed the situation may even be a direct result of this increase in the popularity of local history. As a consequence, it would appear that the time has come for local historians to take stock of the current state of the discipline and evaluate the key substantive issues that require investigation and how these might best be tackled.

To this end the essay that follows is set out in three main sections. It starts by assessing the current position of local history, tracing the development of the subject and its relationship to the academic study of history over the previous twenty-five years. In this discussion attention will focus upon an assessment of the various frameworks which have been proposed for the pursuit of local history as an historical investigation. This is followed by a discussion examining the local in local history. This section explores the relationships that exist between local history and geography, and suggests a framework for geographical investigation, as opposed to historical investigation. Lastly, the importance of place and the concept of regionalism are examined in relation to local historical study. To what extent is locale a central or influencing factor in attempting to understand certain aspects of historical development and behaviour?

T. Lomas, 'The teaching of local history in schools', *The Local Historian*, 18(4) (1988), 174–82. An example of a country record office assisting the teaching of local history is provided by D. Smith and J. Turtle, 'Local history records in schools: the role of the Gloucestershire Record Office', *The Local Historian*, 19(1) (1989), 16–17.

2   See, for example, the editorials to *Local Population Studies*, 45, (1990) and 46 (1991).

Although a distinction between local history and history proper clearly exists, it is far from easy to define or determine. The situation is a particularly curious one. If one thinks in terms of the relationship between local history and what might be called 'academic' history, it would appear that it is not the 'where' (ie., place) which serves as the critical factor, nor indeed the 'what' (ie., subject). Instead it is the way in which a study is carried out that makes it either 'acceptable' or 'unacceptable'. For example, an academic historical demographer interested in population patterns in the past is justified in studying the incidence of baptisms, marriages and burials for a single local parish, yet the practice of family history or genealogy using the same sources and similar but not the same methodology is frowned upon. For many academics undertaking research on historical populations the dividing line between the acceptable and the unacceptable, or desirable and undesirable, is characterised by Postan's notion of a 'microcosmic' study compared to one which is 'microscopic'. The former takes the form of a local based study which regards the situation or issues in question as part of a wider context, while the latter is a study whose outlook, aims and interest are restricted to issues only of local significance.[3] More recently, this notion has been reiterated by Wrigley in his suggestion that:

> What distinguishes a significant from an insignificant piece of historical research is not the size of the unit of investigation, whether in time or space, but the ends in view and the methods used. [4]

Such an approach can be seen, in Finberg's words, as 'national history localised'. Indeed, in his inaugural lecture as head of the Department of English Local History at the University of Leicester in 1952, Finberg seemed to suggest that a distinction between local and general historical studies along such lines was valid. In the lecture be commented that, 'to treat it [local history] as an introduction to national history is to invert the true relationship between them', later suggesting that local historians should approach their subject 'well grounded in the history of England'.[5]

However, the position is far more than a simple matter of approach and relevance to wider issues, with some historical studies being relevant and others less so. In each historical study whether local or otherwise, invariably

---

3   M. M. Postan, *Essays on historical method*, (Cambridge, 1971), 20–21.

4   E. A. Wrigley, *The local and the general in population history*, Sixteenth Harte Lecture, University of Exeter (1985) 1.

5   H. P. R. Finberg, *The local historian and his theme*, Occasional Papers 1, Department of English Local History (1952). See p. 116 above.

there will be a conflict between clarity and comprehensiveness.[6] Ideally, the well informed researcher would wish to display both qualities simultaneously, yet in a micro study the depth of detail may swamp the clarity of understanding. Equally, too much generalisation may generate theories with little or no applicability to the 'real' world. The problem, therefore, is striving to achieve a satisfactory balance between these two opposing forces.

Yet does this mean that in the case of local based historical studies such a balance can only be achieved by viewing particular local events, patterns and features from a national perspective. Quite rightly, this would appear not to be the case. During the late 1950s and 1960s, research work undertaken by disciples of the Leicester school of Local History, and in particular W. G. Hoskins, its founder and first head of department, quite clearly illustrated that local history could be used not only to examine and understand the operation of themes in national history more clearly, but also showed that in-depth local studies sometimes uncovered entirely new themes and issues, all of which pointed to the need for more research to be carried out at a national level. For example, Hoskins's well known work on landscape development and the operation of a 'midland' peasant economy provides a key illustration of what are essentially local based studies giving rise to further undertakings at a more general national level.[7] Consequently, rather than national history being localised, in some cases local history was becoming nationalised.

Following this lead it seems that during the mid-1960s Finberg shifted his ground slightly. Assessing the position of local based studies in a newer and more favorable light he asserted that local history was to be viewed, '... not as an ancillary discipline but as one subsisting in its own right. Those who take up this position draw a distinction between local history *per se* and national history localised'.[8] Unfortunately the distinction between the two does not appear to be particularly clear, yet Finberg's suggestion appears to be that each locality has a history of its own, separate in some respect from national trends, themes and concerns. Consequently, any locality can be studied for historical purpose by itself, in its own right, and for its own sake. In this respect the rationale for research is perhaps best described by Everitt:

No locality or community of course leads a wholly independent life; yet each, like the realm itself, has a life of its own. It will be influenced by national and metropolitan developments; but it will respond to them in its

6   This point is made in Wrigley, *The local and the general*, 12.
7   W. G. Hoskins, *The making of the English landscape* (1955); W. G. Hoskins, *The Midland peasant: the economic and social history of a Leicestershire village* (1957). This second work, as its full title suggests, is a single village study of Wigston Magna.
8   H. P. R. Finberg and V. H. T. Skipp, *Local history: objective and pursuit* (Newton Abbot, 1967), 32.

own way, drawing on its own traditions, its own absorbing historical experience, whenever it is faced with a new challenge or a new opportunity.[9]

More recently this conceptual framework for the historical study of local places and societies has been expanded by Phythian-Adams, the current head of the Leicester School. Concentrating on the network of social relationships experienced by local communities, Phythian-Adams pushes the underlying geographical element of place or locale from the foreground into the background. What really matters, he argues, is an attempt to understand the network of social relationships within a given place.[10] Drawing influence from the French *Annales* school of social historians, and in particular the writings of Braudel, Goubert and Le Roy Ladurie,[11] Phythian-Adams remarks that, 'ideally local history is societal history'. This he defines as:

... history of the component structures of a whole society and the manner in which such structures have been interrelated, both within some simultaneously evolving form of overall social organisations, and within that changing climate of ideas which informs and justifies it.[12]

Given the current state of affairs, it certainly seems desirable for the study of local history to be based within a more theoretical framework, and in this respect, that set out by Phythian-Adams appears to be most appropriate. Yet in adopting such an approach the importance of place becomes somewhat secondary to the theoretical backdrop. Consequently, over the past twenty to thirty years it can be seen that the emphasis on community based historical studies has shifted away from a concentration on place and locale towards one of structure and society. But where does all this leave the geographical component of local history?

---

9   A. Everitt, *Landscape and community in England* (London, 1985), 9.
10   C. Phythian-Adams, *Re-thinking English local history*, Occasional Papers, 4th series, number 1, Department of English Local History (Leicester, 1987), 17.
11   See, for example, F. Braudel, *On History* (1980); F. Braudel, *The Mediterranean and the Mediterranean world in the age of Philip II* (2 vols, 1972/1973); P. Goubert, *Beauvais et le Beauvaisis de 1600 a 1730: contribution a l'histoire sociale de la France du XVIIe siècle* (Paris 1960); E. Le Roy Ladurie, *The peasants of Langudoc* (1974); E. Le Roy Ladurie, *The territory of the historian* (Hassocks 1979). See also H. C. Prince, 'Fernand Braudel and total history', *Journal of Historical Geography*, 1 (1975), 103–106 and A. R. H. Baker, 'Reflections on the relations of historical geography and the Annales school of history' in A. R. H. Baker and D. Gregory (eds), *Explorations in historical geography: interpretative essays* (Cambridge, 1984), 1–27.
12   Phythian-Adams, *Re-thinking*, 19.

Throughout much of the early years of the Leicester School of local historians, the main thrust of research was often directed at the investigation of
landscape history, colonisation and the evolution of settlement, place-name
analysis and the development of agricultural systems.[13] Due to this combination of research interests, it was both convenient and natural to import the
concept of *pays* from France in order to explain and understand the regional
divisions of England more clearly.[14] The delineation of such *pays* was based
primarily on features of physical geomorphology: maps showing such regional divisions equate approximately to the major divisions on a geology
map, with appropriate adjustments being made to take account of settlement
colonisation. Such a framework for spatial investigation may fulfil the requirements for a study of an economy and society heavily engaged and
reliant on agriculture, with an agrarian based infrastructure, yet to what
extent can its purpose be served in relation to an industrialising, or post-
industrial society? A much over-simplified and general view would suggest
that although historic regional diversities in accordance with the concept of
pays can be observed relating to separate agro-ecological production areas,
these were gradually eroded via the process of growing industrial and capitalist infrastructures which in turn generated a trend towards homogeneity.
Parallel to this process, the role of the state increased as the nation moved
toward a single integrated economic unit or entity. In turn, focus centres
more sharply upon the capital, which acts to influence, if not dominate, all
political, cultural and social developments. Yet this orthodox view of regional transition has recently been called into question. In particular, Langton
has suggested that the early phases of industrialisation served to *increase*

13   W. G. Hoskins, 'Regional farming in England', *Agricultural History Review*, 2
(1954), 3–11; J. Thirsk, 'The farming regions of England', in J. Thirsk (ed.), *The Agrarian
history of England and Wales, Vol. IV, 1500–1670* (Cambridge 1967), 1–112; W. G. Hoskins
and H. P. R. Finberg, *Devonshire Studies* (1952); H. P. R. Finberg, *Roman and Saxon
Withington: A study of continuity*, University College of Leicester, Department of English
Local History, Occasional Papers, number 8 (1955); H. P. R. Finberg, *The early charters of
Devon and Cornwall*, University College of Leicester, Department of English Local History, Occasional Papers, number 2 (1953); K. J. Allison, *et al*, *The deserted villages of
Oxfordshire*, University of Leicester, Department of English Local History, Occasional
Papers, number 17 (1965); A. Everitt, *Continuity and colonization: The evolution of Kentish
settlement* (Leicester 1986); R. A. McKinley, *Norfolk Surnames in the sixteenth century*,
University of Leicester, Department of English Local History, Occasional Papers, 2nd
series, number 2 (1969).
14   The chief exponent of the concept of *pays* was the great geographer P. Vidal de la
Blache. For an anglified version of the concept see A. Everitt, 'River and wold: reflections
on the historical origin of regions and *pays*' and A. Everitt, 'Country, county and town:
patterns of regional evolution in England'. Both of these essays are reprinted in A. Everitt,
Landscape and Community in England (1985), respectively 41–59 and 11–40.

rather than *decrease* regional differences.[15] The diversities of regional infra-structures were highlighted by the initial processes of industrialisation, weakening regional variation and solidarity. Moreover, since much initial industrial development was based on canals and water-borne traffic, the network of which was far from being nationally integrated, this process further emphasised regional differences.[16]

If one can detect separate regional identities in the social and economic structures of both, the pre-industrial and industrialising nation state, then this would suggest a need to take 'regions' as the basic geographical unit for local analysis.[17] However, despite the fact that the study of 'whole' regions may be both desirable and profitable, such practice would seem to stand at a tangent to the study of 'local history *per se*' as suggested by Finberg. Irrespective of the desirability of examining 'regions', the unit of investigation, or locale, most commonly identified for the purposes of historical study is undoubtedly the parish 'community'. Yet what is the relevance of such small and localised spatial units? Moving between 'national history localised' and 'local history *per se*', and falling somewhere between the two, Finberg commented that:

We may picture the family, the local community, the national state and the supra-national society as a series of concentric circles. Each requires to be studied with constant reference to the one outside it... but the inner rings are not the less perfect for being wholly surrounded and enclosed by the other.[18]

The need to relate the structures and processes identified at a local level to a broader historical context is clear and 'academic' historians seem to be most aware of this fact. For example, witness the justifications voiced most strongly in the introduction to Spufford's classic study of Fenland communities:

---

15   J. Langton, 'The industrial revolution and the regional geography of England', *Transactions, Institute of British Geographers*, new series, 9 (1984), 145–167.

16   See G. Turnbull, 'Canals, coal and regional growth during the industrial revolution', *Economic History Review*, 2nd series, 4(4), (1987), 537–560. Although this article appears to support Langton's notion of regional development, the Langton thesis has been much criticised. See, in particular, the debate between D. Gregory, 'The production of regions in England's Industrial Revolution', *Journal of History Geography*, 14.1 (1988), 50–58 and J. Langton, 'The production of regions in England's Industrial Revolution: a response', (with reply by D. Gregory), *Journal of Historical Geography*, 14.2 (1988), 170–176.

17   See J. D. Marshall, 'The study of local and regional "communities": some problems and possibilities', *Northern History*, 17 (1981), 203–230; J. D. Marshall, 'Why study regions? (1)', *Journal of Regional and Local Studies*, 5(1) (1985), 15–27; J. D. Marshall, 'Why study regions? (2)': some historical considerations', *Journal of Regional and Local Studies*', 6 (1986), 1–12.

18   H. P. R. Finberg, 'Local history', in H. P. R. Finberg and V. H. T. Skipp, *Local history: objective and pursuit* (1967), 39.

The ideal basis for a study of this kind would not be a number of contrasting village communities, but a number of contrasting neighbourhoods or 'social areas', each extending over a group of parishes within approximately an eight-mile radius of a focal village centre.[19]

Yet simply altering the unit of study does not overcome the basic problem of explaining the relationship and interactions between one type or size of spatial unit and its neighbour or neighbours. The Ptolemic model of relationships as put forward by Finberg (or for that matter a Copernican model) illustrates the problem, yet offers very little in terms of a solution. In the Ptolemic model each identified unit of investigation or spatial type is isolated in an abstract form. The only point of reference for each level within the system is to move along a single artery leading out from the centre, either up or down, to the next order in the hierarchy. The result is that each level is superficially linked to the next within an abstract framework. Such an artificial situation has been attacked most strongly by Schofield, who remarks that:

> ... it does not follow that the relationships involved can only be properly understood at a regional or local level, even if the experience of the national aggregate proves not to have been typical of any part of the country. For 'nation', 'region', and 'locality' are abstractions and each level of abstraction has its own meaning. To move from a national investigation to a regional one is, therefore, to add a new level of understanding. The latter need neither negate nor supersede the earlier.[20]

In place of the solar system of concentric circles suggested by Finberg, it would seem appropriate to substitute the notion of central place theory, as formulated by the German economic geographer Walter Christaller.[21] In its classic form Christaller's central place network takes the guise of an interlocking mesh of hexagons, as depicted in Figure One. The main assumption of the classic formulation of the theory is that six small settlements or hamlets will be served by one village (hence the use of hexagons), six villages by a town, six towns by a city, and so on. Therefore, unlike the

19   M. Spufford, *Contrasting communities: English villagers in the sixteenth and seventeenth centuries* (Cambridge, 1974), 33.

20   R. S. Schofield, 'Through a glass darkly: the population history of England as an experiment in history' in R .I. Rotberg and T. K. Rabb, (eds), *Population and economy: population and history from the traditional to the modern world* (Cambridge, 1986), 31–32.

21   W. Christaller, *Central places in southern Germany* (Englewood Cliffs, New Jersey 1966). The original was published in German in 1933. See also H. Carter, *The study of urban geography* (1976), 72–142. An example of the application of central place theory in an historical context can be found in I. Hodder, 'The human geography of Roman Britain', in R. A. Dodgshon and R. A. Butlin, *An historical geography of England and Wales* (1978), 29–55.

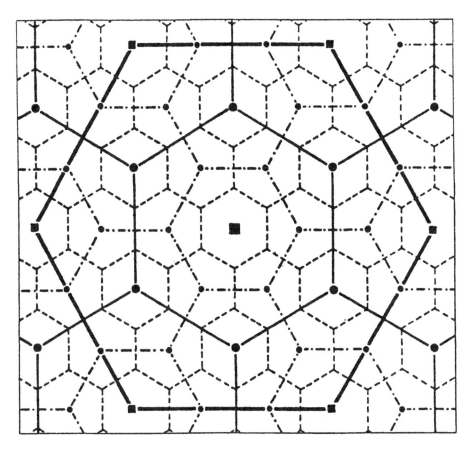

Figure 1: The Christaller central place model
(Example taken from J. H. Johnson, Urban Geography: An introductory analysis, *Pergamon Press (Oxford, 1972), 102.)*

Ptolemic model which suggests a linear hierarchy of settlement, the Christaller model emphases the stepped and overlapping nature of settlement hierarchy. This feature is clearly illustrated in Figure Two, which shows that in contrast to the one to one relationship of the Ptolemic model, the central place model produces a hypothetical relationship between the order of settlements in the ratio 1–6–36–216.[22] Moreover, unlike the concentric circles of the

---

22   Christaller realised that the hierarchy of settlement or ratio between settlements of certain sizes was not fixed. In order to explain this, the size of a settlement's hinterland was represented by what Christaller termed K values. The classic model, as depicted in Figure 1, is drawn with $K=3$, meaning that each settlement serves its own hinterland, plus an area the equivalent to the hinterlands of two other settlements of the same order (6 x 1/3). See H. Carter, *Urban geography*, 77–81.

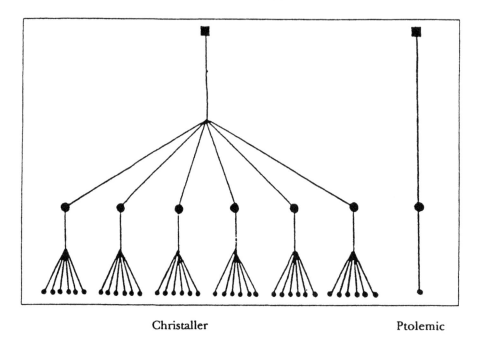

Christaller   Ptolemic

Figure 2: Hierarchy of settlement: Christaller and Ptolemic models

Ptolemic model in which the levels of settlement or organisation rotate in strict hierarchical order, the Christaller model allows settlements of different levels to be intermingled, with lower order settlements adjoining higher order settlements.

The chief importance of the Christaller model for the local historian is that it provides a theoretical framework for investigating spatial relationships. Although the model was initial developed primarily to explain economic behaviour and the location of settlement, the model could equally be applied to social as well as economic relationships. It would be possible to use the model to explain the inter-relationship between various social hierarchies, as well as the economic hierarchies for which it was developed. In addition, the rigidity of the model could be relaxed, perhaps with areas or networks of influence overlapping. In other words, the hexagons of Figure 1 could overlap or alternatively the 'service' area could even take on a form other than that of a hexagon.[23] Indeed, when viewed from an historical perspective it becomes clear that the relationships between the different levels of the model, if anything, must not be viewed as a constant.

23   See, for example, the versions of central place theory put forward in A. Lösch, *The economics of location* (New Haven, 1954). See also Carter, *Urban geography*, 80–87.

The fact that the relationship between the hierarchies or networks will invariably change over time can be seen, for example, by examining the rank-size distribution of settlements in the past. If the number of settlements are counted by size order it can be seen that in the case of England and Wales the distribution underwent a fundamental change in the hundred years between 1650 and 1750.[24] At both dates the first city (London) was clearly dominant, yet at the beginning of the period, middle and lower ranking towns were more evenly distributed in comparison to a century later. Clearly, such a change in the urban structure would also be accompanied by shifts and adjustments in the social and economic relationships between town and their regions.[25] In the case of East Anglia, plotting the distribution of settlements chartered for the purpose of holding a market in the sixteenth century suggests that the normal maximum range of influence for the medieval market was about six miles. This corresponds approximately to an ancient statute which forbade the establishment of a new market within six and two-thirds miles of an existing market. Yet there was much variation according to local conditions. In particular, a concentrated belt of markets with overlapping areas of influence spread out from London through the centre of the East Anglian region – from Braintree to Colchester, to Ipswich and up to Yarmouth – with some markets being located only two to three miles apart. Yet the area to the north-west of the region, around the Fens and Breckland of Norfolk, was served by markets often some eight to ten miles distant from each other. Equally, due to the monopoly operated by the Abbeys of Norwich and Bury St Edmunds, these two towns had no competing market for a considerable distance. However, by the early nineteenth century this pattern was much changed. As a result of developments in transport and communications, as well as the decline of the old traditional industries of worsted and hemp manufacture, a pattern emerged in which a smaller number of select larger markets with areas up to fifteen miles dominated, yet again with concentrations along the central communication routes.[26]

With these examples in mind, it is suggested that the central place model of Christaller might provide a basic framework with which changing temporal relationships between towns and their hinterlands (or vice versa) can be

---

24   J. de Vries, *European Urbanization, 1500–1800* (1984), 118–120. Note that the pattern of urban hierarchy experienced in England was not matched by other European countries. For example, in the case of Spain, the rank-size distributions suggests an 'urban collapse' in the seventeenth-century, see de Vries, 108–109. See also P. M. Hohenberg and L. H. Lees, *The making of urban Europe, 1000–1950* (1985), 217–247.

25   See, for example, E. A. Wrigley, *People, cities and wealth: the transformation of traditional society* (Oxford, 1987), chapter six, and J. C. Russell, *Medieval Regions and their cities* (Newton Abbot, 1972), chapters one and twelve.

26   R. E. Dickenson, *City, Region and Regionalism: a geographical contribution to human ecology* (1947), 80–82.

examined. In addition, it provides a vivid visual illustration of the inter-relationships, both economic and social, between communities and settlements. Lastly, it should be pointed out that the central place theory is clearly not representative of a 'real world' situation. In developing the model Christaller deliberately chose hexagons to illustrate spatial networks due to their special interlocking characteristic. The hexagons all fit together to form a single network, or series of networks, and it is this network of economic and social relationships that is crucial to our understanding of the various forces at work within the local (or regional) community. If a single hexagon is separated out and isolated from its 'neighbours' the network collapses. All one is left with is an abstract impression of the whole picture. Consequently, when studying a local community one needs also to under-stand how it relates to the constellation of communities that surround it, and of which it is a part. The locale of local history must not be separated from its appropriate geographical framework.

It has been argued that in studying a local community the geographical framework and system of spatial networks that surround and encompass it are all important. Yet what do we actually mean by place or region? Quite clearly it is possible to identify regions of various types in the past. It can and has been argued that regions were important in the process of political, administrative, economic, social and cultural development. Yet just because one can identify *regions*, does this mean that *regionalism* was important in the past? To what extent did people or communities identify themselves with a certain place, with a certain locale? To what extent was there a sense at an individual or community level of needing to belong somewhere?

The notion of local solidarity is strongly represented in popular culture and evidence for the displaying of local solidarity is scattered throughout the literature of the nineteenth century. One of the most amusing examples is a cartoon drawn by the well-known illustrator John Leech, published in the satirical magazine *Punch* in the 1850s. This depicts a scene from a 'mining district' with two local workmen in the foreground and a smartly dressed young man, looking distinctly out-of-place, in the background. The caption read: 'First Polite Native – "Who's 'im, Bill?" Second Ditto – "A stranger!" First Ditto – "Eave 'arf a brick at 'im."'[27] Similar expressions of local solidarity can be found in the growing literature of oral history. One example from the pioneering studies of Ewart Evans recalls that upon hear-ing that his daughter was seeing a man from a neighbouring parish less than

---

27   J. Leech, *Four hundred humorous illustrations* (no date), second edition, 192.

half a mile away, an agricultural worker from Needham Market (Suffolk) at the turn of the nineteenth century remonstrated with her, exclaiming: 'You must not do it! I cannot have a daughter of mine a-courting one o'those owd Creeting jackdaws.'[28] Equally, in their anthropological study of the inhabitants of Elmdon, an agricultural village located near the Essex-Cambridgeshire border, Richards and Robin retell the story of Harold (Jake) Reeves, a farmworker born in the village in 1897. Jake recounts that in his youth gangs of young men from Duddenhoe End and Chrishall, hamlets of between two and three miles distant, used to go into the Elmdon pubs only to be chased out again by the local youths, with fighting often breaking out between the two gangs. By way of explanation Jake remarks, 'we did not want strangers coming in here taking our jobs'. Perhaps on a more realistic note, Jake's wife Bertha also adds that, 'they used to fight about the girls. They did not want boys from the villages taking Elmdon girls'. She remembers that one of her own suitors before Jake was chased off having 'to turn round and bicycle back to Walden'.[29]

These are clearly no more than brief and unsubstantiated impressions, yet do they in any way suggest that loyalty or regionalism was operating at a micro-level? Perhaps instead they are the result of extreme parochialism, in which socio-economic and cultural insecurities manifested themselves in an introvert xenophobic vision of society. Whatever the situation, time and time again historians have identified examples of what might be termed local or neolocal-centred behaviour. Perhaps the best known and most quantifiable illustration of limited or restricted geographical horizons can be seen through the study of migration patterns. It is now well known that English society in the past was a very mobile society, the turnover of population in most communities generally being very rapid.[30] This was true not only of urban but also rural areas. Research using the census enumerators' books of the mid-nineteenth century shows that it was not unusual for half of the individuals recorded in one census year to be absent from the community a decade later.[31] Not only was population turnover very rapid, but also migration was a common place phenomenon for all classes of

28   G. E. Evans, *Ask the fellows who cut the hay* (1965), 239.

29   A. Richards and J. Robin, *Some Elmdon families*, privately published (1975), 125. See also M. Strathern, *Kinship at the core: an anthropology of Elmdon, a village in north-west Essex in the nineteen-sixties* (Cambridge, 1981). Saffron Walden is the nearest town to Elmdon, some five miles to the east.

30   A survey of literature on migration is provided in the introduction of P. Clark and D. Souden, *Migration and society in early modern England* (1987).

31   A summary of nineteenth century turnover studies can be found in K. Schürer, *Migration, population and social structure: A comparative study based on rural Essex, 1850–1900*, Ph.D. thesis, University of London (1988), 267–271. See also K. Schürer, 'The role of the family in the process of migration', C. G. Pooley and I. Whyte (eds), *Emigrants and immigrants: a social history of migration* (1991), 106 *et. seq.*

society and was a feature that encompassed all age groups.[32] Yet despite the large volume of movement most of this migration was carried out over short distances. Individuals often tended to move only very short distances, often no more than ten to fifteen kilometres.[33] Equally, the study of marriage registers shows that marriage partners usually experienced geographical horizons which were even more restricted.[34] This source is of course biased towards a narrow age group, yet to a certain degree marriage registers can be seen to depict very accurately the limits and patterns of geographical awareness, reflecting the territory over which the act of courting was undertaken.[35]

Why should the distance travelled by these migrants and courting couples be so restricted? From the mid-nineteenth century at least, it appears that there were few constraints on movement in the form of deficiencies in transportation, nor were there any significant political or administrative restrictions on movement in operation.[36] Perhaps instead the need to retain a sense of local identity acted to restrict and limit the scope and nature of migration and movement. To understand the situation more fully one would need to unravel the perception that individuals in the past had of the geographical environment in which they lived, worked and moved. Although it is very hard, and no doubt in some cases impossible to gather information and evidence which would aid the explanation of this phenomenon, this should not preclude researchers from trying.[37] Scattered and disjointed pieces of evidence, such as those presented here, suggest that concepts such as

---

32   See Schürer, *Migration*, 274–285, 300–306.

33   The predominant short distance nature of internal migration forms the basis of one of Ravenstein's famous 'Laws of migration'. See D. B. Grigg, 'E. G. Ravenstein and the "Laws of migration"', *Journal of Historical Geography* 3.1 (1977), 41–54.

34   Work on marriage horizons is summarized in K. Schürer, *Marriage register analysis of a nineteenth century resort*, Papers in Geography, 14, Department of Geography, Bedford College, University of London (1982) and D. R. Mills, *Aspect of marriage: an example of applied historical studies* (Milton Keynes, 1980).

35   The relationship between marriage horizons and social networks is strongly expressed in R. J. Dennis, 'Distance and social interaction in a Victorian city', *Journal of Historical Geography* 3.3 (1977), pp. 237–250.

36   For a recent review see N. Landau, 'The laws of settlement and the surveillance of immigration in eighteenth century Kent', *Continuity and Change* 3.3 (1988), 391–420. See also K. D. M. Snell, 'Parish registration and the study of labour mobility', *Local Population Studies*, 33 (1983), 29–43.

37   See R. Lawton and C. G. Pooley, 'Individual appraisals of nineteenth century Liverpool', *Social geography of nineteenth century Merseyside project*, Working paper 3, Department of Geography, University of Liverpool; R. J. Dennis, *English industrial cities of the nineteenth century: a social geography*, (Cambridge 1985), 254–255; A. Kussmaul, *The autobiography of Joseph Mayett of Quainton, 1783–1839*, Buckinghamshire Record Society, 23 (1986); J. Boulton, 'Neighbourhood migration in early modern London', in Clark and Souden, *Migration*, 107–149. See also the discussion in R. Lawton, 'Peopling the past', *Transactions, Institute of British Geographers*, 12.3 (1987), 259–283.

locality and regionalism may have been a significant influence on the structure of communities in the past, as well as on the behaviour of their inhabitants. It goes without saying that there is a need for much greater research to be focused in this direction.[38]

By way of conclusion let us return to the central theme of this essay, namely the intellectual framework of local history and its relationship to history proper. If one was to take on the role of devil's advocate, one may be tempted to suggest that there is indeed no such thing as local history, the only thing that matters and is relevant is straightforward history. Such a view may seem somewhat extreme given the nature and history of the journal in which this article is published, but it may help the gap between local history and history proper to be narrowed. It could be argued that what separates or distinguishes local history from history proper ironically has nothing to do with place. Nor for that matter has it anything to do with geography, and it has nothing to do with the subject matter being studied either. If a distinction is to be drawn between the two then I would suggest that the most significant element is the conceptual framework within which the historical study in question was undertaken. If this is indeed the case then it should be relatively clear that in future local historians need to pay more attention to the broader issues and themes of history if the current trend of divergence is to be reversed.

---

38   See the discussion in R. Dennis and S. Daniels, '"Community" and the social geography of Victorian cities', *Urban History Yearbook* (1981), 7–23 and A. Everitt, 'Country, county and town' in *Landscape and Community*.

13

ENGLISH LOCAL HISTORY AND AMERICAN LOCAL HISTORY: SOME COMPARISONS

R.C. Richardson

It behoves every American to be acquainted with the history of the place which gave him birth.
Daniel Ricketson, *History of New Bedford, Mass.* (1858), vi.

There are local and regional histories a-plenty, but few such face up to the natures of local societies in wider contexts over time, or consequently, to such central matters as structure, culture and process at these levels.
C. Phythian-Adams (ed.), *Societies, Cultures and Kinship, 1580–1850. Cultural Provinces and English Local History* (Leicester, 1993), xii.

Americans fear the European past; Europeans fear the American future.
Stephen Spender, *Love-Hate Relations. A Study of Anglo-American Sensibilities* (London, 1974), 47.

There is probably something to be said for the apparently outrageous notion that, except in a merely geographical sense, America is not a continent. Something can also be said in favour of the only slightly less bold contention that America's corporate feeling of nationhood is much stronger in its external manifestations than in its internal realities. America, it might be claimed (and it would be far more than a jest), is fundamentally a collection of islands, some of them very small indeed, jealously defended by inward-looking, parochial populations. According to the 1990 census returns almost 24% of Americans still live in small towns with populations of less than 15,000, far outside the economic, social, political and cultural orbit of the major cities, and for whom small-scale local concerns have an immediacy that the White House and Congress cannot possibly rival. The rural population of the United States accounts for a further 25%.[1] America, all appearances of a mass, homogenised, undifferentiated society notwithstanding, is still

---

1   For assistance in accessing US census data I am much indebted to Professor Stephen MacDonald of the University of Southern Maine.

intensely localised. Local identities, local loyalties are strong – perhaps partly as a reflex reaction to the fact that the whole country is so huge. One very obvious feature of that cultural outlook is a strong commitment to local history. It would be instructive to examine the foundations and expressions of that deeply rooted local historical consciousness and compare them with the changing face of English local history. Strangely, such a task never seems to have been undertaken before. What shared characteristics can be identified, what shared subject matter and other common denominators do the two communities of historians deal with? What are the principal dividing lines and points of contrast between them?

The shared subject matter connecting England and the United States is an enormous field of its own, far too vast to be addressed here in any detailed way. Investigations of it need to take account of the different phases of an imperial connection – exploration, settlement, colonisation, growth, government and administration, commercial, social and cultural interchange – which for two centuries literally bound the two countries together.[2] The sharing of three revolutions – in the 1640s, 1688 and 1776 – must also be considered.[3] The paradoxes of later industrialisation also claim the historian's attention. The historian would recognise, on the one hand, an economic process which made America Britain's most effective late nineteenth-century competitor but which also, in the course of the same century provided massive opportunities for British overseas capital investment.[4] Travel writing, produced by commentators and tourists moving in both transatlantic directions, has become a

---

2   D.B. Quinn, *Explorers and Colonies. America 1500–1625* (London, 1990); D. Cressy, *Coming Over. Migration and Communication between England and New England in the Seventeenth Century* (Cambridge, 1987); N. Canny (ed.), *The Origins of Empire. British Overseas Enterprise to the Close of the Seventeenth Century*, Oxford History of the British Empire, I (Oxford, 1998); P.J. Marshall (ed.), *The Eighteenth Century*, Oxford History of the British Empire, II (Oxford, 1998); I.K. Steele, *The English Atlantic 1675–1740* (New York, 1986); B. Bailyn, *The Peopling of British North America. An Introduction* (New York, 1985) and *Voyagers to the West. Emigration from Britain to America on the Eve of the Revolution* (London, 1987). See also D.H. Fischer, *Albion's Seed. Four British Folkways in America* (Oxford, 1990).

3   R.M. Bliss, *Revolution and Empire. English Politics and the American Colonies in the Seventeenth Century* (Manchester, 1990); J.G.A. Pocock (ed.), *Three British Revolutions: 1641, 1688, 1776* (Princeton, NJ, 1980); J.M. Sosin, *English America and the Restoration Monarchy of Charles II* (Lincoln, NE, 1980); D.S. Lovejoy, *The Glorious Revolution in America* (2nd ed., Middletown, CT, 1987); P.S. Haffenden, *New England and the English Nation, 1689–1713* (Oxford, 1974); C. Bonwick, *English Radicals and the American Revolution* (Chapel Hill, NC, 1977); Margaret and J. Jacob (eds.), *The Origins of Anglo-American Radicalism* (London, 1984); Mary Beth Norton, *The British Americans. The Loyalist Exiles in England, 1774–1789* (London, 1974).

4   F. Thistlethwaite, *The Anglo-American Connection in the Early Nineteenth Century* (Philadelphia, PE, 1984); P.S. Bagwell and G.E. Mingay, *Britain and America. A Study of Economic Change 1850–1939* (London, 1970); A.R. Hall, (ed.), *The Export of Capital from Britain, 1870–1914* (London, 1968).

growth area of research.[5] The blending of English aristocracy and American wealth in the late nineteenth/early twentieth centuries has proved another rewarding field of research, and brings in Churchills amongst others![6] The many dimensions of the shared experience of two World Wars have also frequently come under review.[7] Each of these topics is sufficiently large to have been the subject of many book-length studies. But very noticeably each of them rests on intricate substructures of essentially local connections. Two examples, chosen almost at random from very different points in time, will suffice to illustrate the general point being made.

The first concerns the migrations of the 1620s and 1630s from England to the American colonies. Both the general scale and the specifically puritan contribution to these movements of population have been trimmed down to size in recent studies. In many respects the most significant finding of such investigations has been to recognise that early English settlement in the Massachusetts Bay is best understood in the light of the infinite variety of English local history. What happened, very understandably, as David Grayson Allen and others have shown, was that the distinctive peculiarities of English local economies, structures, culture, institutions, and styles were simply reproduced with intense faithfulness in transatlantic settings.[8] Studying the early settlements of Massachusetts, therefore, partly requires the historian to work in such archives as the Essex and Suffolk County Record Offices in England. What the early colonists built was a new ENGLAND (and their particular part of it at that) and not, emphatically not, a NEW England. Only time, economics and politics brought that about.[9]

The second example comes from Over Wallop, Hampshire, in the 1940s. That village, like so many others, went through substantial social changes in

5   W.L. Sachse, *The Colonial American in Britain* (Madison, WI, 1956); R.E. Spiller, *The American in England during the First Half Century of Independence* (New York, 1926); Allison Lockwood, *Passionate Pilgrims. The American Traveller in Great Britain, 1800–1914* (East Brunswick, NJ, 1981); Jane L. Mesick, *The English Traveller in America, 1785–1835* (New York, 1922); C. Mulvey, *Anglo-American Landscapes. A Study of Nineteenth-Century Anglo-American Travel Literature* (Cambridge, 1983); C. Mulvey, *Transatlantic Manners. Social Patterns in Anglo-American Travel Literature* (Cambridge, 1990).

6   See Maureen E. Montgomery, *Gilded Prostitution. Status, Money and Transatlantic Marriages, 1870–1914* (London, 1989)

7   D. Dimbleby and D. Reynolds, *An Ocean Apart. The Relationship between Britain and America in the Twentieth Century* (London, 1988); K. Burk, *Britain, America and the Sinews of War, 1914–1918* (London, 1985); A.P. Dobson, *US Wartime Aid to Britain, 1940–1946* (London, 1986); D. Reynolds, *Rich Relations. The American Occupation of Britain, 1942–1945* (New York, 1995).

8   D.G. Allen, *In English Ways. The Movement of Societies and the Transferral of English Local Law and Custom to Massachusetts Bay in the Seventeenth Century* (Chapel Hill, NC, 1981); Cressy, *op.cit., passim.*

9   D.J. Boorstin, *The Americans. The Colonial Experience* (New York, 1958); Cressy, *op.cit.,* 292–95.

the first decades of the twentieth century, as patterns of land-owning and employment were modified. During the Second World War a major factor of change at work in the village was the presence of an American airfield. Black as well as white American troops were stationed there and, in line with the current code of military practice of the day, they were carefully segregated. Segregation of black soldiers from the village maidens was another matter, however, and as a result of country copulations the demography of this Hampshire village for a time took a quite unprecedented turn.[10]

The examples of shared subject matter connecting American and English local history could, of course, be endlessly multiplied. We turn now, however, specifically to the historiography of local history and consider first of all its present characteristics. The study of local history in England and the USA, it must be said at the outset, shares a very large number of common features. In each country there is a huge amateur following for the subject. The heritage industry in both countries is on the ascendant and the study of local history is both feeding it and benefiting from it.[11] (Some historians, like J.D. Marshall, see harmful consequences in all this. Heritage promotion strategies, he says in some of his choicest invective, involve a 'dumbing down' through the creation of 'hyper-realities' which both falsify the past and deaden the curiosity and imagination of the public).[12] There are similar infrastructures of museums, historical societies, archives, journals, and similar over-arching bodies concerned with promoting local history and maintaining or improving its standards. In England the Blake Report on Local History was published in 1979 with a formidable array of thirty seven recommendations about the promotion, organisation, training and teaching, sources, research and publication of the subject.[13] The Standing Conference for Local History set up in 1948 was upgraded – under the impact of the Blake Report – to become the British Association for Local History in 1982 with an onerous set of responsibilities. America's Conference of State and Local History Societies was founded in 1904 and was reconstituted in 1940 on a firmer foundation as the American Association for State and Local History.[14] The impact of professionals in both countries has been registered in terms of the assimilation of local history into university curricula, in the development of MA programmes, and in the frequency with which local

---

10   L. Murray-Twin, 'Over Wallop c.1925–1945. Employment and Social Relations. An Oral History', MA thesis, King Alfred's College, Winchester (1998), *passim.*

11   D. Lowenthal, *The Heritage Crusade and the Spoils of History* (New York, 1996); R. Hewison, *The Heritage Industry. Britain in a Climate of Decline* (London, 1987).

12   J.D. Marshall, *The Tyranny of the Discrete. A Discussion of the Problems of Local History in England* (Aldershot, 1997), 5, 56–57.

13   *Report of the Committee to Review Local History* (London, 1979), 53–56. Fourteen of the thirty-seven recommendations were earmarked to have first attention.

14   F.L. Rath et al., *Local History, National Heritage. Reflections on the History of AASLH* (Nashville, TN, 1991), 37, 40.

history topics are now approved as PhD subjects. (In this country about 50% of PhD registrations in modern English history are in local history).[15] The history professionals produce a steady stream of key books in the field of local history and they have effectively captured the leading periodicals in the field of regional and local history. Even in 1955 it was the case that two thirds of the contributors to five of the leading state historical society journals in America were academics.[16] In England all but one of the authors represented in the latest issue of *Southern History* in 1999 are professionals. The trend is undeniable.

The professionals have produced manuals and guidebooks for the amateurs to follow. Pride of place in this country goes to W.G. Hoskins's *Local History in England* (London, 1959) now in its third edition, which offered a magisterial survey of historiography, the structures of local life and their institutional settings, social and economic trends, demography, family names, topography, fieldwork, and the challenges of writing and publishing.[17] Alan Rogers's *Approaches to Local History* (2nd edition, 1977) raised key questions and charted routes through different themes such as population size and distribution, occupational structure, housing, transport, leisure, education, and religion.[18] Maurice Beresford's *History on the Ground* (1957, 3rd ed. 1998) opened up the complex interface between local history fieldwork and documentary evidence. D.P. Dymond, *Writing Local History: A Practical Guide* (1981), W.B. Stephens, *Sources for English Local History* (1981), J. West, *Village Records* (1983), Stephen Porter's *Exploring Urban History. Sources for Local Historians* (1990), J. Richardson's *The Local Historian's Encyclopaedia* (1986), and *The Oxford Companion to Local and Family History* (1996) edited by David Hey are some of the other examples that can be mentioned. Kate Tiller's *English Local History. An Introduction* (Stroud, 1992) has its approximate American counterpart in Carol Kammen's book *On Doing Local History* (2nd ed., Walnut Creek, CA, 1995). Kammen, a faculty member of Cornell University, writes what her publishers describe as 'a wise guide enlivened with examples from the author's experiences' to the problems of researching, writing and publishing local history[19]. It blends utilitarianism, encouragement, optimism and realism and has a second line in its title – *Reflections on what Local Historians Do, Why, and What it Means* – which in fact claims precedence over the first. The academic

---

15   J. Beckett, 'What future for the past in local history?', *East Midland History*, IV (1994), 11.

16   Cited in D.J. Russo, *Keepers of our Past. Local Historical Writing in the US, 1820s–1930s* (Westport, CT, 1988), 203.

17   For the third edition (London, 1984) Hoskins was assisted by David Hey.

18   Kammen brought out a companion volume entitled *The Pursuit of Local History. Readings on Theory and Practice* (Walnut Creek, CA, 1996).

19   Kammen, *On Doing Local History*, back cover.

functions and rationale of local history in the two countries are now very similar though practice has to take account of different politics and different levels of political correctness, as well as the very different scale of the geographical units involved; regional history, for example, in the two countries has different connotations. In both countries a dialectical model of the inter-relationship between local history and national history is in general use; Civil War studies in both countries provide an obvious example.[20] In both countries local history has become one of the principal laboratories for social history.[21] In both countries there has been a very noticeable shift in the working definition of local history – away from a topographical concept of local history entirely defined by place towards a much more overtly sociological concept based on community and culture.[22] Nor has this been the final destination. The need for comparative dimensions has been taken on board. In both countries links between local history and oral history have become very strong.[23] In both countries also as well as the writing of local history being dominated by academics the archives are now in the hands of trained professionals. Most county record offices in England are a product of the period after 1945. In the USA the professional reorganisation of the archives of the state historical societies belongs to the same period.[24] Clearly local history in both countries has a secure base and its necessity and utility are not called into question. The similarities in the present characteristics of local history in the two countries are strong and plain to see. Academically local history is firmly ensconced in historical studies and in a number of ways has positioned itself at the cutting edge.

Historiographically, however, there are some real differences between local history in the USA and in England and these become clearer through

---

20   See R.C. Richardson (ed.), *The English Civil Wars. Local Aspects* (Stroud, 1997). On the American Civil War see, for example, J.I. Robertson, *Civil War Virginia. Battleground for a Nation* (Charlottesville, VA, 1991), M. Fellman, *Inside War. The Guerrilla Conflict in Missouri during the American Civil War* (New York, 1989), and A.M.Josephy, *The Civil War in the American West* (New York, 1991).

21   See, for example, Margaret Spufford, *Contrasting Communities. English Villagers in the Sixteenth and Seventeenth Centuries* (Cambridge, 1974) and D. Rollison, *The Local Origins of Modern Society. Gloucestershire, 1500–1800* (London, 1992); Christine L.Heyrman, *Commerce and Culture. The Maritime Communities of Colonial Massachusetts, 1690–1750* (New York, 1984); R. Hogan, *Class and Community in Frontier Colorado* (Norman, OK, 1987); K.A. Sherzer, *The Unbounded Community. Neighborhood Life and Social Structure in New York City, 1830–1875* (Durham, NC, 1992).

22   See p. 210 below.

23   See, for example, M. Winstanley, *Life in Kent at the Turn of the Century* (Folkestone, 1978); S. Caunce, *Oral History and the Local Historian* (London, 1994); S. Terkel, *Working People Talk About What They Do All Day And How They Feel About What They Do* (New York, 1974); R. Dorson, *Folklore and Folklife* (Chicago, IL, 1956, 2nd ed., 1972).

24   See C.R.J. Currie and C.P. Lewis (eds), *English County Histories. A Guide* (Stroud, 1994), passim; G.C. Fite, 'The Rising Place of Local and State History in American Historiography: A Personal Look at the Last Forty Years', *Locus*, I (1988).

an examination of the pedigree of the subject and the chronology of respective phases of development. What this exposes is different patterns of antiquarianism in the two countries in the past and, in some respects, a different kind of academic leadership today.

The writing of local history in England, though it existed spasmodically in the Middle Ages, effectively originated in the late sixteenth and seventeenth centuries. A very noticeable clustering of activities and outcomes can be found at that time. 1572 saw the founding of the Society of Antiquaries. William Camden's *Britannia* – more than a local history, it is true – appeared in its first Latin edition in 1586. The same author's *Remains Concerning Britain* followed in 1605. John Stow's painstaking *Survey of London* saw the light of day in 1598. There was also, most notably of all, a swelling tide of county studies beginning in 1570 with William Lambarde's *Perambulation of Kent*, continuing with classics such as Sir William Dugdale's *Antiquities of Warwickshire* (1656) and Dr Robert Thoroton's *Antiquities of Nottinghamshire* (1677). County studies of this kind were firmly rooted in the life, culture, and politics of the English gentry. Dugdale and Thoroton both dedicated their antiquarian studies to the gentry communities of their respective counties. Dugdale indeed described his book as a 'monumental pillar [to] the noble and eminent actions of your worthy ancestors', and his topographical survey of the different hundreds which comprised his county gave pride of place to gentry genealogies and to gentry tombs in parish churches.[25] Dugdale's local history, in other words, chiefly served the interests of his own social class. It was all very secular. Heraldry and topography were fused together in his celebratory treatment. Antiquarianism of this kind had a firm social foundation and scarcely concealed political subtext.

The earliest American local histories also belong to the seventeenth century and also had a pronounced memorialising function. But what the first American historians – William Bradford, Edward Johnson, Nathaniel Morton, and Cotton Mather – were doing was to provide memorials of a very different kind from their English counterparts. They provided local histories in a sense – by documenting the first settlements – but they were writing for different purposes, in different ways, and for different audiences. Their memorialising was not secular like Dugdale's but was emphatically puritan in nature and what was being celebrated was not the genealogy and other traces of the gentry – in the nature of things there were not many of this rank in early seventeenth-century New England – but God's work expressed in the colonists' 'errand into the wilderness'.[26] It is a kind of historical writing

---

25   W. Dugdale, *Antiquities of Warwickshire* (1656), epistle dedicatory.

26   P. Gay, *A Loss of Mastery. Puritan Historians in Colonial America* (Berkeley, CA, 1966), chapters 1–3, *passim*. Although in a number of ways the specifically puritan character of the migration has been challenged the loud, forceful voice of puritan writings and government is unmistakable.

that has more in common with the *Acts and Monuments* of John Foxe than with Camden's *Britannia* and Dugdale's *Warwickshire*. This is a form of contemporary history concerned chiefly to document the emergence of churches. Civil government takes a back seat in the accounts. No sense of place is conveyed.[27]

Nathaniel Morton's preface to his *New England's Memoriall* (Cambridge, Mass., 1669) makes all this plain.

> It is much to be desired [he wrote] that there might be extant a Compleat History of the Colonies of New England that God may have the praise of his goodness to his people here and that the present and future generations may have the benefit thereof.[28]

By the time that Cotton Mather's book was published at the very beginning of the eighteenth century the colony had been in existence long enough to merit a different kind of history. But the pattern he adopted for his writing was much the same as Morton's. The chosen title was *Magnalia Christi Americana. The Ecclesiastical History of New England*, and its principal subject matter was 'the wonderful works of God in the late plantation of this part of America'. There were chapters on churches, clergy, divine providences, and on Harvard (at that time still exclusively a theological college). There was an account of Boston, it is true, but the town was presented primarily as a religious symbol and not really as a specific, unique, physical place.[29]

Antiquarianism came later to America than to England. Even in 1739 John Callender's *An Historical Discourse on the Civil and Religious Affairs of the Colony of Rhode Island* is as much sermon as history. But the antiquarian impulse was rising and was driven during the early decades of the eighteenth century by the colonists' determination to assert their right to a proper place in the British Empire and, after 1776, to document the part each colony had played in the Revolution. The new trend can be exemplified in Jeremy Belknap who, though a Congregational clergyman, wrote a three-volume history of New Hampshire in the 1790s that had a pronounced secular ingredient. He deals with agriculture, trade, industry, the growth of towns, communications, and has some forthright comments on the religious intolerance of the early colonists and he is quick to condemn the hypocrisy of their dealings with both native Americans and slaves.[30] Belknap stands out as the leading historian of his generation, not just as a writer but as a proselytiser for his subject, a campaigner for libraries and archives, and for

---

27   D. Van Tassel, *Recording America's Past. An Interpretation of the Development of Historical Studies in America, 1607–1884* (Chicago, 1960), 9–12.

28   Morton, *op.cit.*, To the Reader.

29   Mather, *op.cit.*, attestation, 31.

30   Belknap, *op. cit.*, I, 3–4, 75.

state education. He was the chief driving force behind the Massachusetts Historical Society founded in 1791 and chartered in 1794, the earliest such organisation in America. Connecticut and New York followed suit in 1799 and 1804. The practice spread widely.[31] Maine, Minnesota and Kansas, for example, established historical societies in the very same year that they achieved their designation as separate political territories (1820, 1849, and 1855 respectively).[32] All but two states – Delaware and California – had established historical societies by the time of the American Civil War.[33] L.W. Dunlap and W.M. Whitehill have documented their strivings.[34]

The nineteenth century in America saw local history of an antiquarian kind taken up with unsurpassed zeal; the sheer size of Hermann E. Ludewig's *The Literature of American Local History. A Bibliographical Essay* (New York, 1846) is one contemporary testimony to the bustling activity in this field. The Civil War itself provided a further fillip to local history – of a justificatory kind – as did the first centennial celebrations in 1876 of the Declaration of Independence. Congress added its voice in that year by enjoining that each state, county, and town that had been in existence at the time of the Revolution should organise its own commemoration.[35] Local history became a veritable publishing industry in these decades. Specialist publishers emerged. Some authors, such as George Sheldon of Deerfield, Massachusetts, laboured painstakingly for years on the history of one place.[36] Others prolifically (and sometimes carelessly) churned out several different local histories in rapid succession.[37] Women authors, such as Mary Booth and Abby Maria Hemenway, joined the ranks of amateur historians in substantial numbers.[38] Collaborative projects were launched.[39] Compilations dealing with the history of individual counties appeared in large numbers and followed a well-tried formula.[40] As Richard M.Dorson has argued, these production-line histories

---

31   W.M. Whitehill, *Independent Historical Societies* (Boston, 1962), 3, 10; C.L.Lord (ed.), *Keepers of the Past* (Chapel Hill, NC, 1965), 5–10. See also C.H. Callcott, *History in the US, 1800–1860, its Practice and Purpose* (Baltimore, MD, 1970).

32   Van Tassel, *op. cit.*, 95; Whitehill, *op.cit.*, 269, 279.

33   Whitehill, *op. cit.*, 19.

34   Whitehill, *op. cit., passim*; L.W. Dunlap, *American Historical Societies, 1790–1860* (Madison, WI, 1944).

35   Russo, *Keepers of our Past*, 79–80. The bicentennial celebrations of 1976 had a similar reinforcing effect on local historical studies in the US. (Kammen, *On Doing Local History*, 173–74). See also M. Kammen, 'The American Revolutionary Bicentennial and the Writing of Local History', *Hist.News*, XXX (1975), 179–90.

36   Russo, *Keepers of our Past*, xii.

37   Russo, *op. cit.*, chapter 8, *passim*.

38   Kammen, *On Doing Local History*, 27–28.

39   Russo, *op. cit.*, chapter 10, *passim*.

40   Kammen, *On Doing Local History*, 24–27.

told one rigid, undeviating story. They began with a reference to Indians and the wilderness topography; hailed the first settlers, noted the first churches; the first schools, the first stores; devoted a chapter to the Revolution and the local patriots; swung into full stride with the establishment of the newspaper, the militia, the fire department, and the waterworks; rhapsodized about the fraternal lodges and civic organizations; recounted the prominent citizens of the community, and enumerated famous personages (chiefly Washington and Lafayette) who had passed through; listed a roster of the Civil War dead; and rounded off the saga with descriptions of the newest edifices on Main Street.[41]

What so often this burgeoning nineteenth-century antiquarianism drew attention to and boasted of was the speed of change and progress. J.F. Watson's *Annals of Philadelphia* (1830) proclaimed that 'a single life in this rapidly growing country witnesses such changes in the progress of society and in the embellishments of the arts as would require a term of centuries to witness in full-grown Europe'.[42] America's moving frontier in the nineteenth century and the spread of antiquarianism went together. Local history writing and publishing came to form one aspect (though hardly the most lucrative!) of the United States' dynamic, self-conscious entrepreneurialism in this period. In the short term economic depression in the 1930s might weaken the antiquarian impulse and reduce its audience. And in a perverse kind of way economically opposite conditions later may have had the same kind of effect as the particular forms of post-war prosperity have made the American business classes less settled in one locality and more geographically mobile. Nonetheless the amateur tradition of local history in the States was far too strong, widespread and resilient to submit conclusively to any setbacks. For a long time in America, as in England, the arrival and consolidation of the historical profession made little difference to the antiquarian variety of local history. National history written by professionals and local history written by amateurs simply occupied different, uncontested spaces. Van Tassel in his *Recording America's Past* (Chicago, 1960) is patently wrong to claim that by 1884 'the long age of the amateur historian had ended'.[43]

Significantly Americans seem to have had much less difficulty than the English with the term 'amateur historian' (dropped in favour of *The Local Historian* as a journal title in 1968 in this country). David Russo devoted a whole book – *Keepers of our Past* (1988) – to pay warm and respectful homage to the generations of antiquarians who laboured so productively

41   R.M. Dorson, *American Folklore and the Historian* (Chicago, IL, 1971), 149, quoted in Kammen, *On Doing Local History*, 27.
42   Watson, *op. cit.*, preface.
43   Russo, *op. cit.*, 207–8; Van Tassel, *op. cit.*, 179.

in the field of local history and to stress the vital importance of their legacy.[44]

> The word "amateur"[says Carol Kammen, in similar vein] comes from the Latin *amator* meaning "to love".An amateur historian loves history, both the past itself and the study of the past ... There is no standard apprenticeship that one must follow in order to research and write history ... The past belongs to us all; the language of history is the language we speak. Historical methods ... depend upon intelligence and common sense and most history is not cloaked from view by an arcane jargon and methodology too complex for anyone who is interested but not formally trained to understand.[45]

There are no patronising attitudes in this book. The writer, though a university academic, proclaims a sense of identity with her readers. 'Us' and 'them' do not exist as separate categories, only 'we local historians'.[46] Kammen's belief in a shared community of historians is taken for granted. In England, on the other hand, in a recent, hard-hitting and polemical book on local history J.D. Marshall is obliged to labour his point on this subject to make sure he is not misunderstood.

> This discussion could all too easily be represented as an "attack" on amateur local history, or, worse, as an onslaught on the local historians themselves. On the contrary, the approach set out here refuses to treat such students as second- class citizens, fit only for the bread and circuses of the world of Heritage. It assumes there is one set of painfully agreed standards only, by which all historians must work and regarding which all must ultimately agree. It is most certainly in harmony with the idea of giving amateurs encouragement and support, but it regards the adoption of double or separate standards as a betrayal.[47]

Marshall is clearly of the view that both amateurs and professionals should shun the Heritage industry and turn their backs on antiquarianism in its various forms. Even the best results of antiquarianism are but 'proto-historical'. Marshall does not mince his words. Antiquarianism, he insists, is the great enemy of true local history and he brands it as a 'false trail', even a dangerous 'heresy', 'an inability to distinguish what features of the past are historically significant; an indiscriminately romantic attitude to the past'. He cannot understand why W.G. Hoskins wasted valuable pages on the

---

44   Apart from their own historiographical value, the antiquarian texts, Russo reminds his readers, frequently reprint primary sources that now no longer exist in any other form.
45   Kammen, *On Doing Local History*, 2, 6, 1.
46   *ibid.*, 4.
47   J.D. Marshall, *The Tyranny of the Discrete. A Discussion of the Problems of Local History in England* (Aldershot, 1997), 5.

early antiquarians in his *Local History in England*. Marshall's book abounds with warnings about the dangers which beset both amateurs and professionals in the field of local and regional history. Definitions which are too confining, and which involve a fragmentation of the subject, a fixation with one theme or one place, and a submission to 'the tyranny of the discrete' are to be avoided at all costs.[48]

The separate spaces once occupied by amateur and professional local historians are now increasingly shared. From the 1940s in both the USA and England professionals have taken the lead. Clear differences in that leadership, however, are apparent. First, though some of the big names in the American historical profession, such as Merle Curti, Oscar Handlin, Carl Bridenbaugh and L.B. Wright, wrote works of local history none of them became chiefly identified with that field.[49] There is no American equivalent of the 'Leicester School' of local history, no American equivalent of Hoskins, Finberg, Joan Thirsk, Everitt, and Phythian-Adams, just as earlier there had been no American equivalent of the *Victoria County History*.[50] Certainly there is no theorist of local history in the United States to place alongside Phythian-Adams in England. Second, probably as a consequence of this, there has been less professional evangelism in the States on behalf of local history. Carol Kammen's book mentioned earlier in the course of this essay can, in terms of its content, be seen as a rough equivalent of Hoskins's famous *Local History in England*, but not in terms of its spirit. In this sense the nearest approximation to Hoskins in the USA is probably David Russo's book *Families and Communities* (1974) in which he argues very strongly in favour of loosening, or even ditching, the national history framework in America in favour of a more grass roots kind of history, approached through the development of smaller units.[51] (Even this summary of its contents, however, depicts a very different kind of book in many respects; it is not that close an approximation to Hoskins). Third, local history in the States has become inseparably connected with urban history. Most of the classic twentieth-century local histories in the States deal with towns. Kenneth Lockridge's study of Dedham, Massachusetts *A New England Town. The First hundred*

48   *ibid.*, 55–56, 109, 46, 7.
49   M. Curti, *The Making of a Frontier Community: A Case Study of Democracy in a Frontier County* (Stanford, CA, 1959); C.Bridenbaugh, *Jamestown, 1544–1699* (New York, 1990); L.B.Wright, *South Carolina. A Bicentennial History* (New York, 1976).
50   On American county histories see Russo, *op. cit.*, 178–81. Given the enormous number of counties in the US, let alone all the other geo-political differences, a *VCH* equivalent is inconceivable.
51   D.J. Russo, *Families and Communities. A New View of American* History (Nashville, TN, 1974). Russo's argument is that the 'nation' is a relatively recent construct in America but is arbitrarily imposed as a framework on the country's past. A more richly textured approach to American history is needed, he says, which takes proper account of family life, towns, localities, and regions.

Years (New York, 1970, 1985) is one example that springs immediately to mind. Michael Zuckerman's *Peaceable Kingdoms. New England Towns in the Eighteenth Century* (New York, 1970) and Stephan Thernstrom's study of Newburyport, *Poverty and Progress. Social Mobility in a Nineteenth Century City* (Cambridge, Mass., 1964), are others. Local history significantly shares its space with urban history and community history in the chapter allocated to it in Michael Kammen's edited collection of essays on *Contemporary Historical Writing in the United States* (1980).[52] The patterns of local history studies have clearly been very different in England, with much attention – by Joan Thirsk and others – being specifically devoted to agrarian history.[53] The large-scale, multi-volume *Agrarian History of England and Wales*, significantly, with Finberg and then Joan Thirsk at the helm, grew out of the Department of English Local History at Leicester University.[54]

Finally, there has been relatively little dialogue between local historians in the two countries. In the seventeenth century, as shown above, local historians on each side of the Atlantic pursued a very different kind of memorialising practice. Eighteenth and nineteenth-century American antiquarians studiously avoided following English models. In the twentieth century the 'Leicester School' borrowed some of its sociology from the States. Hoskins drew on Lewis Mumford. The biological model of Finberg's model of English local history clearly tuned in with Hawley's *Human Ecology. A Theory of Community Structure* (New York, 1950). The conceptual apparatus and discourse of sociology and anthropology have clearly influenced the work of Phythian-Adams;[55] Phythian-Adams, it must be said, is the most jargon-laden of English local historians. Two-way traffic between the 'Leicester School' and the USA has been relatively limited. Kammen's useful reader *The Pursuit of Local History* (Walnut Creek, CA, 1996) reprints one of H.P.R. Finberg's essays.[56] Finberg and Hoskins are quoted in the same author's *On Doing Local History* (Walnut Creek, CA, 1995). Joan

52   Kathleen Freils Conzen, 'Community studies, urban history, and American local history', in M.Kammen (ed.), *The Past before Us. Contemporary Historical Writing in the US* (Ithaca, NY, 1980), 270–91.
53   Joan Thirsk, *English Peasant Farming. The Agrarian History of Lincolnshire from Tudor to Recent Times* (London,1957); *The Rural Economy of England. Collected Essays* (London, 1984). See also J. Chartres and D. Hey (eds), *English Rural Society 1500–1800* (Cambridge, 1990).
54   The project was launched in 1956. The first volume in the *Agrarian History* to appear (in 1967) was that covering the period 1500–1640, edited by Joan Thirsk.
55   C. Phythian-Adams, 'Hoskins's England: A Local Historian of Genius and the Realisation of his Theme', *Trans. Leics. Arch. & Hist. Soc.*, LXVI (1992), 149; Marshall, *op.cit.*, 66; C. Phythian-Adams, *Rethinking English Local History* (Leicester, 1987), 48; C. Phythian-Adams (ed.), *Societies, Cultures and Kinship 1580–1850* (Leicester and London, 1993), 7.
56   Finberg, 'How not to write English Local history', 191–99.

Thirsk has become well known on the conference circuit in the States and receives a fulsome tribute in David Grayson Allen's *In English Ways* (Chapel Hill, NC, 1981).[57] But it would be difficult to extend this short paragraph.

The Hoskins version of English local history, predicated partly on alienation from anything taking place since the Industrial Revolution, was not an easy export to the United States. An extended quotation from *The Making of the English Landscape* (London, 1955) gives its essential flavour.

The country houses decay and fall: hardly a week passes when one does not see the auctioneer's notice of the impending sale and dissolution of some big estate. The house is seized by the demolition contractors, its park invaded and churned up by the tractors and trailers of the timber merchant. Down comes the house; down come the tall trees, naked and gashed lies the once beautiful park ... Beyond the park, in some parts of England such as East Anglia, the bulldozer rams at the old hedges, blots them out to make fields big and vacant enough for the machines of the new ranch-farming and the business-men farmers of five to ten thousand acres ...

What else has happened in the immemorial landscape of the English countryside? Airfields have flayed it bare wherever there are level, well-drained stretches of land, above all in eastern England. Poor devastated Lincolnshire and Suffolk! And those long gentle lines of the dip-slope of the Cotswolds, those misty uplands of the sheep-grey oolite, how they have lent themselves to the villainous requirements of the new age! Over them drones, day after day, the obscene shape of the atom-bomber, laying a trail like a filthy slug upon Constable's and Gainsborough's sky. England of the Nissen hut, the "pre-fab", and the electric fence, of the high barbed wire around some unmentionable devilment; England of the arterial by-pass, treeless and stinking of diesel oil, murderous with lorries; England of the bombing range wherever there was once silence, as on Otmoor or the marshlands of Lincolnshire; England of battle- training areas on the Breckland heaths, and tanks crashing through empty ruined Wiltshire villages; England of high explosives falling upon the prehistoric monuments of Dartmoor. Barbaric England of the scientists, the military men, and the politicians: let us turn away and contemplate the past before all is lost to the vandals.[58]

It is instructive to compare two recent re-appraisals of Hoskins from each side of the Atlantic.[59] Phythian-Adams in one of them is reverential. For him Hoskins is a genius with a poetic, highly personalised 'new vision

57   Kammen, *On Doing Local History*, 8, 13, 32, 66; Allen's preface also extends thanks to two other English local historians, Margaret Spufford and Maurice Beresford, xvii.

58   W.G. Hoskins, *The Making of the English Landscape* (London, 1955), 231–32.

59   C. Phythian-Adams, 'Hoskins's England', 143–59. See note 55; D.W. Meinig, 'Reading the Landscape: an appreciation of W.G. Hoskins and J.B. Jackson', in D.W. Meinig (ed.), *The Interpretation of Ordinary Landscapes* (New York and Oxford, 1979), 195–244.

of the whole of English history'.[60] 'To restore the fundamental unity of
human history' was Hoskins's supreme task and its pursuit embraced not
only landscape history but demography, social history and botany.[61] Meinig,
the American commentator, focuses only on Hoskins's pioneering, quintessentially historical contribution to the study of landscapes. Full justice
is done to the historian's poetic sensitivities, the firsthand adventurous,
exploratory nature of his research, and to the many ways in which he was
so alert to the continuities and discontinuities in all he surveyed. 'In all
landscape literature', says Meinig, 'no one has equalled his evocation of
the "many sided pleasures" of his kind of search "to understand" and "to
savour to the full" the English landscape'.[62] Whereas Phythian Adams
recognises, but glosses over, Hoskins's hostility to technology-dominated,
quantitative-minded modernity, the American finds this impossible. For
him Hoskins's vision is flawed on account of it. The Leicester historian's
emotions and prejudices get in the way. However seminal his writings,
therefore, Meinig concludes

> as works of scholarship they stand as incomplete; by militantly, idiosyncrati-
> cally refusing to describe and analyse one of the greatest eras of change,
> Hoskins has arbitrarily truncated the story of the making of the English
> landscape.[63]

The American concept of landscape history, by contrast, is characterised by
its openness to change, and as Meinig shows, has as much to do with
adaptations of the urban form, highways, shopping malls, airports, and
dereliction, as it has to do with time-honoured fields and farms.

More generally, however, the definition of English local history offered
by the 'Leicester School' in the 1950s and 60s as the re-enactment of 'the
Origin, Growth, Decline and Fall of a Local Community' struck few chords
in irrepressibly upbeat America.[64] Carol Kammen, for one, finds the definition 'outmoded' and confining. Part of her advice to today's amateur historians
in the States is 'think about today'.

> All local history is not origins [she says] as interesting as local historians
> have always found origins to be. Today will soon be the past, too. Therefore
> collect materials from the present. Salt the archives with contemporary data.
> Encourage people to write memoirs, keep diaries, write and save letters...

---

60   Phythian-Adams, 'Hoskins's England', 145.
61   *ibid.*, 157. The 'fundamental unity' phrase comes from Hoskins's 1965 inaugural
lecture at Leicester. See p. 137 above.
62   Meinig, *op. cit.*, 209.
63   *ibid.*, 207.
64   The phrase derives from Finberg's 1952 inaugural lecture at Leicester. See p. 115
above.

Consider yourself a source of contemporary history, and write your recollections of living in your community... .[65]

Kammen's critique, in fact, finds echoes in this country. Distancing from,
and criticism of, the Finberg/Hoskins model of English local history is now
not at all unusual. For J.D.Marshall this particular definition is 'somewhat
passé' and for too long it went unchallenged. He devotes a whole chapter in
his recent book to the 'community obsession in English local history' and
takes the Leicester historians to task for their 'rural fixation', their misleading stress on social harmony, shared beliefs and opinions. Finberg's emphasis
on the Elizabethan parish church as a 'rallying point' and the grammar
school of that period as a common resource for 'the young of all ranks' for
Marshall bears little relation to reality. The brutal exercise of power and
social control at village level seem to find no place in the Finberg/Hoskins
organic communities. Marshall's indictment is that these historians indulged
a kind of tunnel vision; they idealised the past and turned their backs on the
present.[66]

The 'Leicester School' itself – never a monolith – has revisited its own
1950s' definitions. Joan Thirsk and Alan Everitt have had different visions of
English local history and have taken it in new directions.[67] So has Charles
Phythian-Adams, above all by explicitly re-addressing the definition of the
subject and its conceptual framework. Indeed there is a case for regarding this
historian as the first significant theorist of local history; in a succession of
substantial articles he has foregrounded the broader theoretical issues with a
seriousness and in ways that Finberg and Hoskins never attempted.[68] Phythian-
Adams pays due homage to the significance of Finberg's 1952 inaugural
lecture on local history (see pp. 110–22 above) as a kind of unilateral declaration of independence for the subject. It 'struck just the right radical note that

65   Kammen, *On Doing Local History*, 4.
66   Marshall, *op.cit.*, 63, 28, 65, 67.
67   Thirsk's collected essays – *The Rural Economy of England* (London, 1984) – give
clear indications of the broad range of her historical interests. Alan Everitt's collection
(from the same publisher) *Landscape and Community in England* (London, 1985) demon-
strates the significantly different scope of his approach to English local history. Keith Snell,
a current member of the Leicester department, is another who has pursued a very distinctive
line of his own. See K.D.M. Snell, *Annals of the Labouring Poor. Social Change and
Agrarian England, 1660–1900* (Cambridge, 1985) and the same author's *Church and Chapel
in the North Midlands. Religious Observance in the Nineteenth Century*, Department of
English Local History, Occasional Papers, Fourth Series (Leicester, 1991).
68   C. Phythian-Adams, *Local History and Folklore* (London, 1975); *Rethinking English Local History* (Leicester, 1987); 'Local History and National History: the quest for the
peoples of England', *Rural History*, 2.1 (1991), 1–20; 'An Agenda for English Local
History' in Phythian-Adams (ed.), *Societies, Cultures and Kinship, 1580–1850* (Leicester
and London, 1993), 1–23; 'Local History and Societal History', *Local Population Studies*,
51 (1993), 30–45.

was needed at that time in order to distinguish subtle local rhythms from crude forms of national periodisation'.[69] Even within its own terms of reference, however, the definition had its drawbacks. It paid scant attention to the active 'middle years' of a community's life-cycle, it was too inward-looking, and insufficiently alert to the periodic realignments of communities 'on the move'.[70] Studying single communities over time, Phythian-Adams insists, can no longer be a sufficient objective for the local historian. 'Congeries of communities', regions, pays, cultural provinces are now taken to be more appropriate subjects for a genuinely societal study. A comparative dimension to English local history should also be present to overcome a preoccupation with the unique. Attention should always be given to the *longue durée* (the influence of the *Annales* School is very obvious here) as well as to time in the short term, to kinship, lineage, neighborhood, social territories, and cultural contexts.[71] There is a recognition in Phythian-Adams's model of 'the crucial role of towns and the manner in which these focus both society and culture'.[72]

The ultimate goal [he argues] is nothing less than a properly grounded understanding of the rich geographical and cultural diversity of the "English" as an ever-evolving people. In striving – however imperfectly – towards such an end, however, we shall have finally to relinquish our still lingering obsession with the uniqueness and centrality of the single place[73]

The wider purposes of English local history should always be kept in view.

For these purposes, I would suggest, are essentially concerned with disentangling the ways in which, down to today, the "English" have related through the local society or societies with which they have most immediately identified, to a more generalised notion of national belonging.[74]

But Phythian-Adams's challenge to his fellow historians is even greater than this.

We should not limit English local history either to the English or to England … The subject cannot be regarded as a series of compartmentalised versions of English national history … Even for local historians there is much to be said for a historical view that supersedes the merely national … We urgently need here a British equivalent of Fernand Braudel.[75]

69   Phythian-Adams,'Local History and National History', 12.
70   *ibid.*, 12–13.
71   *ibid.*, 5
72   'Local History and Societal History', 39.
73   *ibid.*, 44.
74   'Local and National History', 20
75   *ibid.*, 20, 3.

With that kind of refreshingly outward- and forward looking attitude the next chapters in the parallel development of English local history and American local history may well be very different. Local history has to be rooted in particulars – they provide some of its obvious distinctiveness – but it does not have to be confined by them.

FURTHER READING

J. Beckett, 'What future for the past in local history?', *East Midland History*, IV (1994)

M. Beresford, *History on the Ground* (1957, 3rd ed., Stroud, 1998)

C.R.J. Currie and C.P. Lewis (eds), *English County Histories. A Guide* (Stroud, 1994)

D.P. Dymond, *Writing Local History: A Practical Guide* (London, 1981)

F.S. Fussner, *The Historical Revolution. English Historical Writing and Thought, 1580–1640* (London, 1962)

R. Hewison, *The Heritage Industry. Britain in a Climate of Decline* (London, 1987)

W.G. Hoskins, *Local History in England* (1959, 3rd ed., London, 1984)

W.G. Hoskins, *The Making of the English Landscape* (London, 1955)

D. Hey, *Family History and Local History in England* (London, 1987)

D. Hey, (ed.), *The Oxford Companion to Local and Family History* (Oxford, 1996)

Carol Kammen, *On Doing Local History. Reflections on What Local Historians Do, Why, and What it Means* (2nd ed., Walnut Creek, CA, 1995)

Carol Kammen (ed.), *The Pursuit of Local History. Readings on Theory and Practice* (Walnut Creek, CA, 1996)

M. Kammen (ed.), *The Past Before Us. Contemporary Historical Writing in the US* (Ithaca, NY, 1980)

C. Lewis, *Particular Places. An Introduction to English Local History* (London, 1989)

D. Lowenthal, *The Heritage Crusade and the Spoils of History* (New York, 1996)

J.D. Marshall, *The Tyranny of the Discrete. A Discussion of the Problems of Local History in England* (Aldershot, 1997)

D.W. Meinig, 'Reading the Landscape: an appreciation of W.G. Hoskins and J.B. Jackson', in D.W. Meinig, (ed.), *The Interpretation of Ordinary Landscapes* (New York and Oxford, 1979)

S.A.E. Mendyk, *'Speculum Britanniae'. Regional Study, Antiquarianism and Science in Britain to 1700* (Toronto, 1989)

G. Parry, *The Trophies of Time. English Antiquarians of the Seventeenth Century* (Oxford, 1996)

S. Piggott, *Ruins in a Landscape. Essays in Antiquarianism* (Edinburgh, 1976)

S. Piggott, *William Stukeley. An Eighteenth Century Antiquary* (New York, 1985)

C. Phythian-Adams, 'Hoskins's England: A Local Historian of Genius and the Realisation of his Theme', *Trans. Leics. Arch. & Hist. Soc.*, LXVI (1992)

C. Phythian-Adams, *Local History and Folklore* (London, 1975)

C. Phythian-Adams, 'Local History and National History: the quest for the peoples of England', *Rural History*, 2.1 (1991)

C. Phythian-Adams, 'Local History and Societal history', *Local Population Studies*, 51 (1993)

C. Phythian-Adams, *Rethinking English Local History* (Leicester, 1987)

C. Phythian-Adams (ed.), *Societies, Cultures and Kinship, 1580–1850* (Leicester and London, 1993)

Report of the Committee to Review Local History (the Blake Report) (London, 1979)

J. Richardson, *The Local Historian's Encyclopaedia* (London, 1986)

A. Rogers, *Approaches to Local History* (2nd ed., London, 1977)

D.J. Russo, *Keepers of our Past. Local Historians writing in the US, 1820s–1930s* (Westport, CT, 1988)

J. Simmons (ed.), *English County Historians* (Wakefield, 1978)

W.B. Stephens, *Sources for English Local History* (Manchester, 1981)

Rosemary Sweet, *The Writing of Urban Histories in Eighteenth-Century England* (Oxford, 1997)

Kate Tiller, *English Local History. An Introduction* (Stroud, 1992)

Retha M. Warnicke, *William Lambarde. Elizabethan Antiquary* (Chichester, 1973)

INDEX

For Product Safety Concerns and Information please contact
our EU representative GPSR@taylorandfrancis.com Taylor & Francis
Verlag GmbH, Kaufingerstraße 24, 80331 München, Germany

T - #0114 - 160425 - C0 - 219/152/12 - PB - 9781138739956 - Gloss Lamination